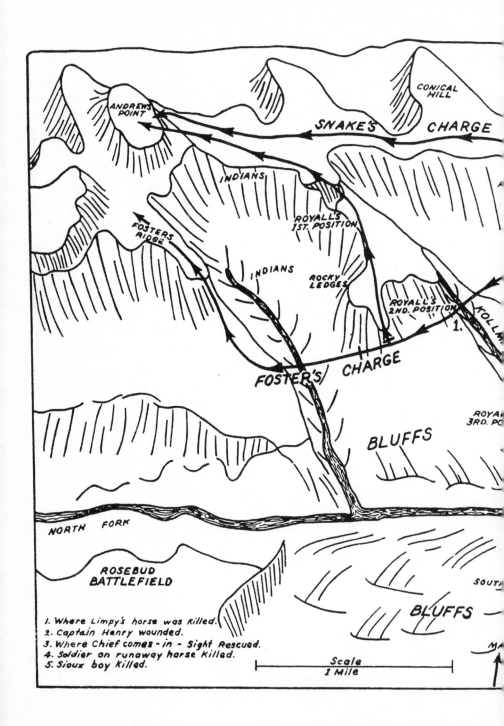

CONICAL HILL

ANDREWS POINT

SNAKES   CHARGE

INDIANS

ROYALL'S
1ST. POSITION

FOSTERS
RIDGE

INDIANS   ROCKY
LEDGES

ROYALL'S
2ND. POSITION

KOLLM

1.

FOSTER'S   CHARGE

ROYA
3RD. PO

BLUFFS

NORTH FORK

ROSEBUD
BATTLEFIELD

SOUT

BLUFFS

MA

1. Where Limpy's horse was killed.
2. Captain Henry wounded.
3. Where Chief comes-in-Sight Rescued.
4. Soldier on runaway horse killed.
5. Sioux boy killed.

Scale
1 Mile

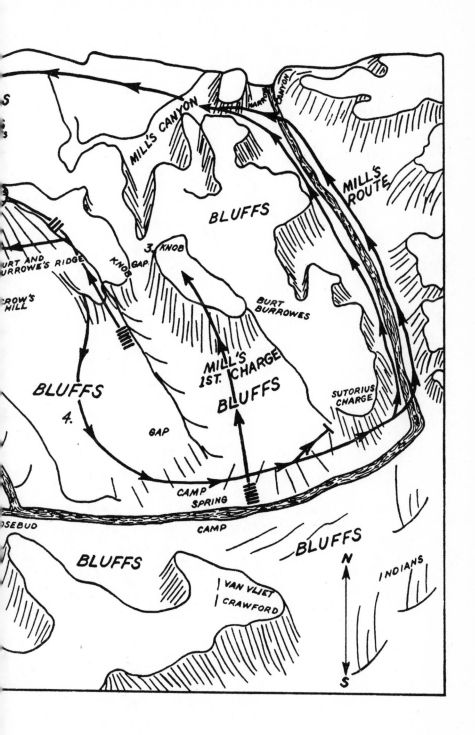

With Crook
at the Rosebud

With Crook at the Rosebud

J. W. Vaughn

New introduction by
Brian C. Pohanka

STACKPOLE
BOOKS

Published by
STACKPOLE BOOKS
5067 Ritter Road
Mechanicsburg, PA 17055

Printed in the United States of America

Second hardcover edition

Originally published in 1956 by the Stackpole Company

10 9 8 7 6 5 4 3 2 1

Library of Congress Cataloging-in-Publication Data

Vaughn, J. W.
    With Crook at the Rosebud / J.W. Vaughn ; new introduction by
Brian Pohanka. — 2nd hardcover ed.
        p.   cm. — (The Custer library)
    Originally published: Stackpole Company, 1956.
    Includes bibliographical references and index.
    ISBN 0-8117-1742-9
    1. Rosebud, Battle of the, 1876.   2. Crook, George, 1828–1890.
  I. Title.   II. Series.
    E83.876.V3   1994
    973.8'2 — dc20   93-46515
                                                               CIP

DEDICATION

To the men and warriors
on both sides of the battle
who fought for the right
as it was given them to see the right

ACKNOWLEDGMENTS

In order to gather all this information, I have found it necessary to enlist the cooperation of many persons and institutions. I am proud to acknowledge my indebtedness to them for various forms of assistance contributed to this work. Among them are the following:

Mr. Elmer Kobold, Kirby, Montana,
Mrs. Rose Kobold, Kirby, Montana,
Mr. Charles Young, Kirby Montana,
Mr. Jesse Young, Kirby, Montana,
Lt. Col. E. S. Luce, U.S. Army Retired, Crow Agency, Montana,
Mr. George G. Osten, Billings, Montana,
Mari Sandoz, New York City,
Mr. Dean F. Krakel, University of Wyoming, Laramie, Wyoming,
Mr. Edwin Pomranka, University of Wyoming, Laramie, Wyoming,
Mr. F. H. Sinclair, Sheridan, Wyoming,
Mr. M. D. Jenkins, Sheridan, Wyoming,
Mr. Harvey Friedberger, Sheridan, Wyoming,
Mr. Fred Colson, Sheridan, Wyoming,
Mr. H. E. Zullig, Sheridan, Wyoming,
Mr. Archie Storm, Sheridan, Wyoming,
Mr. Ben Reifel, Pine Ridge Agency, South Dakota,
Mr. Jake Herman, Pine Ridge Agency, South Dakota,
Mr. Albert Sims, Douglas, Wyoming,
Mr. Henry Bolln, Douglas, Wyoming,
Mr. John F. Henry, Douglas, Wyoming,
Mr. L. C. Bishop, Cheyenne, Wyoming,
Mr. Frank Sibrava, Wilson, Kansas.
Western History Department, Denver Public Library,
Reference and Research Service, Boston Public Library,
Reference Department, New York Public Library,
Patents and Newspapers Department, Chicago Public Library,
Library, Colorado State College of Education, Greeley, Colorado,
Historical Society of Montana, Helena, Montana,
Nebraska State Historical Society, Lincoln, Nebraska,
Colorado State Historical Society, Denver, Colorado,
U. S. Bureau of Reclamation, Billings, Montana,
U. S. Bureau of Reclamation, Hardin, Montana,
Army War College, Carlisle Barracks, Pennsylvania.

PERSONAL ACKNOWLEDGMENTS

My sister has rendered invaluable assistance in preparation of the manuscript.

I am deeply grateful for the help of my wife during many tortuous days on the field where she courageously endured mosquitoes, ticks, rattlesnakes, and J. W. Vaughn.

To all others who have in some manner aided in the preparation of this work "I can no other answer make but thanks, and thanks, and ever thanks."

J. W. VAUGHN

PREFACE

Though the battle of the Little Big Horn, June 25, 1876, received widespread publicity because of the magic personality of General George Armstrong Custer and the mystery surrounding the massacre of half of the 7th Cavalry regiment, the Battle of the Rosebud, thirty miles southeast and occurring one week earlier—virtually unknown except to a few students —involved more troops, had fewer casualties, lasted for most of a day, and was of far greater historical significance.

The Battle of the Rosebud covered an area four miles long east and west and two miles wide north and south along the banks of the little Rosebud River in southern Montana.

Northward into this territory in middle June, 1876, Brigadier General George Crook led a large column of U. S. Cavalry and Infantry. This column numbered in excess of 1325 soldiers, Indian allies, packers and miners besides some Army servants who were made part of the fighting force. Regarded at the time as the main force against the infractious Indians, the command was intercepted by a party of Sioux and Cheyennes under Crazy Horse at the big bend of the Rosebud River. After a battle which lasted nearly a day, General Crook was compelled to return to his base forty miles away on the present site of Sheridan, Wyoming.

Five correspondents from the largest newspapers in the country accompanied Crook's column. Their full description of the campaign affords a valuable source of information. One of the correspondents, John F. Finerty, wrote a book, *Warpath and Bivouac*, in 1890, reporting in detail his experiences in the expedition.

Lieutenant John G. Bourke, one of General Crook's staff officers, kept a diary in which he set forth at the end of each day the most minute happenings. This *Diary* is now in possession of the library at West Point. Later, his book, *On The Border With Crook*, recounted campaign events.

Captain Anson Mills, leader of a cavalry battalion in the Rosebud fight, gave additional details in his book, *My Story.*

Frank Gruard, General Crook's head scout, told his experiences in the campaign, *Life and Adventures of Frank Gruard,* edited by Joe De Barthe.

These and other eye witness accounts, together with the official reports of the battle, furnish sufficient material to piece together the highlights of the action.

In September, 1952, I made my first trip to the Custer battlefield in southern Montana and spent four days roaming over its historic hills and ravines. Before going, I had read all the books I could find on that engagement, and all mentioned vaguely an Indian battle on the Rosebud River which occurred a week before the Custer fight. Yet no one seemed to know much about the affair or where it took place. So I decided to visit this field on my way back to Colorado.

In order to get to Rosebud Valley, I took the old Busby road leading east over the Wolf Mountains, following the trail that Custer took to the Little Big Horn River. As I drove along, I passed the fork in Reno Creek where he had found the lone tepee with the dead Sioux Indian in it, and farther on, the bog where several of the pack mules had got stuck. Nearing the divide or crest of the mountains, I saw to the south the "Crow's Nest" from which Custer's scouts had discovered the large Indian village fifteen miles to the west.

On the east side of the mountains the road followed down Davis Creek to the point where it ran into Rosebud Creek. Looking several miles to the north, I could see the little Indian settlement of Busby where Custer made his last camp. This was a beautiful little valley with conical hills of red rock covered with pine trees lining it on the east, green bluffs on the west, the picturesque stream meandering from one side to the other—no wonder the Indians fought for it!

Turning south on the road to Decker, I learned that near Kirby, the Indian village which Crook vainly sought was said to have been located. Seven miles south along the stream I found the small valley where the Rosebud came in from the west. The stream ran east for two and three-fourths miles after coming down from the divide on the south, forming the "Big Bend."

In this peaceful setting occurred one of the largest Indian battles ever waged in this country, a hard fought engagement with fierce charges and counter-charges, where two equally gallant commanders met to alter the destiny of many lives. A cavalry fight, it covered a large area, yet the terrain was so cut up with ravines and ridges that Crook's soldiers become separated and were compelled to fight in detachments. Also, since it was a cavalry fight, there were comparatively few casualties. Confederate General Longstreet's statement that he had never seen a dead cavalryman, was illustrated to a certain extent by the Battle of the Rosebud.

I returned to this scene many times with a metal detector. In spite of the terrific cloudbursts to which this country is subject, I found many shells, both empty and loaded, and shell fragments. The types of shells found enabled me to locate action sites and verify various positions on the field. While much research through old Army magazines and newspapers brought to light accounts of the battle, the old maps were very inaccurate. I soon learned there was no action at a place unless shells could be found with the metal detector. For I had determined to make a thorough study of this obscure but fascinating battle which may have changed the history of the west. I have written down the story in the hope that it will prove interesting to others.

J W Vaughn

INTRODUCTION

On the afternoon of Sunday, June 25, 1876, Lieutenant Colonel George Armstrong Custer led six hundred troopers of the Seventh United States Cavalry to disaster on the banks of Montana's Little Big Horn River. In a daring offensive gone tragically awry, Custer and more than a third of his soldiers perished at the hands of counterattacking Sioux and Cheyenne warriors.

On that same Sunday afternoon, fifty-five miles south of the carnage unfolding at Little Big Horn, a military force twice as large as Custer's contingent idled in their camp on Wyoming's Goose Creek while their officers went fishing. By day's end one captain had hooked no fewer than one hundred trout; a catch of fewer than twenty would have been considered an embarrassment. The commander of the Big Horn and Yellowstone Expedition, Brigadier General George Crook, was an avid hunter and outdoorsman who encouraged this sport as a means to supplement unsavory commissary rations. It also served to alleviate the monotonous routine while his force awaited reinforcements. Crook himself was contemplating an exploring and hunting excursion into the nearby Bighorn Mountains.

Stolid and taciturn by nature, George Crook appeared outwardly oblivious to the fact that eight days earlier his troops had waged a desperate day-long battle, the most significant event in his twenty-four years as an officer, and the largest engagement of the frontier Indian Wars. Though Crook did not realize it at the time, the strategic implications of the Battle of the Rosebud—particularly his decision to delay his column's advance northward—held crucial, perhaps fatal import for Custer and the Seventh Cavalry.

In the spring of 1876 George Crook was given command of the largest of three military contingents deployed to coerce the so-called "hostiles" onto their allotted reservations. The assignment made a great deal of sense, for at age forty-seven Crook was one of the Army's most experienced Indian fighters.

The ninth of ten children, Crook was born September 8, 1828, on a farm near Taylorsville, Ohio. At age nineteen Crook was offered an appointment to the United States Military Academy by Congressman Robert Schenck, a family friend. The congressman seems to have been motivated more by the desire to benefit the son of a fellow member of the Whig Party than by his appointee's character. Indeed, Schenck, who later served as a general in the Union Army, remembered the young man as "exceedingly non-communicative" and "quiet to reticence."

George Crook's four years at West Point were undistinguished, and despite a paucity of demerits he graduated near the bottom of the class of 1852. One of the introverted Ohioan's few friends at the academy was a diminutive cadet of Irish extraction named Philip Henry Sheridan. Though held back a year because of poor academic performance, Sheridan would eventually be posted to Crook's regiment, the 4th U.S. Infantry.

Despite his unpromising career at West Point, Lieutenant Crook began to prove his metal in a grueling series of campaigns against the Indians of the Northwest frontier. Utterly indifferent to military pomp, and openly contemptuous of the widespread drinking and gambling indulged by his fellow officers, Crook soon displayed what would thereafter be the hallmarks of his soldierly skills—gritty determination, physical endurance, a love of the outdoors, and an acute appreciation of the Indian way of warfare.

Some writers and historians have made the mistake of confusing Crook's demonstrated knowledge of Indian language, customs, and lore with an innate sympathy for the Native Americans. Although in his unfinished autobiography Crook recognized white avarice and duplicity as the underlying cause of most Indian outbreaks, he nonetheless declared: "It is an easy manner for anyone to see the salient points of Indian character, namely that they are filthy, odiferous, treacherous, ungrateful, pitiless, cruel, and lazy." A participant in dozens of clashes in California, Oregon, and Washington Territory, Crook killed at least six native warriors with his own hand. In one battle he suffered a potentially fatal wound that left an arrowhead imbedded in his right hip for the remainder of his life.

At the outbreak of the Civil War Crook was on garrison duty in San Francisco, but he soon found a role in the conflict as colonel of the 36th Ohio. Promoted to brigadier general of volunteers, he commanded an infantry brigade in the Antietam Campaign and a cavalry division at Chickamauga. Returning to the Eastern Theater at the behest of Sheridan and Grant, Crook served in the mountains of West Virginia and in Virginia's Shenandoah Valley.

As leader of the division-sized "Army of West Virginia," Crook contributed mightily to General Sheridan's September 19, 1864, victory at the Battle of Winchester, but a month later endured the misfortune of having his command routed by a surprise Confederate assault at Cedar Creek. The tensions that emerged between George Crook and Phil Sheridan in the course of the Valley Campaign soured their longstanding friendship and embittered their future relations.

On February 21, 1865, Crook and another Federal general were captured by Rebel partisans in Cumberland, Maryland. What could have been a humiliating conclusion to a rather uneven Civil War career was averted by a rapid exchange of prisoners that allowed Crook a chance to participate in the final weeks of the conflict. Commanding a division of cavalry, he served creditably with the Army of the Potomac during the campaign that culminated in Union victory at Appomattox.

With the muster-out of the volunteer forces, Major General Crook was fortunate to find a place in the postwar Regular Army as lieutenant colonel of the 23rd U.S. Infantry. Returning to the scenes of his former exploits in the Northwest, Crook maintained his reputation as a gritty field officer in a series of campaigns against the Paiutes in Idaho and Oregon. Following a two-year stint at Portland as commander of the Department of the Columbia, Crook, at President Grant's behest, was transferred to the Department of Arizona. There his Indian-fighting skills were put to the test against the most formidable of guerrilla fighters, the Apaches.

Beginning in 1871 and continuing through the next two years, Crook led numerous military expeditions through the rugged vastness of the arid Southwest in pursuit of his elusive opponents. He expected his soldiers to travel light and to keep the field until the enemy was cornered and vanquished. Crook set the example for his officers and men by his own spartan simplicity and stoic indifference to hardship. His spare six-foot frame habitually clad in a threadbare private's blouse or civilian hunting jacket, with torn trousers and a ragged slouch hat, Crook was about as far removed from military foppery as it was possible to be. His eccentricity was accented by the habit of braiding his scraggly beard with ribbons or string. Lieutenant Charles King, a noted chronicler of Crook's campaigns, claimed the only time he ever saw George Crook in full uniform was when "he lay garbed for the grave."

To some officers, Crook's approach to Indian warfare was as unorthodox as his appearance. Perhaps the most innovative of Crook's stratagems was a potent combination of intimidation and negotiation that convinced numbers of Apaches to join forces with the bluecoats against other, hostile, bands. This use of Indian scouts enabled Crook to track and bring his foes to bay, at which point he was equally prepared to negotiate or to fight. "The Indians feared him," said one of his aides, "but they respected him."

Crook's success in a region that had proven a graveyard for military reputations won him promotion from lieutenant colonel to brigadier general. He was thus jumped over the heads of numerous regimental commanders—a reward that Lieutenant Colonel Custer may well have been seeking when he made his ambitious and reckless attack at Little Big Horn.

In the autumn of 1875 Crook was given command of the Department of the Platte, with headquarters at Omaha, Nebraska. On March 1 of the following year, he led a nine-hundred–man force out of Fort Fetterman, Wyoming, in an attempt to locate and destroy the snowbound encampments of the hostile Sioux and Cheyennes. On March 17, Crook's advance guard, led by Colonel Joseph J. Reynolds, surprised a large Cheyenne village on southern Montana's Powder River. But Reynolds failed to exploit his initial success, and the winter campaign foundered in blunders and recriminations. Despite his demonstrated abilities, Crook seemed out of his element in this theater of war. "He has chiefly become famous as an Indian fighter among the Apaches in Arizona," a cavalryman noted, "but the mounted and nomadic Sioux are a more difficult proposition."

On May 29, two months after his abortive effort at Powder River, Crook again sallied forth from Fort Fetterman with nearly a thousand troops—a force soon augmented by several hundred Crow and Shoshone auxiliaries. Crook headed north, bound for Yellowstone country, where contingents led by Colonel John Gibbon and General Alfred Terry were similarly converging on the vast and rugged landscape known to contain several thousand tribesmen who had coalesced around the charismatic Hunkpapa medicine man, Sitting Bull.

Formidable as Crook's force was, on June 17, 1876, the soldiers and their Indian allies would meet their match on the banks of a narrow, winding stream called the Rosebud.

Though largely eclipsed by the more decisive and far bloodier clash at Little Big Horn, by Indian Wars standards the Battle of the Rosebud was fought on an epic scale. The contending forces each numbered more than one thousand men, and the combat ebbed and flowed across a six-mile-wide front of ridges, hills, and valleys. It is no wonder that the fluid nature of the fighting and the vastness of the terrain proved an almost insurmountable challenge to historians seeking to reconstruct the sequence and course of events. It was seventy-five years after the battle before a clear picture of the affair began to emerge thanks to the dedication of a Colorado lawyer named J. W. Vaughn.

Jesse Wendell Vaughn was born in Dadeville, Missouri, on March 4, 1903, the son of Rose and Samuel Jesse Vaughn. In his youth he moved to DeKalb, Illinois, where he attended the local high school. In 1925 he graduated from the University of Missouri, and three years later received a law degree from the University of Denver. Vaughn settled in Windsor, Colorado, where he was a practicing attorney for thirty-nine years, excepting a brief stint in the Army during World War II. Vaughn served as Windsor town attorney, was active in the local Methodist church, and was a member of the Masonic Fraternity. At the time of his death, on September 29, 1968, he was secretary of the Windsor-Severance Fire District.

Wendell Vaughn was forty-nine years old, when, in the fall of 1952, he made his first visit to the Little Big Horn and Rosebud battlefields. Unlike most students of the 1876 campaign, it was Crook's standoff at the Rosebud, not Custer's last stand, that seized Vaughn's imagination. He began to gather primary data—the memoirs, recollections, and testimony of survivors, both published and unpublished—as well as microfilmed after-action reports and troop returns from the files of the National Archives. But it was Vaughn's on-site use of a metal detector to locate bullets, ejected shell cases, and other Indian and soldier artifacts that provided uncontrovertible evidence of the fighting. "I soon learned," Vaughn stated, "that there was no action at a place unless shells could be found with the metal detector."

Retired National Park Service historian Don Rickey, a noted authority on the Indian Wars, remembers Vaughn as "one of the most dedicated, persevering metal-detecting field workers I ever knew; persistence was his long suit." Although Vaughn was in poor health for the last decade of his life, and was particularly susceptible to the heat, the companionship and patience of his wife, Florence—who toted a gallon water jug on their excursions to the battlefield—helped keep him going. Still, it was hard and often frustrating work. "It is very discouraging to swing a ten-pound metal detector around in the hot sun for hours at a time without finding anything," Vaughn confessed, "but when something eventually turns up, enthusiasm is renewed until the next long dry spell." By the time he finished his survey of the Rosebud battlefield, Vaughn had unearthed some eight hundred shell cases from twenty different types of firearms.

With Crook at the Rosebud, published by the Stackpole Company in 1956, was the first of J. W. Vaughn's book-length studies of Indian Wars engagements. Three more followed over the next decade: *The Reynolds Campaign on Powder River* (1961), *The Battle of Platte Bridge* (1963), and *Indian Fights: New Facts on Seven Encounters* (1966), all published by the University of Oklahoma Press. Each work reflected Vaughn's singular ability to synthesize archival and artifactual data in a thorough, informative, and impartial fashion. There was, moreover, a sense of mission to Vaughn's undertaking. "My purpose has been to develop and record all the factual details," he wrote in his last book, "together with convincing proof of its exact location before these sites are lost forever before the relentless onslaught of time and modern civilization."

George Crook survived the Battle of the Rosebud for fourteen years—he died suddenly, of a heart attack, on March 21, 1890—and in 1876 much campaigning yet lay before him. To his dying day, Crook claimed the Rosebud as a victory, insisting that "My troops beat those Indians on a field of their own choosing." Yet the fact remains that despite minimal losses—ten killed and twenty-one wounded—Crook removed his own force from the larger campaign for a crucial six weeks. If victory it was, then Sheridan was quite correct when he termed the affair "barren of results." Emboldened by their success, Indian veterans of the Rosebud—warriors like the Oglala leader Crazy Horse—undoubtedly went into the fight at Little Big Horn with no small amount of confidence.

J. W. Vaughn admitted, "One could spend a lifetime in the study of the Rosebud battle and still not cover all of the various angles and details." In a manner befitting his legal training, Vaughn wished to let his voluminous research speak for itself. His history of the fight incorporated lengthy verbatim narratives from men who were present on the field. "Where the evidence is conflicting," he wrote, "an opinion is expressed as to which is correct." And Vaughn's final opinion was that Crook had been "out-scouted, out-surprised, out-maneuvered," and had "lost control of the situation."

Vaughn thought that the Battle of the Rosebud "was of far greater historical significance" than Little Big Horn. While students and historians of the Indian Wars still ponder and debate the "what ifs" of Crook's stalemate at the Rosebud—could Crook, for instance, have marched on and struck the Indians before Custer did—J. W. Vaughn made no secret of his own damning conclusion. Had Crook truly won a decisive victory, "Without doubt, the disaster at Little Big Horn would have been averted."

Brian C. Pohanka
Alexandria, Virginia

CONTENTS

Chapter 1

THE CAMP AT FORT FETTERMAN

GOLD! Yellow kernels of lode for which men of all nations have fought and died, fired the adventurous hearts of this country when discovered in the Black Hills, 1874, bringing an invasion of prospectors into the Dakotas. This was indian territory; and the eyes of the warriors glaring across the council circle at White River, September 20, 1875, were hot and resentful. Retaliation they had had. The murdered bodies of their victims were legion. The Government officers, attempting to settle differences peacefully at this council near Fort Robinson, realized by the bitter words spoken that they had failed. Neither white nor red man could know this was the prelude to the decisive battle of the Rosebud,[1] the companion battle to Custer's fight on the Little Big Horn.

By the terms of the treaty of Fort Laramie, 1868, the Sioux and Cheyenne tribes were given control over wide territory in Montana, Wyoming, Nebraska, and western portions of the Dakotas. The Government had agreed to vacate the territory, abandoning its forts, including Fort Reno and Fort Phil Kearney, and endeavor to keep out white men. However, because of the influx of gold-mad miners, encroaching European immigrants from all directions and the continual use of the Bozeman Road, the attempt had been unsuccessful. Therefore, the Government's commissioners at the Peace Council sought to purchase the Black Hills.

Captain Anson Mills, in command of the soldiers present told of the Council:

"On June 18, 1875, Mr. Ed. P. Smith, the Commissioner of Indian Affairs, organized a commission to treat with the Sioux. It was composed of very distinguished men. Senator William B. Allison was the president, and General Terry among the thirteen members who met at Fort Robinson, September 20,

1

1875. I commanded the escort, consisting of my own and Captain Eagan's white horse company of the 2d Cavalry.

"The majority of the Indians refused to enter the post, declaring they would make no treaty under duress. The commission agreed to meet in a grove on the White River, eight miles northeast of the post. Spotted Tail, who accompanied me from Fort Sheridan, warned me it was a mistake to meet outside the post, and kept his best friends around my ambulance.

"The commission sat under a large tarpaulin, the chiefs sitting on the ground. Senator Allison was to make the introductory speech, and Red Cloud and Spotted Tail were scheduled to reply favorably to the surrender of the Black Hills for certain considerations.

"There were present an estimated 20,000 Indians, representing probably 40,000 or 45,000 of various tribes. Probably three-fourths of the grown males of the consolidated tribes were present and might have subscribed to a new treaty in accordance with its provisions, that it be with the consent of three-fourths of the Indians, which supposedly meant the grown people, although the treaty did not so state. The Indians were given to understand that the whites must have the land, so that they became alarmed, and most of them threatened war.

"Eagan's Mounted company, drawn up in single line, I placed on the right of the commission, my own on the left. Allison began his address, during which hostile Indians, well armed, formed man for man in the rear of Eagan's men. "Young-Man-Afraid-of-His-Horses," a captain of a company of friendly Indians, asked permission to form his men in the rear of the hostile Indians, to which I consented.

"When Red Cloud was about to speak, "Little-Big-Man," astride an American horse, two revolvers belted to his waist, but otherwise naked save for a breech clout, moccasins and war headgear, rode between the commission and the seated Indian chiefs and proclaimed, "I will kill the first Indian chief who speaks favorably to the selling of the Black Hills."

"Spotted Tail, fearing a massacre, advised that the commission get back to the fort as quickly as possible. General Terry consulted with Allison, and then ordered the commission into ambulances to make for the post. I placed Eagan's company on each flank and my own in the rear of the ambulances, At least half the men warriors pressed about us threatening to kill some member of the commission.

"One young warrior in particular, riding furiously into our ranks, frenziedly declared that he would have the blood of a commissioner. Fortunately we reserved our fire.

"A friendly Indian soldier showed him an innocent colt grazing about one hundred yards away and told him he could appease his anger by killing it. Strange to say, he consented, rode out and shot the colt dead, and the whole of the hostile Sioux retired to the main body at the place of our meeting. Thus ended the efforts of this commission to formulate a treaty."[2]

It was now necessary for the Bureau of Indian Affairs to adopt regulations demanding that all Indians in the northwest live on reservations, setting January, 1876, as the final date for infractious tribesmen.

The Crows, having lost their territory by the terms of the treaty, had moved to the western side of the Big Horn Mountains, where they lived neighbors with the Shoshone. These two tribes, on friendly terms with the U. S., were long standing enemies of the Sioux and Cheyenne, who refused to return to their reservations. Under the leadership of Sitting Bull of the Hunkpapa tribe of Sioux, these latter tribes, concentrated for mutual protection, moved north and westward into eastern Montana.

Helpless, the Indian Bureau turned the problem over to the military and Lt. General P. H. Sheridan, Commander of the Division of the Missouri, wherein the hostile tribes were located.

Subsequently, Brigadier General George Crook, an Ohioan, in his 48th year, on orders from the War Department, March, 1876, led a column of infantry and cavalry north from Fort Fetterman by the Bozeman Road, then northeastward to the Powder River. A portion of his command under Colonel J. J. Reynolds surprised a large village believed to be Oglala Sioux under the leader Crazy Horse. Reynolds captured and destroyed the village and supplies, but was driven back after the Indians rallied and recaptured their horses. Though the Indians claimed this was a village of Cheyenne under Chief Two Moon, who after the battle sought refuge in Crazy Horse's village, there was public ridicule of the defeat.

General Crook, mortified, critical of Reynold's failure, arranged a court martial upon his return to Fort Fetterman:

"Owing to the age and feebleness of Colonel Reynolds," wrote Mills, "and the bitter feud that existed in the regiment (similar to that in the 7th Cavalry between Colonel Sturgis and his friends and Colonel Custer and his friends, that proved so disastrous at the Little Big Horn), this attack on the village on Powder River proved a lamentable failure. Reynolds disobeyed

Crook's order to hold the village until his arrival, abandoning the field and retiring in the direction of Fetterman."[3]

Failure of Crook's expedition meant all-out war. General Terry commanding the Department of Dakota, and General Crook, commanding the Department of the Platte, were instructed to organize large commands for the purpose of pursuing and punishing derelict Sioux.

General John Gibbon left Fort Ellis, near the present site of Bozeman, Montana, to move southeast, with 450 men, including six companies of infantry and four troops of cavalry. Descending the Yellowstone River, he kept his men stationed at various points to see that the Indians did not escape to the north.

From Fort Abraham Lincoln, near Bismarck, North Dakota, General Alfred H. Terry set out in a westerly direction with a column composed of 950 men, May 17. A portion of this force, composed of three companies of infantry and a battery of Gatling Guns (early rapid fire machine guns), met the advance forces of Gibbon on June 8 at the mouth of Glendive Creek, where the balance of Terry's command, 650 men of the 7th Cavalry under General Custer, did not arrive until several days later.

The third column of cavalry and infantry under General Crook was destined to leave Fort Fetterman, May 29th, following the Bozeman Road northward into hostile territory.

Thus, the three commands were acting in concert to complete a pincers movement closing in on the concentration of Sioux and Cheyennes, believed to be somewhere west of the Rosebud River.

All during May, Crook's column was assembling and outfitting at his base located ten miles northwest of where Douglas, Wyoming, now stands. Situated on a small plateau, Fort Fetterman was a quarter mile from the south bank of the North Platte River near the point where the old Oregon Trail running east and west intersected the Bozeman Road. Named for Brevet Lt. Col. W. F. Fetterman, Captain in the 27th Infantry, who was massacred with his whole command near Fort Kearney, December 21, 1866, it was one of the larger western forts with accommodations for three infantry companies, four cavalry troops and one hundred citizen employees.

A small column of troops under the command of Major Evans,[4] an old classmate of Crook's, assembled at Medicine Bow Station on the Union Pacific Railroad, marched across country to join Crook at Fort Fetterman on May 25th.[5] But the main body of troops with wagons, supplies and pack train assembled at Fort Russell near Cheyenne, Wyoming, under command of Colonel Royall, that "tall handsome Virginian," marching via Fort Laramie and the old Mormon Emigrant Trail to Fort Fetterman. They went into camp on the north side of the river across from the fort and east of Major Evans' men, waiting for the other troops to be brought over for the anticipated march.

There were however, no bridges across the stream, and the North Platte River, swift and running from bank to bank, presented the first major obstacle to General Crook.

"The Command Was Taken Over On a Ferry Boat"

Lieutenant Daniel C. Pearson, 2nd Cavalry, a young officer appointed to the Military Academy from Massachusetts and graduated in the class of 1870, describes in his article "Military Notes, 1876, U.S. Cavalry Journal, September 1899," the difficulties encountered:

"Below, and near at hand to the fort, swiftly ran the North Platte River, bank-full at that time of year. The command was, with the exceptions of horses that could be made to swim, taken over on a ferry boat, which was propelled to and fro by presenting sides, alternately, obliquely to the current, with the help of ropes, blocks and pulleys operating upon a cable that was stretched from bank to bank.[6] The process of swimming the horses was interesting, more particularly when it came to those of one troop which positively refused to take the water. With that mount, as was the case with all, the men of the troop formed a semi-circle about the horses, the ends of the circle resting at the waters edge, to force the horses into the river. The particular mounts referred to were young and new to the service. They broke through the line of men; they turned tail to the river; they sailed past the fort like the wind, and then they disappeared in the mountains southward, the most of them never to be recovered.[7]

"This column having collected on the north bank of the river, was then inspected. As a result of this inspection, a car-load of the personal effects of officers and men had to be sent back to the fort, to be left in the quartermaster's warehouse. In fact, many of these effects were yet on the river bank as the column pulled out to the north. Every pound that could be dispensed with was left behind. Currycombs and brushes were not allowed to the cavalry. Clothing, blankets, and equipage were closely scanned, and reduced by an inflexible rule in the case of every individual. Herein the infantry suffered most. Many nights were spent by them hovering over camp-fires, while the cavalryman was sleeping well under the additional cover afforded by saddle blanket and another extra blanket, which was carried beneath the saddle in the daytime with no detriment to the horse."

"Bustle and Activity Prevailing In Camp"

Lieutenant John G. Bourke, aide-de-camp to General Crook, wrote in his diary about the enormous task of getting men and supplies over the river:

"*May 26*. The hausers of the ferry broke this morning about 11 o'clock. Not much trouble was made because most of the supplies and all the troops had already crossed. By hauling the slack of the rope across the stream the break was repaired in a few hours.

"*May 28*. Bustle and activity prevailing in camp; officers, orderlies and detachments of men passing constantly to and from the garrison; the ferry repaired during the past night found no respite all day. Wagon loads of grain, ammunition, subsistence and other stores crossed the Platte to the camp on the other side which spread out in a picturesque panorama along the level meadows, surrounded by a bend of the stream. The long rows of shelter camps, herds of animals grazing or running about, trains of wagons and mules passing from point to point, made up a scene of great animation and spirit. The allowance of baggage for the present expedition has been placed at the lowest limit. Shelter tents for the men and "A" tents for the officers all trunks and heavy packages ordered to be left at the fort.

"The ferry worked constantly during the day, transporting quantities of stores so that by night fall but little was left on the Fetterman side. Between 8 and 9 in the evening, the cable, the new one ordered up from Laramie, snapped in twain, letting the boat swing loose into the current. It was soon recovered and the toilsome work resumed of splicing the ruptured hauser. Our ferrymen were well nigh exhausted and with much difficulty exerted themselves to restore communications.

"*May 29*. Left Fort Fetterman at one o'clock and joined Col. Royall's[8] column which was then slowly defiling out from its camp on the left bank of the Platte."

According to John F. Finerty, one of the newspaper correspondents attached to the command, writing in 1890 after the Fort had been vacated, the men were more than happy to quit the post:

"Fort Fetterman is now abandoned. It was a hateful post—in summer, hell; and in winter, Spitzbergen. The whole army dreaded being quartered there, but all had to take their turn. Its abandonment was a wise proceeding on the part of the government."

There had been little to amuse Crook's men at the post with the exception of the *Hog Pasture*, a rip-snorting, bawdy saloon and dance hall located across the river a mile to the north. Far from their homes where wives and sweethearts waited, his men had found macabre romance in the arms of the raucous-voiced lusty girls who, too old, too degraded for elsewhere, had sought this last refuge in the west.

Fort Fetterman, built under the supervision of Major William McE. Dye of the 4th U.S. Infantry, was to be abandoned shortly as a military post. All that remains today of that historic garrison are several buildings, including a large log structure, one of the officers' quarters, on the extreme south portion of the post. An adobe building, used for Ordnance, later as a guard house, is enclosed by a wooden barn. At the edge of the plateau just south of the river are the wall remains of a small stone water storage tank with the end of pipe leading up from the river. Other foundation remains, broken pieces of bottles, iron stoves, nails and spikes made by blacksmiths have stood the ravages of time.

Southeast of the fort was the cemetery, now the picture of desolation. The bodies of soldiers buried there were removed to the National Cemetery in Washington, D. C.,[9] but weather-beaten headboards with printing long-since obliterated, mark the remains of civilians who were unable to survive those rugged surroundings. Beyond the south side of the cemetery are three Indian burials with rocks marking the outlines of the graves.

In surveying the fort site, it is difficult to believe that this stretch of barren waste and desolation was the scene of teeming activity that May day in 1876 when Crook moved out his column toward that ill-fated battle.[10]

Though Crook was seemingly cold, undemonstrative, the stigma of having been bested by Crazy Horse and his savage horde had stung his pride. The censure rankled deep. Determined to avenge the Powder River defeat, Crook meant to devastate the village of Crazy Horse. Plans of his own had formulated in his mind, though he was not the man to talk. He had the reputation of being very reserved, uncommunicative and withdrawn. An Indian chief described him once as being more Indian-like than the Indians themselves. His officers knew him as a man unaffected by privation or vicissitude. His aide, Lt. John G. Bourke, in an 1890 *Century* article, said of him:

"He was, at that period of life, fond of taking his rifle and wandering off on his trusty mule alone in the mountains at sunset, he would picket his animal to a mesquite bush near grass, make a little fire, cook some of the game he had killed, erect a small 'wind break' or brush and flat stones such as the Indians make, cut an armful of twigs for a bed wrap himself up in his blanket, and sleep till the first peep of dawn."

In personal appearance, Crook was impressive. He was six feet in height, broad shouldered, and straight as an arrow. Despite his blue gray eyes and quick penetrating glance, he was as plain as an old stick, and looked, as Bourke described him, "more like an honest country squire than the commander of a warlike expedition."

A graduate of West Point in the class of 1852 and a famed Civil War cavalry leader, Crook had the reputation of being one of the foremost Indian fighters.[11] Yet he was to find before the end of that disastrous campaign that the Sioux and Northern Cheyenne were better fighters than any he had met and the best cavalrymen in the world. The Northern Cheyenne warriors from Nebraska were repaying the debt they owed for help rendered by the Sioux when in 1868 they opposed the building of the Union Pacific Railroad through their territory.

The command that followed Crook northward on the old Bozeman Road consisted of 10 troops from the 3rd Cavalry, 5 troops from the 2nd Cavalry, 2 companies from the 4th Infantry and 3 companies from the 9th Infantry, comprising an army of 47 officers and 1002 men.[12] Many were seasoned Civil

War veterans but there "was a great ratio of recruits in the command."[13] This force was officially designated as "Big Horn and Yellowstone Expedition."

Uneasy at the persistent reports that all able bodied male Indians had left the Red Cloud Agency, Crook was handicapped by lack of means of communication with General Gibbon and General Terry. Swarming with hostile Indians as the intervening country was, couriers could not get through.

The distance on the Rosebud River where Custer was to turn westward over the divide to the Little Big Horn is only twenty miles north of the Rosebud battlefield. But Custer was not to hear in time of Crook's defeat. Custer was to meet the full force of the combined Indian tribes thirty miles northwest of the "big bend" on June 25, where he and all his command would be killed.

What might have occurred had General Crook been able to defeat the Indians at the Rosebud? History would read differently today had he been able to maintain his position and complete his role in the pincers movement. Without doubt, the disaster at the Little Big Horn would have been averted.

Chapter 2

THE MARCH TO GOOSE CREEK

CROOK left Fort Fetterman with the promise of a contingent of Crow warriors to come to his aid but with an ominous warning from Crazy Horse not to cross the Tongue River. Yet his hopes were high. A spirit of adventure had also seized his troops. As they left the hated post for a campaign against the Sioux, excitement soared among them. After an endless wait, the actual start of the march was thrilling. Lt. Bourke describes the spectacle in his *Diary,* May 29:

"The long black line of mounted men stretched for more than a mile with nothing to break the sombreness of color save the flashing of the sun's rays back from the arms of the men. A long moving stretch of white told us our wagons were already well under way and a puff of dust just in front indicated the line of march of the infantry battalions. After moving NW for eleven or twelve miles camp was made on Sage Creek . . . At a late hour, we served supper and then gave some time to an examination of the mail which had overtaken us from the post."

Bourke goes on to state the list of companies and officers serving with the expedition:

"1. The undersigned assumes command of the troops comprising the Big Horn and Yellowstone Expedition.

"II. Lieut. Col. W. B. Royall, 3rd Cavalry, will command the Cavalry of the expedition.

"III. Major Alex Chambers,[1] 4th Inf. will command the Battalion composed of 4th and 9th Infantry.

"IV. Major A. H. Evans, 3rd Cavalry, is assigned to the command of the Battalion composed of Companies of the 3rd Cavalry, reporting to Colonel Royall.

"V. Capt. H. E. Noyes,[2] 2nd Cavalry is assigned to the command of the Companies of 2nd Cavalry, reporting to Colonel Royall.

"VI. The following named officers will compose the staff of the Expedition:

Captain A. H. Nickerson, 23rd Inf. A.D.C. ADG.

Lieut. John G. Bourke, 3rd Cavalry, A.D.C.

Captain Geo. M. Randall,[3] 23rd Inf. Chief of Scouts.
Capt. W. S. Stanton,[4] Eng. Corps. Chief Eng. Officer.
Capt. J. V. Furey,[5] AGM, Chief QM.
Lieut. J. W. Bubb,[6] 4th Inf. Act. Comm. Subsistence.
Asst. Surgeon Albert Hartsuff,[7] Med. Director.

Company A	3rd Cavalry.		Lt. Morton.
„ B	„	„	Capt. Meinhold, Lt. Simpson.
„ C	„	„	Capt. Van Vliet, Lt. Von Leuttwitz.
„ D	„	„	Capt. Henry, Lt. Robinson.
„ E	„	„	Capt. Sutorius.
„ F	„	„	Lt. B. Reynolds.
„ G	„	„	Lt. Crawford.
„ I	„	„	Capt. Andrews, Lt. Foster, Lt. A. King.
„ L	„	„	Capt. P. D. Vroom, Lt. Chase.
„ M	„	„	Capt. Anson Mills, Lt. A. C. Paul, Lt. Schwatka.
Company A	2nd Cavalry.		Dewees. Lt. Peirson.
„ B	„	„	Rawolle (Lt)
„ E	„	„	Capt. Wells. Lt. Sibley.
„ F	„	„	Capt. Noyes.
„ G	„	„	Swigert. Huntington.
Company C	9th Infantry.		Capt. Sam Munson. 1st Lt. Capron.
„ H	„	„	Capt. A. S. Burt. 2nd Lieut. Robertson.
„ G	„	„	Capt. T. B. Burrowes, 1st Lt. W. L. Carpenter.
Company D	4th Infantry.		Capt. A. B. Cain. 1st Lt. Henry Seton.
„ F	„	„	Capt. Gerhard Luhn.

Surgeons Patzki, Stevens, (McGillicuddy), & Powell. Charles Russell and Thomas Moore. Masters of Transportation. Frank Gruard, Louis Richaud,[8] and Big Bat,[9] Guides. Joseph Wasson,[10] R. E. Strahorn,[11] J. Finerty, W. C. McMillan,[12] and R. B. Davenport,[13] Reporters for Public Press."

Bourke, one of Crook's aides-de-camp, was himself a veteran campaigner, having served with Crook in the Indian wars in the southwest. A private with the Pennsylvania Cavalry during the Civil War, Bourke had been appointed to West Point at its conclusion and graduated in the class of 1869. In his *Diary* he kept a daily detailed description of events, as the following excerpts show:

"*May 30th.* Two companies of Cavalry under Captain Meinhold,[14] 3rd Cavalry, sent forward this morning to find a better road and a better ford across Powder River than the one followed by last expedition. Frank Gruard, our guide accompanied them. Command moved twenty miles to the South Cheyenne River, a shriveled stream of muddy and alkaline water standing in pools.

"*May 31st.* Moved 20 miles NW to N Fork of Wind River, a confluent of the South Cheyenne, during day. This day's march was very monotonous: day very cold and bleak. All the officers and men wrapped in overcoats. A man was brought in from Meinhold's command accidentally wounded in thigh (gunshot).

"*June 1st.* A cold miserable day; heavy clouds laden with rain hanging over us; snow and sleet falling during the morning. Road pursued today follows along a back bone between ravines and gulches, running down towards the 'Dry Fork of the Powder River.' Country very broken and destitute of timber, except in the 'brakes' where a few scrub juniper trees can be found secreted. Distance marched today 21½ miles in a direction generally NW., but extremely tortuous. Grass improving in quality. Passed to the South and West of the Pumpkin Buttes, four in number, some 15 or 20 miles distant . . .

"At this camp found wood, water and grass in plenty and were rejoined by Meinhold's command returning unsuccessfully from a search after a new road to Reno. A party of (65) sixty five miners, travelling from Montana to the Deadwood District in the Black Hills, left an inscription on a board stating they had camped here on the 27th. Van Vliet's[15] command had been here on the 29th."

Sleet or sunshine made little difference to seasoned trooper Crook. His old battered hat awry, coat flapping, he weathered wind or rain. He was notorious throughout the Army for his inattention to personal appearance. In later years one officer said that the only time he ever saw General Crook dressed in full uniform was in his coffin. As a matter of fact, his aide John G. Bourke was little better. Both men were described by Captain Charles King, 5th Cavalry:

"This utterly unpretending party—this undeniably shabby looking man in a private soldier's light blue overcoat, standing ankle deep in mud in a far-gone pair of soldier's boots, crowned with a most shocking bad hat, is Brig. Gen. George Crook, of the United States Army. . . . Bourke, the senior aide and Adjutant General of the expedition, is picturesquely gotten up in an old shooting coat, an utterly indescribable pair of trousers, and a crown without a thatch."[16]

As the command approached Fort Reno, a woman known as "Calamity Jane" was found dressed like a man and driving a team in the wagon train. When first discovered, she claimed to know Captain Anson Mills, much to his embarrassment.

"In organizing the wagon train at Fort Fetterman," writes Mills in *My Story*, "the wagonmaster had unintentionally employed a female teamster, but she was not discovered until we neared Fort Reno, when she was suddenly arrested, and placed in improvised female attire under guard. I knew nothing of this, but being the senior Captain of Cavalry, having served as a Captain for sixteen years, and being of an inquisitive turn of mind, I had become somewhat notorious (for better or for worse).

"The day she was discovered and placed under guard, unconscious of the fact, I was going through the wagon-master's outfit when she sprang up, calling out 'There is Colonel Mills, he knows me,' when everybody began to laugh, much to my astonishment and chagrin, being married.

"It was not many hours until every man in the camp knew of the professed familiarity of 'Calamity Jane' (as she was known) with me, and for several days my particular friends pulled me aside, and asked me 'who is Calamity Jane?' I, of course, denied any knowledge of her or her calling, but no one believed me then, and I doubt very much whether they all do yet.

"We carried her along until a force was organized to carry our helpless back, with which she was sent, but she afterwards turned out to be a national character, and was a woman of no mean ability and force even from the standard of men. I learned later that she had been a resident of North Platte, and that she knew many of my soldiers, some of whom had probably betrayed her. Later she had employed herself as a cook for my next door neighbor, Lieutenant Johnson, and had seen me often in his house, I presume."

Calamity Jane was kept at the supply camp during the Rosebud battle and was returned to Fort Fetterman with the wagon train several days after the battle. She later became quite a notorious frontier character.

The weather was to be as uncertain as events. Both were unpredictable. Yet Crook continued his drive into hostile territory. Following the Bozeman Road in a northwesterly direction, he reached the site of old Fort Reno on the Powder River, about ten miles northeast of the present town of Sussex, Wyoming. Lt. Bourke mentions this in his *Diary:*

"*June 2.* Road followed down the Dry Fork of Powder River, 7½ miles to old Fort Reno, and was generally good and of easy grade. Found Powder River low, not more than two feet deep and one hundred feet wide. Had no trouble crossing."

General Crook was to greet Van Vliet's command here but not his Crow allies. The assistance of the Crows would equal the strength of another regiment, and he was unable to account for their delay. Consequently, he made camp on the site of the abandoned fort and sent out to the west his three scouts, Frank Gruard, "Big Bat" and Louis Richaud to locate the Crows and bring them in.

While there, Lt. Bourke investigated the desolated garrison, once active in the war with the Sioux.

"This afternoon, in company with Mr. Davenport of the NY Herald and Mr. Jos. Wasson of the NY Tribune and Alta, California, visited the ruins of old Fort Reno. We first wended our way to the cemetery, a lonesome spot on the brow of a squatty bluff overlooking the valley of the Powder. It would be hard to compress within the limits of a note book, an adequate description of the utter desolation now prevailing in this Sacred Field, or to analyze the emotions to which the sight gave rise. Not a head board remained in place, not a paling of the fence which once surrounded the tombs was now in position: a rude cenotaph of brick masonry, erected by the loving hands of the former garrison to commemorate comrades who had fallen in the war with the Sioux, lay dismantled, a heap of rubbish at the entrance.[17] A line of graves covered with rough boulders held the remains of the brave who in the dark days of 1866 and '67 gave up their lives to protect the emigrants and freighters traveling to Montana. A few feet beyond these, a promiscuous heap of boards held inscribed the names of some at least whom the graves had sheltered. Curiosity impelled me to attempt a transcription from those upon which the inscription were still legible:

No. 12

Private C. Slagle, Co. F. 27th Inf. Killed May 30th-67.

Clure	8	No. 10
Killed	C. Riley	L. T. Morner
Mar 27,	7th Inf.	27th Inf.
'67	Killed	Mar. 31
	By Indians	'67
	27, '67	

"From the beams, stones, bricks, and old iron of the (fort) ruins, the party of Montana miners[18] who passed here a few days ago, had hastily improvised a number of lunettes and redoubts to check any attack the Sioux might make. As we looked down from this desolate solitude where the wary pickets secreted behind the tombs and chimneys afforded the only sign of animation, we saw outspread before us the well ordered camp of the command and the bustling air of readiness visible in everything, the thought would rise in my mind that perhaps the year 1876 would witness the revenge of the horrible scenes of 1866 and '67 and the humiliation of the savages who had participated in the slaughter of our feeble garrisons."

There is nothing left today of the buildings of the Fort, nothing to mark their location except a few sunken places where the Fort bastions had been. Bodies of the soldiers buried here have been removed to the Custer National Cemetery near the Crow Agency, Montana.

Crook did not linger here. His desire to locate Crazy Horse's village spurred him to activity. He ordered his column on the march again, still following the Bozeman Road, to make camp that night at Clear Creek. In his book, *On the Border With Crook*, Bourke entertainingly describes the site:

"Clear Creek, upon which we made camp, was a beautiful stream, fifty feet wide, two feet deep; current rapid and as much as eight miles an hour; water icy cold from the melting of the snow banks on the Big Horn . . . Birds, antelope, and fish began to figure on the mess canvas; the fish, a variety of sucker, very palatable, were secured by shooting a bullet under them and stunning them, so that they rose to the surface, and were then seized . . .

"Here we were visited by messengers from a party of Montana miners who were traveling across country from the Black Hills back to the Yellowstone; the party numbered sixty five, and had to use every precaution to prevent stampede and surprise; every night they dug rifle-pits, and surrounded themselves with rocks, palisades, or anything else that could be made to resist a charge from the Sioux, whose trails were becoming very thick and plenty.

"To prevent any stampede of our stock which might be attempted, our method of establishing pickets became especially rigid; in addition to the mounted vedettes encircling bivouac, and occupying commanding buttes and bluffs, solid companies were thrown out a mile or two in advance and kept mounted, with the purpose of holding in check all parties of the enemy which might attempt to rush down upon the herds and frighten them off by waving blankets, yelling, firing guns or other tricks in which the savages are adepts."

On June 5th the command reached the site of old Fort Kearney and camped along the Big Piney east of the fort. Near the hill five miles north of Fort Kearney, where Captain Fetterman had been killed with all his command, Crook left the Bozeman Road and turned to the northeast and followed down Prairie Dog Creek, arriving at its confluence with the Tongue River on June 7th.

General Crook intended to follow down Little Goose Creek to its juncture with Big Goose Creek, but instead swung his command eastward over the small divide to the next valley and followed it northeasterly, believing it to be Little Goose Creek. It took two days to march to the mouth of this stream where permanent camp was made. The mistake however was not discovered until the command unexpectedly arrived at the Tongue River. This error appears in Bourke's *Diary*:

"*June 6*. Our camp tonight is on a tributary of Goose Creek. (We afterwards discovered that we had reached Prairie Dog Creek at its junction with Tongue River), one of the head waters of the Tongue River, 17¾ miles from the site of our last night's bivouac. Owing to the sultriness of the day and the bad road running over steep grades, this march has told upon both men and animals."

In *On The Border With Crook*, Bourke describes activities in camp:

"On the 7th of June we buried the soldier of Meinhold's Company who had accidentally wounded himself with his revolver while chopping wood. Besides the escort prescribed by the regulations, the funeral cortege was swollen by additions from all the companies of the expedition, the pack train, wagoners, officers, and others reaching an aggregate of over six hundred. Colonel Guy V. Henry,[19] Third Cavalry, read in a very feeling manner the burial services from the "Book of Common Prayer," and as cavalry trumpets sounded taps, a handfull of earth was thrown down upon the remains, the grave was rapidly filled up, and the companies at quick step returned to their tents."

Late on the night of June 7th, shouting by an unknown

Indian on the bluff to the north across the river caused General Crook to send Ben Arnold, a courier, down to the river to find out what the excitement was all about. With Louis Richaud, the Sioux interpreter and "Big Bat," the Crow interpreter gone, Arnold was the only man in camp having any understanding of either language. Arnold, befuddled with sleep, answered the Indian *in the Sioux language,* and the Indian fled. General Crook was very angry, fearing that the Indian was a runner from the long-expected Crows.[20]

Crook needed the Crows to scout for him. Though rumor said Crazy Horse and his forces were somewhere west of the Rosebud River, he did not know where Crazy Horse was. And he did not want Crazy Horse to know where he was. But as he viewed his well-equipped large command, a feeling of confidence filled him. He could whip Crazy Horse or any other Indian. Surprise was the element he sought, and what he was sure he would have. However, Crook was shortly to be disillusioned as Bourke reported:

"*June 9, 1876,* the monotony of camp life was agreeably broken by an attack upon our lines made in a most energetic manner by the Sioux and Cheyennes. We had reached a most picturesque and charming camp on the beautiful Tongue River, and had thrown out our pickets upon the hill tops, when suddenly the pickets began to show signs of uneasiness, and to first walk and then trot their horses around in a circle, a warning that they had seen something dangerous. The Indians did not wait for a moment, but moved up in good style, driving in our pickets and taking position in the rocks, from which they rained down a severe fire which did no great damage but was extremely annoying while it lasted.

"We had only two men wounded, one in the leg, another in the arm, both by glancing bullets, and neither wound dangerous,[21] and three horses and two mules wounded, most of which died.[22] The attacking party had made the mistake of aiming at the tents, which at the moment were unoccupied; but bullets ripped through the canvas, split the ridge poles, smashed the pipes of the Sibley stoves, and imbedded themselves in the tail boards of the wagons. But, Munson,[23] and Burrowes[24] were ordered out with their rifles,[25] and Mills was ordered to take his own company of the Third Cavalry and those of Sutorius, Andrews,[26] and Lawson,[27] from Royall's command, and go across the Tongue and drive (away) the enemy which they did."[28]

"They Got Out Of The Way With Much Celerity"

John F. Finerty, correspondent for the Chicago *Times,* was attached to Company E of the 3rd Cavalry, Captain Mills' battalion. Known as the "Fighting Irish Pencil Pusher," he tells of accompanying Mills to the bluffs in his book, *Warpath and Bivouac:*

"A young staff-officer, excited and breathless, rode into the camp of the Ist Battalion of the 3rd Cavalry.

" 'Colonel Mills! Colonel Mills!' he shouted.

" 'Here, sir,' replied the commander of the battalion.

" 'General Crook desires that you mount your men instantly, Colonel, cross the river, and clear those bluffs of the Indians.'

" 'All right,' said Col. Mills, and he gave the order.

"All at once the four companies of our battalion-A, Lieutenant Lawson; E, Captain Sutorius;[29] Captain Andrews and Lieutenant Foster;[30] and M, Lieutenants Paul[31] and Schwatka,[32] were in the saddle.

" 'Forward!' shouted the Colonel, and forward we went.

"A company of the 2d Cavalry was extended among the timber on the left, to cover the attack upon the bluffs. In a minute our charging companies were half wading, half swimming, through Tongue River, which is swift and broad at that point. The musketry continued to rattle and the balls to whiz as we crossed. Partially screened by cotton-wood trees in the bottom-land, we escaped unhurt. In another minute we had gained the base of the bluffs, when we were ordered to halt and dismount, every eighth man holding the horses of the rest. Then we commenced to climb the rocks, under a scattering fire from our friends, the Sioux. The bluffs were steep and slippery, and took quite a time to surmount. Company A had the extreme right; M, the right center; E, the left center, and I, the extreme left.

"We reached the plateau almost simultaneously. The plain extended about 1000 yards north and east, at which distance there arose a ridge, and behind that, at perhaps the same distance, another ridge. We could see our late assailants scampering like deer, their fleet ponies carrying them as fast as the wind up the first ascent, where they turned and fired. Our whole line replied, and the boys rushed forward with a yell. The Sioux gave us another salute, the balls going about 100 feet above our heads, and skedaddled to the bluff further back. There, nothing less than a long-range cannon could reach them, and we could pursue them no farther, as the place was all rocks and ravines, in which the advantage lay with the red warriors. . . .

"To say the truth, they did not seem very badly scared, although they got out of the way with much celerity when they saw us coming in force. Our firing having completely ceased, we could hear other firing on the south side of the river, far to the left, where the 2nd Cavalry had their pickets. This, we subsequently learned, was caused by a daring attempt made by the Indians to cross a ford at that point and take the camp in rear, with the object of driving off the herd.[33]

"After the Indians retired, Mills' men were withdrawn to camp, and the bluff was garrisoned by Captain Rawolle's[34] company of the 2nd Cavalry, who had a most miserable experience, as they did not bring their tents to the other side and had to endure in the open a pitiless rainfall all through the night."

The troops enjoyed the excitement of the attack, believing it to be a bluff of Crazy Horse's to drive them away. In fact, the men regarded the whole expedition as something of a picnic, despite a large number on sick call.[35] Crook, however, remembered Crazy Horse's warning that if he crossed the Tongue River he would be attacked. His confidence temporarily shaken, Crook must have reviewed with misgivings his campaign thus far. His three scouts had been gone over ten days. Nothing had been heard from the Crow allies. He had blundered down the wrong valley and gone on a needless wide detour to the east. Crazy Horse knew now of his presence; the chance of surprising him was slim, indeed. And he had received no word from Gibbon or Terry, with whom he was to cooperate in the pincers movement.

However, there was prospect of other aid. On the eighth of June he had received word that the Fifth Cavalry had been ordered up from Kansas to take post in his rear. The sixty-five miners had attached themselves to his command. In addition, one hundred and twenty Shoshone warriors were crossing the mountains from their reservation in the Wind River Range in the Rockies to join him. Geared for battle against their hated Sioux enemies, the Shoshones were expected any day.

In defiance of Crazy Horse, Crook moved his command to the confluence of the two forks of Goose Creek—on a branch of Tongue River—to wait for what the morrow would bring.

Chapter 3

THE ARRIVAL OF THE CROW AND SHOSHONE ALLIES

H E would wait; but he would not wait too long. He might miss the Sioux, and the honor of defeating the hostiles. He might miss the converging columns, Terry, Gibbon, Custer. He might run short of rations and ammunition. His 1800 mules had grass now, but it would not last. Besides, somewhere beyond that inverted V made by the junction of Big Goose Creek[1] and Little Goose Creek[2] where sprawled his camp, lay the village of Crazy Horse. Where were his scouts?

After days of anxiety for himself and his men, Crook was soon to learn. Lt. Bourke, his friend, wrote in his *Diary* of their arrival:

"*June 14th.* Great joy was diffused through camp when Frank Gruard and Louis Richaud came back this afternoon, bringing with them an old Crow Indian. They reported to General Crook that they had proceeded on their journey as far as the site of old Fort C. F. Smith, on the Big Horn River. On the other side, discerned a camp of many lodges, but were not assured of their identity as Sioux or Crow. Rested at that point a short while, making dinner and giving feed to animals. The smoke from their fire probably attracted the attention of the Indians who galloped out in great numbers across the broad plain stretching along the other side of the river, boldly swam its torrent and charged up the acclivity after our messengers, one of whom narrowly escaped a bullet from one of the Crows.

"Our men followed the Crows to their town, found to consist of two hundred and odd lodges. At the beginning, difficulty was experienced in persuading the Crows to let a detachment of their young warriors join General Crook. Their chiefs alleged many reasons. Their families were starving and they wanted to get them meat. The buffalo was in the vicinity and they could not lose the opportunity of a big hunt. They were afraid we wouldn't stay out to fight the Sioux or that we might remain out longer than the summer. Much palavering followed, our

20

guides neglecting no persuasion to induce them to agree to come. They appeared suspicious of some plot at first, but finally consented to send a band of (175) One hundred and Seventy-Five picked warriors to aid us as scouts and spies."

Disappointed that his scouts had returned with but one Indian, an old chief, Crook demanded the reason and learned the cause. When the warriors crossed Tongue River and found Crook gone from Prairie Dog Creek camp, they thought he had abandoned the campaign. Also, the night of June 7, when Ben Arnold answered *in Sioux* the shouting Indian from the bluff, he had frightened away a Crow scouting party. Big Bat was bringing in a party of fifteen or sixteen, but the rest of the Crow warriors were too suspicious of a plot to follow.

Immediately General Crook directed Major Andy S. Burt[4] to go after the Crows, taking Louis Richaud and the chief, and endeavor to bring them in.

Lt. Bourke reported the outcome of the affair:

"The mission of Major Burt was a perfect success. Before dusk he was with us again, this time riding at the head of a long line of savage retainers, whose grotesque headdresses, variegated colored garments, wild little ponies and warlike accouterments, made up a quaint and curious spectacle. While the main column halted just inside our camp, the three chiefs, Old Crow, Medicine Crow and Good Heart were presented to General Crook. . . ."

Mrs. Tom La Forge, a Crow woman raised by Chief Old Crow, told F. H. Sinclair of Sheridan, Wyoming, that the old chief pointed out to her the spot where Crook formed his 15 troops of cavalry and five companies of infantry in regimental front to greet the Crows, on a flat now covered by the north end of Sheridan.[5]

It was natural that General Crook would use the flat just north of camp for a parade ground, all other sides being bluffs. "Mounted at 'close order' troopers are touching stirrup to stirrup or a distance of about 5 feet from horses' heads in a troop front," wrote Lt. Col. E. S. Luce, 7th Cavalry, U. S. Army, retired.[6] With the cavalry front occupying about 4000 feet, exclusive of troop intervals, and the infantry in double line taking up 300 feet, the regimental front was close to a mile in length, an imposing sight.

The activities of the Crows were described by Lt. Bourke:

"Our newly arrived allies bivouacked in our midst, sending their herd of ponies out to graze alongside of our own horses. The entire band numbered one hundred and seventy-six, as near as we could ascertain. Each Indian had two ponies. The first thing to be done was to erect their war lodges of saplings, covered over with blankets and shreds of canvas. Fires were next built and a feast made ready of the supplies of coffee, sugar and hardtack, dealt out from our Commissary Train. These are the prime luxuries of an Indian's life. A curious band of lookers-on, officers, soldiers and teamsters, congregated around the little squad of Crows, watching with eager attention their every movement. The Indians seemed proud of the distinguished position they occupied in popular estimation and were soon on terms of easy familiarity with our soldiers, some of whom can talk a few words of Crow and others a little of the 'sign language.'

"In stature, complexion, dress and general demeanor, a marked contrast was observed between our friends and the Sioux Indians-contrast decidedly to the advantage of the former. The Absaraka or Crow Indians, perhaps as a consequence of their residence along the elevated banks and in cool, fresh mountain ranges between the Big Horn River and the Yellowstone, are somewhat fairer than the other Indians about them. They are all above medium height, not a few being quite tall and many have a noble expression of countenance. The dress of the members of the tribe consists of shirt of flannel, cotton or buckskin; breech-clout, leggings of blanket, moccasins of Deer, Elk, or Buffalo hide, coat of bright colored blanket, made with sleeves and hood and a head-dress fashioned in divers shapes, but most frequently formed from an old black army hat, with top cut out and sides bound round with feathers, fur and scarlet cloth.

"Their arms were all breech loaders, throwing metallic cartridges, most of them Caliber .50, with an occasional .45. Lances, medicine poles and tomahawks figured in the procession. The Tomahawks, made of long knives inserted in shafts or handles of wood or horn, were most murderous weapons. Accompanying these Indians were a few little boys, none of them over 15 years old: their business will be to hold horses and other unimportant work while their elders conduct the dangerous operations of the campaign."

Crook, as disheveled as ever, good humoredly watched these gaudy, barbaric activities. Display, ostentation—whether personal or otherwise—meant little to him, as Henry R. Daly recorded in "The Warpath," *American Legion Monthly*:

"In a populous place General Crook would have worn the regulation uniform, but it probably would have needed pressing. A battered slouch hat would have been carelessly thrust on his head and his boots would have been dusty. In the field, except that everybody knew him, General Crook might have been taken for a Montana miner. The only part of his uniform he wore was an old overcoat. Except in wet weather he wore moccasins, and his light bushy beard would be gathered in a series of braids. He was a silent man, but good natured and philosophically humorous. I have seen him walk up to a cook fire, where the troops were getting their coffee, take his turn for a cup, and then walk away and sit down on the ground and blow it off and drink it without saying a word."

If Crook was a man of action rather than words, he yet gave ear to the thoughts of his men. In an 1890 *Century* article, Bourke explained that:

"He was at all times accessible to the humblest soldier or the poorest 'prospector' without ever losing a certain dignity which repelled familiarity but had no semblance of haughtiness."

Unknown to General Crook, the Shoshone warriors under Washakie, had reached Fort Bridger, where they had assembled with a few Utes, preparing to join him. Among the spectators who saw them line up near Sutler's store was a correspondent of the Salt Lake Herald:

"In advance of the party was a swarthy temporary chief, his face covered with vertical white streaks that made him look like---. In his right hand, hanging to the end of a window blind rod, were the two fingers of a dead Sioux, another rod had a white flag nailed to it—a precaution necessary to preserve them from being fired upon in proceeding to the seat of war. The faces of the rest had on a plentiful supply of war paint. Once in line they struck up a peculiar grunting sound on a scale of about five notes. Some persons might call it singing, but all such must have the tinpanum of their ears out of joint. One of the braves, afflicted with a malady peculiar to the Caucasian race, began to brag what he'd do when he got to the seat of war, and winding up in broken English, 'Me little mad now; bime by me heap mad.' Old Washakie, their chief, wants to die in battle and not in bed!"[7]

Old Washakie, still anxious to fight the Sioux, shortly greeted Crook, himself. And Crook, in a magnanimous gesture, turned out a second regimental formation in his honor. Stationed at headquarters, Lt. Bourke was in a good position to see and hear everything when the new allies joined the command.

"Resplendent In All The Fantastic Adornments"

"A long line of glittering lances and brightly polished weapons of fire announced the anxiously expected advent of our other allies, the Sho-Sho-Nees, or Snakes, who to the number of (86) Eighty-Six came galloping rapidly up to Hqrs., and came left front into line in splendid style. No trained soldiers ever executed the evolution more prettily. Exclamations of praise and wonder greeted the barbaric array of these fierce warriors, warmly welcomed by their former enemies, but now strong friends, the Crows. General Crook came out to review their line of battle resplendent in all the fantastic adornments of feathers, beads, brass buttons, bells, scarlet cloth and flashing lances. The Shoshones were not slow to perceive the favorable impression made and when the time came for them to file off by the right, moved with the precision of clock-work and the pride of veterans. A Grand council was the next feature of the evening's entertainment . . .

"Around a huge fire of crackling boughs, the officers of the command ranged themselves in two rows, the interest and curiosity depicted upon their countenances acting as a foil to the stolidity and imperturbable calmness of the Indians squatted upon the ground on the other side. The breeze blowing the smoke aside would occasionally enable the flames to bring out in bold and sudden relief from the intense blackness of the night, the sepulchral whiteness of the tents and wagon-sheets, the blue coats of the officers and soldiers (who thronged among the wagons behind their superiors). The red, white, yellow and black banded blankets of the savages, whose aquiline features and glittering eyes had become still more aquiline and still more glittering, and the small group in the center of the circle, composed of General Crook, Captain Nickerson, the interpreters, Frank, Louis and Bat, and the Indian Chiefs. One quadrant was reserved for the Shoshones, another for the Crows. Each tribe selected one spokesman who repeated aloud to his people the words of the General as they were made known to him by the interpreter. Ejaculations of "Ugh! Ugh!" from the lips of the Chiefs were the only signs of interest betrayed upon their faces, thus it was easy enough to see nothing was lost that was addressed to them. Pipes, of same kind as those the Sioux have, were kept in industrious circulation . . .

"The Crows and Snakes showed a great eagerness to commence the campaign which they hoped would break the spirit of their hereditary and cruel enemies, the Sioux. They asked however, the privilege of scouting in their own way, a privilege

General Crook very willingly conceded, confident that nothing would be lost by so doing. . . .

"The council ended at 10:20 P. M., General Crook shaking hands with the more prominent chiefs as they passed. The supposition was these tired Indians would without delay retire to rest. Their day's ride had been over 60 miles in length and the night was already far advanced. The erroneousness of this assumption was disclosed very speedily. A long series of monstrous howls, shrieks, groans and nasal yells, emphasized by a perfectly ear-piercing succession of thumps upon drums improvised from 'parflech,' (dried buffalo skins) attracted nearly all our soldiers and many of our officers not on duty, to the allied camps. Peeping into the different tepees was much like peeping through a key hole to Hell. Crouched around little fires, not affording as much light as an ordinary tallow candle, the swarthy figures of the naked and half naked Indians were visible, moving and chanting in unison with some leader. No words were distinguishable; the ceremony partook of the nature of an abominable incantation and as far as I could judge had a semi-religious character."

"Crook Was Bristling For a Fight"

Before the evening was over Crook had outlined his plans to move the morning of the 16th to the allies and troops. The morale of the troops had previously been high; but when the Indian allies came into camp with such an imposing array of strength, there was a feeling of invincibility. Enthusiasm reached a high level. "They are numerous as grass," Finerty said, "was the definite Crow manner of stating the strength of the enemy," yet Crook's men, in jovial mood christened the Goose Creek camp, which was on a branch of Tongue River, Camp Cloud Peak—after two snow-capped peaks of the nearby Big Horn Mountains. And Crook, like Custer after him, became over-confident in his command and abilities. Though his words were characteristically soldierly, it was apparent to all, Finerty wrote, that "Crook was bristling for a fight."

"By Hook Or By Crook"

Captain Azor H. Nickerson,[8] 23rd Infantry, one of Crook's aides-de-camp wrote later of Crook's stringent requirements in a sketch entitled 'Major General George Crook and The Indians, the undated, unpublished manuscript of which is in the custody of the Army War College Library, Carlisle Barracks, Penna.

"Immediately upon the arrival of our Crow Allies," wrote Nickerson, "Crook packed his wagons in such a manner that they could easily be defended by the teamsters and other citizen employees as were attached to the quartermaster's department; the quartermaster remaining with them, and in command of the whole, they were left behind. He then took all the mules belonging to the train, and mounted our infantry upon them. Our subsistence stores and surplus ammunition were carried by the pack train.[9]

"Officers and men alike were restricted to the same quantity of personal baggage, if one overcoat each can be so designated, for that was all any one was permitted to carry. No tents were taken, and neither wagons or ambulances. Besides the regular subsistence stores carried by the pack train, many of the officers, as well as the soldiers and newspapers correspondents, took the precaution to carry in their saddle pouches, or fastened to the saddle, by hook or by Crook, a good sized piece of dried elk meat, some hard bread, sugar, coffee[10] and at least one hundred rounds of ammunition, so that in the event of their being separated from the command, they could subsist for several days and offer reasonable defense, for capture meant slow, but positively certain death."

The orders had been terse and spare as Crook's speech. As the entertaining Bourke said, "the General meant business."

Shabby Crook may have lacked the theatrical qualities of the glamorously groomed Custer, but he was a man of action and iron determination. He had learned three things from his allies that day:

Gibbon was on the banks of the Rosebud near the Yellowstone, unable to cross for the Sioux were holding him at bay.

The main body of the Sioux were encamped on the Tongue River at the mouth of Otter Creek.

And the village of Crazy Horse was thought to be located on the Tongue River.[11]

He would strike at once without further delay.

Chapter 4

THE MARCH TO THE ROSEBUD

W HILE General Crook was determined to strike quickly against the hostiles, he was "particular in having his command in perfect shape" before ordering it on the march.

"I Never Saw So Much Fun in All My Life"

Crook had mounted the infantry upon mules so that it could move faster and keep up with the cavalry in the march ahead. Col. Chambers, his old friend, Major Burt, Captain Luhn,[1] and his other officers who had seen mounted service, went through the ordeal of breaking the infantry and animals to the saddle—to the number of 200. This proved as amusing to the men as it was to Crook, yet to Chambers' demurs, the General was adamant that the order be followed. His head scout, Frank Gruard, told of the mounting in *Life and Adventures of Frank Gruard*, written by Joe De Barthe:

"During my absence, General Crook had given an order to mount the infantry and the only animals available were the mules belonging to the wagon train. On the day following the arrival in camp of our Indian Allies (June 15) the work mules were turned over to the tender mercies of the infantrymen (or vice versa) and the first circus Goose Creek valley ever beheld began. Many of the infantry (Walk-a-heaps, as the Indians called them) had never been in a saddle in their lives, while none of the mules had ever had a saddle on their backs, and, under the supervision of experienced riders, the officers prepared to give the infantry a lesson in equestrianship.

"I never saw so much fun in all my life. The valley for a mile in every direction was filled with bucking mules, frightened infantrymen, broken saddles and applauding spectators. Having nothing else to do, the entire command took a half holiday to enjoy the sport, and some of the most ludicrous mishaps imaginable were witnessed. But the average soldier is as persevering as the mule is stubborn and in the end the mule was forced to surrender. The City of Sheridan is now located on the immense flat where this incident occurred and I never pass down the

27

streets of the place but what the memories of those ludicrous scenes are brought vividly to mind, and I laugh as heartily as I did on that bright June day in the memorable year of 1876."

Gruard himself was a colorful character, one of the controversial figures of the period. Tom Colsen, Sheridan, Wyoming, said Gruard told him that when he was captured by the Indians in the winter he had on a big coat made of bearskin and the Indians thought he was a bear. They named him "The Grabber," a term descriptive of the principal motions of a bear when fighting. Gruard's pedigree was a source of never-ending speculation. He had such dark complexion that he gave out the story that he was from the Sandwich Islands and became a mail carrier after coming to this country; that he was captured by the Sioux and lived in the villages of Sitting Bull and Crazy Horse for many years, but after some misunderstanding escaped to civilization.

However, Mrs. Nettie Goings a half breed Oglala, gave a different account of his origin at Pine Ridge Agency, March 13, 1907, which may be found in the *Ricker Interviews*, tablet 13, p. 107. Mrs. Goings says that:

"She and Frank Gruard are children of the same father by different mothers. The brother of Frank Gruard's mother was named 'Black Lodge Pole.' The name of her father and Frank's was John Brazeau. He was a French Creole. He was from St. Louis and worked for the American Fur Company. He came up and settled at Fort Pierre some twenty years; he and Popineau were companions and chums, and he was associated with the Pecots (Picottes).

"Mrs. Goings is the mother of Frank Goings, Agency interpreter at Pine Ridge. She says that Frank (Gruard) and three other boys were in school and the four got into difficulty and she says that there was something about a killing but she was young and does not know just how it was, etc.!! He got on a boat going up the river and the father boarded the same boat to bring him back, but did not succeed in doing so. His right christian name was 'Walter'—full name Walter Brazeau. His Indian name was 'Grabber.'

"Mrs. Goings 'Indian name is money.' Her father had money and she may have used money in a way to draw to herself that name. She does not doubt that he may have been in the family of Parley Platte in Salt Lake; she says that he told her that he lived in the family of some white man away off north or west, and he showed her the picture of this man. She says her family was acquainted with the Pratts in St. Louis. Choteau Pratt was killed at the Lower Brule Agency on the Missouri."

It appears from this that Gruard was the offspring of a French Creole father and an Oglala squaw. That Gruard was a mail carrier who took to scouting is attested to by William Garnett, *Ricker Interviews*, Tablet 1, Nebraska State Historical Society:

"Garnett is confident that Mrs. Goings at Pine Ridge is a sister of Gruard. Gruard came to Red Cloud in early spring of 1875 costumed in a G string. One of the Derres who were traders at Red Cloud said he knew Gruard as a mail carrier 4 or 5 years before in the Fort Peck country. He was a strongly built muscular man weighing over 200. He was not excessively sociable, and seemed somewhat shy at first, and it was several months before his nakedness was covered by the ordinary apparel of civilization and the first suit of such garments was provided by the generous purse of Ben Tibbits . . . He had worked around the agency for a little, and when the commissioners came out later in the season to begin negotiations for the Black Hills Gruard was one of the men who went as a guide. His familiarity with the country so recommended him that he had no difficulty in drifting right into the service."

Quiet, shy, naked; Gruard had the ways of an Indian. That he had lived among them is verified by Louis Bordeau in the *Ricker Interviews*, Tablet 11, p. 74, who says:

"Gruard was afraid of Crazy Horse after having lived among his band for years as a refuge from trouble on the Missouri where he killed . . . mail carriers and robbed the mail and carried letters into the Indian camp and read them to Crazy Horse, the contents describing information as to the whereabouts and movements of the soldiers in all of which the Indians were keenly interested."

Gruard's colorful account of the mule episode was only one of several humorous incidents of Crook's campaign. Finerty, the inveterate scribbler, described Crook's men as always ready for a laugh, in *Warpath and Bivouac*:

"The great mass of soldiers were young men, careless, courageous and eminently light hearted. The rank and file, as a majority were of either Irish or German birth or parentage, but there was also a fair sized contingent of what may be called Anglo-Americans, particularly among the noncommissioned officers. Taken as a whole, Crook's command was a fine organization, and its officers, four-fifths of whom were native Americans and West Pointers, were fully in sympathy with the ardor of their men."

All that day (June 15) every man in camp had been actively engaged in preparation for the big movement against Crazy Horse, leader of the Oglala Sioux. "Arms were cleaned,[2] horses reshod, haversacks and saddle bags filled." Crook was taking his pack train only so that he would be unhampered by impedimenta. He had directed Major John V. Furey, Quartermaster, to remain with the wagons and 100 men as guards, on an island strategically located near the junction of Big and Little Goose Creeks.[3] Crook told of his plans in his official report:

"The Crow Indians were under the impression that the hostile village was located on Tongue River[4] or some of its small tributaries and were quite positive we should be able to surprise it. While I hardly believed this to be possible as the Indians had hunting parties out who must necessarily become aware of the presence of the command, I considered it worth while to make the attempt. The Indians (ours) of course being expert in the matter I regulated movements entirely by their efforts to secure this end.

"I did not believe that any fight we could have would be decisive in its result, unless we secured their (the Sioux) village supposed to be in close proximity. I therefore made every effort to make a surprise attack on their village."

Failure, defeat, never entered his head. Nor did it weigh on his men. Secure in their might, the command rested, even if all did not sleep, satisfied that nothing could hamper the success of the movement of the morrow. Bourke summed up the situation confidently:

"No one now doubts we shall be victorious; the only discrepancy of opinion is in regard to the numbers we may find."

If Crook dreamed that night of the daring Oglala's war cry, he was to be awakened by warwhoops of another sort.

"It must have been soon after daybreak," wrote Nickerson, "that I was startled by a series of groans and cries as though the author was enduring excruciating torture. I jumped up, ran to the front of my tent, turned back the flap and peered out. Riding down through the camp, came an old Crow warrior, nearly as naked as when he was born, but painted and tattooed in approved form, and carrying his rifle which, from time to time, he swung in the air, as a drum major would handle his baton or staff. His wild eyes appeared to be fixed on objects, invisible to the outer world, and which he seemed to think were hovering about him, great tears rolled down his cheeks, as he pleaded, prayed and exhorted—the empty air. He was going through that species of savage incantation known as 'crying for scalps'."

Finerty, the correspondent, sleepily clutched his pen as the loud exhortations of the Crow and Shoshone medicine men went on, the morning of June 16, 1876.

"The harangues," he wrote, "lasted for nearly an hour, and then the Indians breakfasted to satiety on the government rations issued the previous day, because it is a rule with the savages never to miss a good opportunity of making a meal, especially when on the war path.

"The bugles of our command were silent, but, notwithstanding, everything worked like magic. Tents were abandoned to the quartermaster, and every man of the expedition, except the hundred detached, was in the saddle, having barely swallowed a tin full of black coffee and a hard tack, as the sun rose redly on the eastern horizon.

"Our course was north by west, and lay through a fine 'buffalo grass' region, on which signs of the bison were recent. The cavalry, fifteen companies of the 2nd and 3rd under Royall, Noyes, Henry, Mills and Van Vliet, led the van. Then followed the splendid mule pack train, commanded by Chief Packer Tom Moore,[5] as bold a frontiersman as ever looked at an enemy through the sight of his rifle; and, in rear, galled, but gallant, rode, on muleback, the 200 hardy infantry, under Col. Alex. Chambers and the brave Major Andy Burt. The Indians, with war bonnets nodding, and lances brilliant with steel and feathers, headed by their favorite chiefs, rode tumultuously, in careless order, filled with barbaric pride of arms, on our flanks. I felt a respect for the American Indian that day."

The breakdown of the command accompanying Crook is as follows:

Second Cavalry (Noyes' official report)	269
Mills' battalion 3rd Cavalry (Mills' official report) ..	207
Infantry (Bourke's account[6])	175
Royall's battalion 3rd Cavalry [7]	327
Shoshone Indians	86
Crow Indians	176
Packers	20
Montana Miners	65
	——
Total	1325

In addition, there were the guides, surgeons, executive officers, and an unspecified number of teamsters and volunteer civilian employees.

The equipment they carried was described by Dr. Thomas B. Marquis in the Hardin (Montana) *Tribune Herald*, January 20, 1933, from an interview with James Forrestell, a trooper in Troop D, Second Cavalry:

"The Springfield 1873 Model was our rifle equipment. It was a single shot cartridge gun, .45 caliber and using 50 grains of powder. It would shoot and kick hard, carrying up to 500 yards very well. The infantry had the same kind of gun, except their's had a longer barrel. Our form of the rifle was known as 'carbine,' theirs was known as the 'Long Tom.' Their gun would carry farther as it's cartridge held 70 grains of powder. The standard revolver equipment was the same all through. It was the Colt six shooter .45 caliber."

"Through a Country Green as Emerald"

Upon leaving Camp Cloud Peak, Crook forded Big Goose Creek and ordered his command north and a little west following approximately the present route of Highway 87 for six miles and fording the stream now called "Tongue River." With the Big Horn Mountains slowly receding, his column rode the plateau, paralleling the river, through "the finest game country in the world."

During the day, Crook's Chief of Scouts, Major Randall of the 23rd Infantry, while in advance, sighted a small herd of buffalo which "ran like the wind" as the column approached.

"There will be music in the air now, sure," remarked Captain Andrews to Sutorius. "Whenever you see buffalo, there, too, you will find Indians."[8]

In the meantime, the scouts had come to the conclusion that Crazy Horse's village was located in a canyon of the Rosebud River. While Crook hardly believed he could surprise the village, he still had hopes. The last thing he wanted therefore—the last thing he expected—was to have his usually dignified cavalcade turn into a rout. Yet fate was to play a part in Crook's campaign.

Buffalo!

"All at once we ascended to the crest of a grassy slope," Finerty wrote, "and then a sight burst upon us calculated to thrill the coldest heart in the command. Far as the eye could reach on both sides of our route the somber, superb buffalo were grazing in thousands. The earth was brown with them.

"'Steady men, keep your ranks!' was the command . . . as many of the younger soldiers . . . made a movement as if to break from the column in wild pursuit.

"Then arose on our right and left such a storm of discordant shouts as can only come from savage throats. The Crow warriors on the west, and the Shoshones on the east . . . dashed off like mounted maniacs, and made for the gigantic herd of bisons.

"Then rang out the crack of the rifle, the whoop and the yell of triumph, as buffalo after buffalo went down before the fire of those matchless horsemen and superb shots. The bison, for great, lumbering, hump backed, short headed creatures, ran like the wind, but the fleet Indian ponies soon brought their wild riders within range, and the work of destruction proceeded apace.

"The iron discipline of the army kept the soldiers in their ranks, but their glowing cheeks and kindling eyes proclaimed the feverish excitement the Nimrod passion that consumed them. For at least five and twenty miles this strange scene was continued, our dark mass of regulars and mules, moving at quick time through a country green as emerald."[9]

The General's eye, blazing with indignation, swept over this chaotic scene from time to time. Strict disciplinarian that he was, he had no patience with men, whether red or white, who stupidly exposed their heads to a rain of Sioux arrows; worse, to call attention of the cavalcade to some wandering scouts of Crazy Horse. Finerty spoke of his growing anger:

"General Crook, who desired to surprise the village of the Sioux, supposed to be situated in the canyon of the Rosebud, at the point near its northern debouch called 'Indian Paradise,' was annoyed by the conduct of his savage allies, which could not help alarming the wary foe with whom he had to contend; but nothing could check the Indians."[10]

With such a spectacle disturbing the sereneness of the countryside, it is little wonder that they were seen by sharp hostile eyes. Perturbed as he was, Crook mentions it but briefly in his official report:

"Marching from our camp on the South Fork of Tongue River or Goose Creek as sometimes called, towards the Yellowstone, on the end of the first day's march we came to a small stream near the divide that separates the waters of the Tongue and Rosebud we discovered a small party of hunters had seen us."

The column moved steadily on, despite heat, buffalo, sagebrush and the delightfully tempting multi-colored prairie flowers, toward the unsuspected but impending bitter conflict. Having arrived at a· little valley coming in from the north, two miles west of the present site of Decker, Montana, the column had turned north up the valley, followed the bluffs, crossing several little tributaries full of water, crossed the south fork of the stream—now called "Spring Creek"—and turned northwest to ride along the divide between the south and north forks. Reaching the head of the creeks, Crook halted the column for some time, sending his scouts to the ridge north which formed the divide between the Rosebud and tributaries ,of the Tongue River.

After ascertaining that there were no hostile Indians on the north side of the divide, except for "the hunting party," Crook crossed his men over the divide and they came down to the south fork of the Rosebud.[11]

It is apparent from looking at a topographical map of the area that General Crook took the route he did because he was at all times near water and had the advantage of a more direct route along the plateau; and that by swerving to the northeast, he avoided the crest of the low mountains directly in his path straight north.

"They Began to Bray as Loud as They Could"

All the while, rumors of the exact whereabouts of the Sioux and the location of Crazy Horse's village were rife among the troops. Crook's overconfidence in the lack of positive knowledge made Captain Anson Mills uneasy.

"I did not think that General Crook knew where they (Crazy Horse and the Sioux) were," Mills chronicled in *My Story*, "and I did not think our friendly Indians knew where they were, and no one conceived we would find them in the great force we did."

Mills, commander of Company M, 3rd Cavalry, was leader of a battalion of that regiment. A Texan, who had served in the infantry throughout the Civil War, he had been brevetted for meritorious services in many campaigns. He eventually became a general and designed many articles of military equipment which bore his name in the post First World War period. He described the end of the day's journey:

"We marched thirty-five miles the first day until we came to a lake or swamp of about five hundred yards diameter, the headwaters of the Rosebud. We left Chambers' command several miles in the rear, and when we had bivouacked our camp on three sides of the lake, leaving the fourth side of the rectangle for Chambers when he arrived, the officers and many of the men walked over to observe the military movements of the 'Mule Brigade' as it was called.

"Chambers was proud and ambitious to do his duty, how-ever humiliating and disagreeable; as well as he could, so when the leading company came near the line designated, he gave the command, 'Left front into line' in military style, and the first company came into line, but no sooner had the mules halted, when, after their custom, they began to bray as loud as they could, making extra effort in accord with the extra effort they had made to carry their strange burden into camp. The cavalry officers began to laugh and roar . . . Chambers lost courage and with oaths and every evidence of anger, threw his sword down on the ground and left the command to take care of itself as best it could."

I had a hard time finding this campsite. For several years I assumed it was up on the divide straight south of the west bend as indicated by Mills' map. Closer study showed it could not have been at this point. From various descriptions the site was "between the forks," at a place where the Rosebud ran nearly straight east.

In the summer of 1955 I met Jesse Young, son of Burt Young, owner of much of the land around there, who gave me an old weather-beaten McClellan saddle found beside a spring north of the divide. The saddle consisted of the front piece and back, but the kidney board which connected them was broken. All brass rings and attachments were there, but the leather had disappeared except for a strap along the back of the rear piece.

Jesse took me to this place, which fits the description of the camp. It is about two miles west of the dry lake on the divide

where I first thought it was located, according to Mills' map,
and at the foot of white rocky bluffs which mark the north
edge of the divide. There is a little valley commencing at the
divide extending northeastward for about two miles where it
joins another valley coming in from the west, known as the
South Fork. The camp was on both sides of this tributary of
the South Fork a short distance down from the divide. The
site is surrounded by bluffs on all sides except on the east,
and resembles the amphitheater in the place where the attack
occurred, farther down the stream.

Crook said in his official report that he marched about five
miles from camp to his bivouac, and the site pointed out by
Jesse Young is close to five miles.

About a mile east of the camp site Charles Young found in
a ravine south of the creek a brass belt buckle rectangular in
shape with leather belt evidently dropped during the march
down the creek. The belt buckle had "U. S." stamped on it
and had undoubtedly belonged to an officer. Farther down the
fork a table knife stamped with "U. S.", part of a soldier's mess
equipment, has been found.

As this tributary of the South Fork was the camp site, then
it is very probable that the soldiers came up the middle prong
of Spring Creek which has its beginnings due south of the
camp. The north prong of Spring Creek heads out immediately
south of the west bend while the west prong runs far to the
northwest.

Charles Young, the early settler, told the writer that the
country has changed a great deal since his arrival. The large
rocks and rocky formations have disintegrated, the hills and
ridges somewhat levelled off by cloudbursts washing the light,
sugary gray soil down the slopes. He cited his homestead smoke
house on the hillside, built upon log piles five or six feet off
the ground. The earth has washed down the slopes so that
now the smoke house seems to rest upon the ground.

In like manner, the McClellan saddle may have been exposed
from debris. One can almost imagine one of Crook's horses or
a *Pegasus* of Chambers' brigade so overwhelmed with gladness
in reaching the spring that late afternoon of June 16 that it
rolled over and over in the long grass breaking its saddle.

Humor again with the mule brigade pulling into position. But beneath the laughter, wrath at the unruly Crows and Shoshones. Correspondent Finerty shared Crook's justifiable condemnation of their continuing debauchery:

"The sun was low when we approached the Rosebud valley, but still in the distance, right, left, and in front, we could hear the rapid crackling of the Indian guns, as they literally strewed the plain with the carcasses of the unfortunate bison. Quiet reigned only when the sun had set, and we went into camp in an amphitheatrical valley, commanded on all sides by steep but not lofty bluffs. Pickets were posted along the elevations, and the command proceeded to bivouac in a great circle, with the horses and pack mules in the center, for fear of a sudden attack and possible stampede.

"The General gave orders that no fires should be lit, for fear of alarming the Sioux, but the Indian allies paid no attention to them, they lit what fires they listed, and proceeded to gorge themselves with fresh buffalo meat, roasted on the cinders. They also, when they had feasted sufficiently, set up one of their weird, indescribable war chants, of which they never seemed to tire.

"General Crook called upon the Crows and Snakes to furnish men to scout ahead of our camp during the night but he could induce a few only of the latter tribe to go forward under Tom Cosgrove and Frank Gruard. The General was angry enough to punish the recalcitrant savages severely, but it would never have done to make them enemies at that stage of the game. He therefore, submitted with characteristic philosophy to the inevitable."

Finerty had a magic way of being everywhere, of seeing everything; a magic pen to draw the scenes he saw. He ended his day with these words:

"The whole command sank early to repose, except those whose duty it was to watch over our slumbers, and the boastful, howling Indians, who kept up their war songs throughout most of the night. Captain Sutorius, lying on the ground next to me, with saddle for pillow, and wrapped in his blanket, said,

"'We will have a fight tomorrow, mark my words—I feel it in the air.'"[12]

Chapter 5

IN THE SIOUX CAMP

MEANWHILE back in the Sioux camp, Crazy Horse awaited Crook.

All the spring, while General Crook was getting his forces ready for the campaign at Fort Fetterman, the young Indians had slipped away to join Sitting Bull's[1] camp, leaving the women and children on the reservations where they were safe.

This large encampment first traveled northwesterly into eastern Montana in the vicinity of the Tongue River, following it almost to the Yellowstone. Then it moved westward to the Rosebud River near its confluence with the Yellowstone and came up the Rosebud. Here the Indians paused for three days from June 7th to June 10th in order that the Hunkpapa tribe might have its annual sun dance.[2]

This was the sacred ceremony during which the medicine men and chiefs sought visions and religious help for their people. According to their ritual, Sitting Bull had a hundred small pieces of flesh cut from his arms with a sharp knife and, bleeding from his wounds, gazed at the sun from dawn to dusk seeking a vision for the guidance of his people. While lying exhausted and unconscious, he saw a vision of *many soldiers falling into camp upside down*. He proclaimed this vision to the Indians as an omen of victory, and they were convinced that victory over the soldiers was certain. It was this inspired and abiding faith in their destiny which sustained them during the following two weeks, enabling them to turn back General Crook at the Rosebud and thus crush Custer's command at the Little Big Horn.

After the Sun Dance, they moved south to Davis Creek, which comes into the Rosebud about three miles south of present Busby, Montana. Here they camped from June 12th to June 14th. Turning westward again, they followed Davis

38

Creek to the divide and down Reno Creek into the valley of the Little Big Horn River.

The Indians took this route because they were following the vast herds of roaming buffalo upon which they were dependent for survival in this northern climate. These herds provided not only food and clothing but winter fuel. Also, this country was rough and broken, making it easy to defend against an aggressor.

"Long ago a frontier scout named Hank Clifford, who had taken a squaw from the Sioux Nation, said that he had often heard them declare that if ever the antagonism between them and the whites grew to a final struggle there was a country in the north where they could take refuge and could never be conquered nor dislodged," wrote R. B. Davenport, *New York Herald*, July 13, 1876. "They would wait there to receive the force sent against them, and could hope to destroy it before it could escape. This region they described as extremely rough, where steep ridges, precipices and deep canyons formed a chaotic surface upon which the force first in possession could fight successfully three times their own number. Clifford believed that it was the Rosebud Mountains to which they referred, as they are nearly impregnable to an invader. . . .

"They expected a great victory, a harvest of white scalps and their freedom from dependence on the Great Father."

After June 14th the main Indian encampment was located at the forks of Reno Creek, 22 miles northwest across country from the Rosebud's big bend. The west part of the camp was on land now known locally as the Jones Ranch, four and one-half miles east of the Little Big Horn River. The South Fork of Reno Creek came in from the southeast down a little valley and ran into Reno Creek near the site of the present bridge, about the center of the combined camps.[3]

At this main camp, extending two miles east and west along the valley of Reno Creek, six different tribes had their camp circles. The Hunkpapa Sioux, most numerous, were under Sitting Bull, their old man chief, also the old man chief of the combined tribes. The Oglala Sioux were under Crazy Horse,[4] an old man chief but also war chief of the combined tribes. Hump or Hump Nose was the leader of the Arrows-All-Gone Sioux. A few Blackfeet Indians, late arrivals had no leader of consequence. The Cheyennes were under Old Bear, Dirty

Moccasins and Crazy Head. Lame White Man was regarded as a warrior chief, but being a Southern Cheyenne visiting Northern Cheyenne relatives, did not have actual authority.[5] Little Big Man,[6] an Oglala sub chief, was Crazy Horse's right hand man.

Lt. John G. Bourke described Crazy Horse at the time he returned to the Agency in the spring of 1877:

"I saw before me a man who looked quite young, not over thirty years old, five feet eight inches high, lithe and sinewy, with a scar on his face. The expression of his countenance was one of quiet dignity, but morose, dogged, tenacious, and melancholy."

Mr. Louis Bordeau, whose description is in the *Ricker Interviews*, Tablet 11, p. 72, Nebraska State Historical Society, testified that:

"Crazy Horse was slight in form, tall, very light complexion, hair long and hung down to his hips."

Of his character, Lt. John G. Bourke, in *On The Border With Crook*, states:

"All Indians gave him a high reputation for courage and generosity. In advancing upon an enemy, none of his warriors were allowed to pass him. He had made hundreds of friends by his charity towards the poor, as it was a point of honor with him never to keep anything for himself, excepting weapons of war. I never heard an Indian mention his name save in terms of respect."

In an excerpt from a letter from Major General Hugh L. Scott, National Archives, this opinion is substantiated:

"I have lately (1920) talked to his (Crazy Horse's) brother-in-law Red Feather and his head soldier 'He Dog' or 'Male Dog', Oglalas at Pine Ridge who still mourn his death. They say they knew of nine horses being killed under him and that when he came on the field of battle he made everybody brave. He was the most prominent soldier in the Sioux tribe."

Though not a Medicine Chief, Crazy Horse had a medicine of his own. William Garnett, Cane Creek, South Dakota, testified January 10, 1907, in the *Ricker Interviews*, Tablet 1, that his medicine began with a dream or trance in the vicinity of the Rosebud:

"Crazy Horse told the story that he was near a lake. A man on horseback came out of the lake and talked with him. He told Crazy Horse not to wear a war bonnet; not to tie up his horse's tail. . . . So Crazy Horse never tied his horse's tail, never wore a war bonnet. It is said he did not paint his face like the other Indians. The man from the lake told him he would never be killed by a bullet, but his death would come by being held and stabbed; as it was actually. Crazy Horse was known and accounted a brave man before this vision.

"Crazy Horse before going into battle observed this ceremonial. . . . Taking some of the dirt thrown up by the pocket gophers, he would rub it on his horse in lines and streaks, not painting him, but passing this dirt over him in this way in a spot or two; and put in his hair also two or three straws of grass 2 or 3 inches long . . . The man from the lake told him to use the dirt and straws."

Garnet goes on to say in his interview with E. S. Ricker, that:

"Crazy Horse considered himself cut out for warfare, and he therefore would have nothing to do with affairs political or social or otherwise, like making treaties, scheming, laying plans, moving camp, disciplining the people and soldiers, etc.

"He had no ambition to be chief, disdained the compliment of being great—a great leader, or anything of that sort. He depended simply and solely on himself and cared nothing for the applause of others. He was great in his ability to follow his own ideas and to resist the allurements of other people and their cheap homage and noise."

Crazy Horse is said to have made his boast that his image would never be taken by the white man's little black box, and it has long been a question of controversy as to whether his picture was in fact ever taken. On July 10, 1924, a picture purporting to be of the great Oglala chief was received by the National Archives and numbered 83158 in its files. This picture widely published shows a tall Indian in full warbonnet with hands folded in front, with a small boy in background. In an effort made to establish its authenticity, this picture was sent to a number of authorities, who returned it with their comments.

D. F. Barry, 1316 Tower Avenue, Superior, Wisconsin, photographer of many old Indians, said in a letter dated January 15, 1926:

"Crazy Horse was never photographed; an unprincipalled photographer, I think the name Moorehouse from Washington, sent out a photo claiming to be 'Crazy Horse'." Later, Mr. Barry asserted in a letter dated February 19, 1926, the photograph was of 'Race Horse.'

E. W. Jermark, Superintendent, Pine Ridge Agency, South Dakota, wrote to General Hugh L. Scott, March 1926:

"Interviewed your old friend 'He Dog' and other old timers re picture. These Indians are agreed that the picture is not a likeness of the Oglala Chief Crazy Horse. . . ."

On March 4, 1955, Ben Reifel, then Superintendent, Pine Ridge Agency, reported:

"Moses Two Bulls, Pres. of the Oglala Sioux Tribe, and I interviewed Dewey Beard (only living participant in the Custer Battle) on Feb. 24, 1955. Mr. Beard was positive that no picture was ever taken of Crazy Horse. And, certainly, he said, 'with war bonnet and other colorful regalia such a picture could not be one of Crazy Horse. He never wore more than two feathers'."[7]

Jake Herman, the Fifth Member of the Executive Committee, Oglala Sioux Tribal Council, at Pine Ridge, also reported March 4, 1955:

"This picture I showed a few older Indians and they identified him as a man by the name of Bald Eagle from Pine Ridge, who at one time travelled with the Buffalo Bill show. It is not the authentic picture of Chief Crazy Horse."[8]

This opinion is corroborated by Mari Sandoz, author of *Crazy Horse* and the acknowledged authority on the history of Oglala Sioux:

"Now to the most frequently encountered picture labeled Crazy Horse—the very dark little man in warbonnet, with his hands folded—The Indians told me this is of Greasy Head, known as Crazy Horse No. 2 after, by good Sioux custom, he took the name of his illustrious predecessor when he married Crazy Horse's widow, the Larrabee woman. The war chief was light coffee colored, never wore a warbonnet, and died before this type of photography was discovered. And look at the clothing of the white men—long after 1877."[9]

Of another photograph labeled Crazy Horse, published in

Fighting Indians of The West, by Schmitt and Brown (1948), photographer, S. J. Morrow, Mari Sandoz also expresses doubt:

"There was a Hunkpapa Crazy Horse contemporaneous to the Oglala war chief (see Vestal's *Sitting Bull*). This may be the subject of the Morrow photograph at South Dakota, the one in Brown and Schmitt. Their man is plainly part white and wears the slip knot hair tie of the northern Indians, brought south by the returning Sioux from Canada in '81. The blanket coat is also northern. I am told that the Morrow picture is of *Crazy in the Lodge.*"[10]

However, new evidence has recently been brought to light. Ellen Howard, Pine Ridge Agency, one of the daughters of Baptiste Garnier, the famous scout Little Bat, dug up from her mother's trunk some old tin types taken near Fort Laramie, Wyoming, about 1870. One was the picture of Little Bat's wife, who was cousin of Crazy Horse. Another was of Frank Gruard, the Grabber, and Little Bat. The third was to cause instant excitement and speculation. It was a picture of an Indian of medium height and build, with light complexion, and long hair coming down to his waist.

This picture answered the description of Crazy Horse, but how came it here? Ellen Howard tells the story as it was told to her by her mother and father. One day Little Bat and Frank Gruard coaxed Crazy Horse into having his picture taken and —as a family lark—they all went together and had their pictures taken.

The fact that it was found among the effects of a close relative was significant. Yet the Sioux were cautious. Only after careful study of the picture and much checking among the older Indians at the Agency, did Jake Herman, the Fifth Member of the Oglala Sioux Tribal Council, announce that he believed it to be the authentic picture of Chief Crazy Horse who led the Sioux at the Battle of the Rosebud and Custer's massacre at the Little Big Horn.

Crazy Horse knew about the presence of the soldiers in the region even before the skirmish at Prairie Dog Creek on June 8.[11] There were always blue-coated soldiers following, pushing the Sioux on, on. Was the Sioux' tragic story not easy to follow? Now, they had been crowded westward to their last stronghold.

It was the domination of the reservation where food was scarce, or it was the final stand to retain their freedom.

The General from Fort Fetterman had not heeded his warning. Therefore scouts from the main encampment had been sent out to watch for his advance. Preparations had been made in the Sioux camp for the coming encounters with the white soldiers which Crazy Horse and every Indian knew to be inevitable.

Medicine men of the Cheyenne tribe had already devised magic medicine horns for their warriors. It was their belief that a warrior who wore a pair of these horns, taken from buffaloes, was bullet proof. A pair was mounted on a sort of cap with the two horns in the same positions as on the head of the buffalo. (Since the Rosebud fight came sooner than expected there were only 59 sets of these horns ready. By the time of the Custer battle, one week later, there were horns for all Cheyenne warriors. There is a set of these horns in the collection of the late Jim Gatchell of Buffalo, Wyoming, given to him by Weasel Bear, Limpy and Yellow Dog, Cheyenne warriors who were in both battles.)

His Indians had also made eagle's wing whistles as a charm against death. (Later, after the battle, some of Crook's soldiers said that above the roar of conflict could be heard the shrill whistles of the enemy during their charges.)

And now, Little Hawk and his Cheyenne scouts had thundered into the Sioux camp with the alarm. They had discovered General Crook and his soldiers near the divide between the Tongue River and Rosebud River valleys. The end of the story, then, was to be written with a bloody arrow.

Although the council of chiefs advised the excited Indians to wait until they were actually attacked, this was shouted down by the warriors and plans were made to attack the soldiers immediately, who, they guessed, were coming down the Rosebud.

Crazy Horse, the acclaimed war chief, made a speech before the council with the warriors in the outer circle in the background. He told them his plans in words as terse and sparse as Crook's, for both men were reserved. A strong force under the older chiefs would be left to guard the women, children and old men in camp. A strong party would be sent to drive the soldiers away. This would be different from fighting Indian tribes where the important thing was to count coup[12] on the enemy by touching the person or dead body with their coup sticks. Always before, this had been regarded as the height of bravery, the subject of long recitals at the victory dance. But these soldiers, warned Crazy Horse, were in the business of killing. The only way the Indians could fight them would be to kill also.

Shortly after the council meeting, the warriors whipped out for the Rosebud, in different parties, each under its own chief.[13] There were many bands of Cheyennes, Oglala, Miniconjou, Sans Arc, and Brule Sioux.[14] Young Two Moons' band and the Cheyennes rode east and a little south across the divide to the Rosebud, then southward to the big bend. Others followed up the south fork of Reno Creek to arrive at the field through Sioux Pass. These were the young hot heads who could not be restrained by the older chiefs. Other warriors, including the Hunkpapas, started later and kept coming in all morning reinforcing the earlier arrivals. Gall and Crow King had not yet joined the encampment,[15] but Sitting Bull, still very weak from the tortures of the Sun Dance, was present, giving the warriors encouragement and urging them on.[16]

Many of the war party were armed with 1866 repeating Winchester rifles of .44 caliber, obtained from white traders; others had muzzle loaders, Spencer carbines, Henry rifles and old Sharps military rifles. Some soldiers' accounts state that the Indians were well armed with the latest model rifles, mentioning the tremendous fire power obtained against Royall's men during the battle.

In the fall of 1955 I arranged with John Stands-In-Timber, the Historian and Custodian of the records of the Cheyennes, to go over the battlefield with me pointing out where the various incidents took place. John, a grandson of Lame White Man, who attended Haskell Institute, had several relatives in the battle, among whom were Tall Bull and Wolf Tooth. As John had never heard the Cheyenne warriors mention Chief Dull Knife at the Rosebud, he believes he was not in the battle. Spotted Wolf was the leader of the Cheyennes that day, the sub chiefs being American Horse, Little Wolf, Chief Two Moon and Young Two Moon, his nephew.

John confirmed the number of Sioux and Cheyenne in the battle which Crazy Horse estimated at 1500, with 100 being Cheyenne warriors.[17]

Thus while Crook and his soldiers, all unknowing, were sleeping in their camp on the headwaters of the Rosebud the eve of the battle, Crazy Horse with his Sioux and Cheyenne forces was riding through the night so that he would arrive in the vicinity of the big bend about daylight.

Pine Ridge, S, D,

Statement.

I Ellen Howard A member of the Ogalla Sioux tribe of Pine Ridge S, D, Certify that i am the daughter of Bat Garnier an Ogalla Sioux, Who was an Indian Scout Station At Fort Robinson. Neb in 1876 and 1877 And my father and mother are dead. My father left a tin type picture and always told me that it was the picture of Chief Crazy Horse And i am letting Jake Herman giving him the rights to have him printed in a book or to whom ever he degnigated it to.

I further state that my mother is dead and she left the picture to me.

Signed,
     Ellen Howard

A signed copy of this statement which is in the possession of the writer, attests to the authenticity of the picture of Crazy Horse.

Chapter 6

OUTLINE OF THE BATTLE

IT was the morning of June 17, 1876, near the headwaters of the Rosebud. At 3:00 a.m. Crook ordered his camp awake. By 6:00 he had his men on the march. A line of blue against the azure sky, his cavalcade flanked the south fork of the stream swollen by melting snows from the divide. Daintly, his big black charger picked his way along the sodden bank. Green were the pines above him and greener yet the grass, a "country green as emerald" but for the pink dotted hills where the rosebuds bloomed.

Thirty-five miles behind him lay his supply base, and miles beyond Fort Fetterman, from which he had come. Ahead, among the hills and canyon of the Rosebud, perhaps five miles, perhaps fifteen, was the village of Crazy Horse. Would he find it today, tomorrow, the day after? Even before daylight he had sent Humpy, the little Shoshone and the Crow scouts on ahead to try to locate it.

While the hilarious mule brigade led the way, it was soon overtaken by the cavalry.

"We began a rapid but alert descent along the east bank of the Rosebud," wrote Henry W. Daly, in "The Warpath," *American Legion Monthly,* April, 1927. "It was hard going. The Rosebud was as crooked as a corkscrew, and the country is very rough. Now we would be hugging the bluffs through the narrow, winding valley, unable to see fifty feet ahead; now passing through an open glade, which though difficult underfoot, presented fewer perils of surprise."

Eastward two miles, Crook led his column, then followed the turn of the south fork down the slope a mile and a half to the bend where the North Fork came in from the west, and the stream turned down the valley. Two and three-fourths miles to the east, the Rosebud resumed its course to the north—forming the big bend. It was 8:00 o'clock when the head of

47

Crook's column, having gone five miles, arrived between the two bends in the streams.

The march of the 16th to the headwaters of the Rosebud had been long and tiring. Crook, a humane man, halted the column to give his men a short rest and ordered the heated, still-tired horses and mules unsaddled and put out to graze.

John F. Finerty gives an account of the surroundings:

"At about 8 o'clock, we halted in a valley, very similar in formation to the one in which we had pitched our camp the preceding night. Rosebud stream, indicated by the thick growth of wild roses, or sweet briar, from which its name is derived, flowed sluggishly through it, dividing it from south to north into two almost equal parts. The hills seem to rise on every side, and we were within easy musket shot of those most remote."

Suddenly the excited Crow scouts were among them, requesting General Crook to keep the men under cover while they investigated further. Evidence had been found that Sioux were in the vicinity.

At this news, Crook immediately ordered pickets thrown out to the north along the foot of the bluffs and his camp went into bivouac.

Nothing happened. All was quiet—deceptively so. Fifteen minutes—thirty, passed. The men relaxed. The sun rose higher and hotter in the clear blue western sky. Finerty, the Fighting Irish Pencil Pusher, threw aside his note book and sprawled upon the cool ground. Near by Captain Sutorius, the Swiss, sat smoking calmly with Lt. Von Leuttwitz, the affable German recently transferred to Company E. The hearty laugh of Captain Dewees telling one of his inimitable stories floated across the water. Reynolds, the Beau Brummel of the outfit, fastidiously flicked particles of dust from his sleeve.

Drifting softly on the warm breeze came the wisp of a song from Major Burt, mingled with one of Nickerson's droll remarks, and the cheery voice of Tom Moore, Chief Packer, recounting one of his exploits. The young Crows were racing their ponies against the young Shoshones to the amusement of a group of onlooking soldiers. Reassured, and overconfident as he was, Crook sat down by the spring a quarter mile west of the head of the column for a hand of cards with Lt. Bourke and several other officers.

On the north side of the stream was stationed Captain Noyes' battalion of five companies of the 2nd Cavalry. Just behind him was Van Vliet's battalion of two companies of the 3rd. The mule brigade—five companies of mounted infantry came next, while the packers were in the rear to the west with most of the Crows and Shoshones.

Across, on the south side of the stream, Captain Anson Mills' battalion of four companies of the 3rd Cavalry headed the column. Behind him was stationed Captain Henry's battalion of four companies of the 3rd Cavalry.

The rest of the command was still coming in, the line of march being so long that the rear had not yet left camp at the headwaters of the Rosebud.[1] Indeed, for half an hour after the halt, the rear was still closing up. When the action started, it was attacked by Indians coming from the northwest through Sioux Pass. Numerous articles of equipment and mess gear found on the south side of the west bend testify to the unseemly haste of the rear hurrying to join the command.

Crook had bivouacked his command in an amphitheater hemmed in by a line of bluffs a half-mile south, paralleling the stream, and a low range of bluffs north, from two to six hundred yards from and paralleling the stream. North of the low bluffs was a level plateau varying in width from several hundred yards at the east end, to a half-mile at the west end. North of the plateau, about a mile from the creek was the main crest where much of the battle was to take place. This ridge commencing a mile west of the east bend ran west and north for three miles, extending more than a mile beyond the west bend, where it was joined by another ridge from the southeast, forming an acute angle in which was located Kollmar Creek, a tributary of the Rosebud.

Kollmar Creek runs two miles southeasterly through a little valley between the ridges, emptying into the Rosebud a mile east of the west bend and parallel with the south ridge two to three hundred yards from its crest.

Immediately north of the head of the column in the high ridge and lower bluffs was a large ravine three hundred yards across, its mouth opening into the valley at the line of bluffs. East of the ravine, the area was extremely rough, covered by many small rocky hills and gullies, while to the west the land was open and rolling.

This was the setting then, that hot June morning at 8:30 when shots were heard beyond the ridge to the northeast.

"*Lakota!* Lakota!" Humpy, the Shoshone scout, dashed wildly into camp, shouting hoarsely.[2]

"Lakota! Lakota!" yelled the Crow scouts just behind him, one of whom was severely wounded.

Crook's scouts had run into the scouts of Crazy Horse on the bluffs eleven miles to the north.

Already, Indians were attacking the pickets—hand to hand fighting. Then a volley of shots, a sprinkling of arrows, harsh cries of surprise from the troops struggling to mount frightened horses, howling savages boldly plunging from the bluffs after the scouts—and the battle of the Rosebud had begun.

Shortly afterwards, hostile Indians appeared all along the high ridge to the north; they poured out from the small hills to the west. *Sioux!*

Down near the rear of Crook's column, the Crows and Shoshones were quickly rallied by Chief of Scouts, Major Randall, who led them directly against the oncoming force. Randall's line, facing west and a little north, met the enemy on the plateau north of camp. Here, for twenty minutes—within 500 yards of the troops who were endeavoring to get in organized positions—the Crows and Shoshones held the insurgents, fighting fiercely, charge against countercharge.

Meanwhile, General Crook, who had been unable to see what was happening at the spring, because of the low bluff to the north which obstructed his view, mounted his black charger and rode north to a small hill to learn the extent of the force against him. At the same time, Captain Mills rode southward to higher ground to obtain a view of the approaching Indians. Before going, Crook had given orders to Mills to hold the bluffs. In Crook's absence, Colonel Evans, that "melancholy, philosophically inclined officer,"[3] confronted with immediate decisions, made the disposition of the troops.

Captain Van Vliet with his two companies was sent to guard the rear, occupying the bluffs to the south. Mounting the crest, he met and turned back an oncoming Sioux force attempting to take the ridge from the east. In the meantime, two companies of the 9th Infantry (G, under Burrowes and Carpenter, and H under Burt and Robertson) were ordered to advance dismounted to hold the low bluffs to the north. Four companies of the 2nd Cavalry, dismounted, were sent to support them. Captain Dewees'[4] company of that regiment was ordered to guard the horses in the valley for the other four companies.

To the west of these forces, the remaining company of the 9th Infantry and the two companies of the 4th Infantry were directed forward as a skirmish line. This line reached the plateau where the friendly Indian allies were so valiantly contesting the enemy.

The enemy was in full battle array. Nickerson, one of Crook's aides-de-camp, who was with this line, wrote:

"When we reached the crest of the plateau, there appeared in our front a formidable band of those justly celebrated Sioux and Cheyenne warriors, magnificently mounted, and in all the splendor of war paint and feathers. Every hill appeared to be covered with their swarming legions, and up from every ravine, and out of every little vale, more seemed to be coming.

"Many wore the long Sioux war bonnet of eagle's plumes, which floated and fluttered in the air, back of the wearer, to the distance of five or six feet; while others wore half masks of the heads of wild animals with the ears and sometimes the horns, still protruding, giving them the appearance of devils from the nether world, or uncouth demons from the hills of Brocken."

As the troops reached the rear of the "friendlies," the Sioux made a surprise move. Crazy Horse cleverly divided the forces sending them around both flanks of the Crows and Shoshones. One force came around to the east down the big ravine intent on routing the cavalry and capturing the horses in the valley. However, the men of the 9th Infantry and 2nd Cavalry, using the very tactics of the enemy they fought, had hidden themselves behind a small rise near the ravine's mouth and surprise met surprise. Waiting till the Sioux were within 150 yards, they poured forth a sudden hot volley. Against this barrage, the Sioux dissipated into two forces, retreating northward up either side of the ravine, where they spread out on the ridge contesting the advancing troops and Captain Mills' direct charge east of the ravine.

The other Sioux force split off to the west, south of the Crows and Shoshones, flinging themselves against the three infantry companies. The infantry, armed with their Long Toms, were quick in dispersing this force, but seeing the exposed west flank of the infantry, Indians swarmed around it.

Quick to sense the seriousness of the threat, Colonel Evans, still in command, ordered Captain Henry to send two companies of his battalion to the south side of the stream to occupy a low ridge to keep the Sioux from flanking the camp from this direction.

To obey this order, Henry was compelled to split his battalion, taking his own company and that of Lt. Bainbridge Reynolds[5] to the low ridge 500 yards to the west. He held this position until Colonel Royall, deploying two companies mounted, cleared the Sioux from the west flank of the Infantry.

The fight was getting hotter. More Sioux were appearing as if from nowhere. They whipped out of every crevice, over every ridge. Royall left the men behind a knoll—on the extreme left of the line—and went back to camp to order the advance of the remaining companies of the 3rd Cavalry, for the Crows and Shoshones had withdrawn with their wounded.

The maneuvers had been so sudden and unexpected that General Crook had not yet returned from the hill where he was studying the situation.

Now, the three companies of infantry on the west and the four companies of 2nd cavalry on the east commenced a general advance northward. Though progress was slow—all were dismounted—the enemy fell back before the advance, yet kept up a brisk fire upon the approaching line.

Captains Burt and Burrowes, after checking the Sioux advance down the big ravine, concealed their men at the foot of the bluffs in ambush, some distance apart. The Shoshones and the Crows were to pretend retreat and draw the Sioux down between the two companies. This too failed, when the latter were discovered. Rallying, the men took the led horses to the crest, leaving Captain Burt to bring up the wounded.

Meanwhile Colonel Evans ordered the remaining two companies of Henry's battalion under Captains Meinhold and Vroom,[6] together with the four companies of Mills' battalion under Captain Sutorius, Lt. Paul, Captain Andrews and Lt. Lawson, to mount, cross the stream and take position behind a low bluff. Moving by the right flank towards the east, they cleared the east end of the 2nd Cavalry line which had been in their front. Under command of Colonel Royall they charged that portion of the high ridge east of the big ravine by a flank movement from the southeast.

The six companies were now in column, Lt. Lawson's leading, followed by those of Captain Sutorius, Lt. Paul, Captain Andrews, Captain Meinhold and Captain Vroom. Before this headlong cavalry charge with its blasting carbines spewing death, the Sioux fled. The troops sped on, mounting the crest east of the gap at the same time that the infantry and 2nd Cavalry occupied the gap and portion of the ridge to the west of the gap.

"Company 'B' 2nd Cavalry under Lt. Swigert[7] was posted on the knob to the right of this ravine or gap," wrote Captain Henry E. Noyes, later, "which was very rough and rocky and afforded cover for quite a number of Sioux. Company 'E' (Captain Wells)[8] was posted on the knob and crest to the left of this ravine, and the other two companies (Co. 'B' under Lt. Rawolle, and 'I' under Lt. Kingsbury)[9] were on the ridge to the left of Co. 'E.' Co. 'D' reached the crest just before the arrival of the Sioux, who were found in force just beyond. The Companies to the left of the ravine found the Sioux on the crest, but drove them from it, and they retreated toward our left along the crest, whence they were subsequently driven by troops further to the left. The command was halted on the crest to await orders: the only casualties attending the occupation of this ridge were the wounding of First Sergeant Thomas Meager, Co. 'I', 2nd Cavalry, and Sergeant Patrick O'Donnell, Co. 'D' 2nd Cavalry, each of whom was wounded in the arm."[10]

The forces of Crazy Horse retreated westward along the ridge to a hill on the crest rising 600 yards west of the gap which jutted southward into the valley. This hill is one of the key points on the field. For convenience it might be called Crook's Hill in honor of the General commanding. The Sioux occupying this hill raked the troops with a brisk fire.

General Crook meant to clear out the insurgents and take that hill. He ordered Captain Mills, with his four companies, and the two companies of Captain Henry's Battalion to reform for another charge. Facing west on the crest east of the gap, in column same as previously formed, they charged westward under Crook's direct orders, "to take that hill."

In order to deploy, the column moved to the open ground south, in the valley, where the order was given, "Left front into line." The leading three companies charged northwest back onto the crest taking Crook's Hill as ordered. Under the heavy fire, Crazy Horse's warriors retreated to a "large cone shaped mound" 1200 yards northwest, from which they delivered a desultory long range fire.

Just as he was about to advance upon the conical mound, Captain Mills received another order. General Crook had decided on a different course of action. Mills was to advance no farther but was to throw out dismounted skirmishers to hold his position. Fortifications were therefore made by Mills' men along the southwest rim of Crook's Hill by piling up flat rocks.

Action now shifted from Mills to Royall. While deploying in the valley, Royall, fortified by Captain Henry and his two companies from behind the knoll, saw that the Sioux had gained a lower ridge a half mile south, across Kollmar Creek and parallel with the main crest. So, at the same time that Mills was charging Crook's Hill, Royall with Andrews', Meinhold's and Vroom's companies was charging southwest to the Sioux-covered ridge. He pushed westward along it, the hostiles retreating before the rifled advance, till he reached a ridge near the head of Kollmar Creek, where he remained with four companies.

Sioux were now swarming over the next ridge to the left of his position, delivering an enfilading fire. Captain Andrews detached Lt. Foster with one platoon of 18 men with orders to charge south and drive the Sioux from that ridge. Andrews himself advanced with one platoon to a high rocky point at the head of Kollmar Creek which commands the valley and ridge adjacent.

By this time, Foster had been victorious in his mission. Driving the enemy from the ridge to the south, he charged west along its crest to a rocky knoll. Here he dismounted his men to deliver a volley at Sioux forces occupying a wooded ridge in his front. Charging again, he gained the ridge, riding some distance along its crest only to be forced back to the rocky knoll by the enemy who were trying to cut him off.

At this point, Lt. Foster received an order from Captain Andrews to rejoin his company—without delay—on the ridge where Royall was forming a line. Foster obeyed but while crossing the valley between, two of his men and one horse were wounded in the withering fire of Crazy Horse's men, even though Andrews' men covered his crossing. Captain Andrews was then ordered to retreat from his perilous position, to rejoin Colonel Royall's command, where he was placed in line on the ridge with the other four companies.

Now, this ridge, so occupied, was 600 yards southeast of the high rocky point, just vacated by Captain Andrews, and "was lying adjacent to but separated by a wide cañon from the main crest"[11] to the north, the valley at the head of Kollmar Creek where the two ridges came together. It was a very exposed position, being almost a mile west of Crook's Hill and beyond supporting distance. Indians surged upon this rocky point, so lately abandoned by Andrews, forming a line along a spur 600 yards to the west.

The main crest to the north was by this time also occupied by Indians. From these three vantage points they obtained a raking, plunging fire on the troops. Swarming like flies to the Blue-coated honey, an estimated 500 hostiles were soon congregated in the rear and left rear of the soldiers. The hills and ledges—so prevalent in this area—concealed them from Colonel Royall. For two hours these troops were to hold their position against the heavy fire.

Mounted on his black charger between Mills and Noyes, Crook ordered the gap closed between the two commands. Royall sent Captain Meinhold's company down a ravine eastward to rejoin the main command on Crook's Hill. To accomplish the order, Meinhold braved the heavy, sweeping Sioux fire from the main crest to the north. One of his men was wounded, one horse killed. The line was then extended to occupy that portion of the ridge thus vacated by Meinhold. The horses were protected on the south slope of the ridge, where they were held by every fourth man of the command.

Three actions were now going on simultaneously, three battles within a battle—Royall towards the west, Crook on the crest with the main command, and Van Vliet's two companies on the bluff to the south. Royall and Crook were obscured from each other by the rough ground, boulders and rocks, innumerable crevices and ledges, and distance, but Van Vliet had a perfect view of the whole field.

During the three parallel cavalry charges to the west, the troops on the crest were not engaged but were consolidating their positions. The led horses and mules which had been left in camp with horseholders were sent for, saddled up, and taken close to the crest, where the men remounted and occupied it. It took about an hour to bring up the horses and remove the wounded to a field hospital established in a gully.

Now the Shoshones were placed on the left of the line on the south slope of Crook's Hill. The Crows were posted in intervals between the other battalions along the crest to the east, in reserve. Captain Cain's[12] infantry company occupied Crook's Hill together with some of Mills' cavalry. Captain Luhn's infantry company was deployed east of Cain, while Captain Sam Munson's infantry company was east of Luhn. Then came the four companies of the 2nd Cavalry in order previously stated, while Captain Dewees brought the led horses of the battalion close to the crest. Captains Burt and Burrowes with their 9th Infantry companies were posted in reserve just below the crest on the south slope of the extreme east end of the high ridge east of the gap.

General Crook now saw what he thought to be his chance to end the fight. Above all else he was determined to seek out and destroy the village of Crazy Horse, a plan he had never lost sight of. Moved by this pressing desire, he ordered Colonel Evans to withdraw Mills' three companies from Crook's Hill, to mount them on the eastern crest, to make a demonstration downstream and prepare for a movement upon the village which he now believed to be eight miles north down the dark Rosebud canyon.

Up to this time, Crook still was under the misapprehension that he could whip any Indian force. He did not seem to realize the enormity of the attack. He had such a poor opinion of the Sioux strength that he told Captain Mills not to press the engagement further. He had ordered all the troops assembled on the crest, he said, for a movement by the whole command upon the village. His words were terse and sparse as usual. Mills was to lead the column, pushing as rapidly as the horses would stand. Mills was to pay no attention to the assaults of the Sioux. Mills was to take the village and hold it until he, Crook, came to his support with the rest of the command.

Twenty men from Lt. Lawson's Company A were to accompany the friendly Indians who would flank the command on the march down the canyon, not only for safety's sake but to keep up connections.

The whole command was therefore under order to move on the village. Crook sent one of his staff to call in Royall's men to proceed as ordered. Royall did not comply.

Mills however, complied immediately, withdrawing his two and one-half companies. The position he had occupied on Crook's Hill fell to Van Vliet's two companies, Captain Meinhold's Company and some packers and miners. Five companies of the 2nd Cavalry were soon sent after Mills in support.

This move was instantly observed by the sharp eye of Crazy Horse. At the withdrawal of troops from Crook's Hill, his Indians charged upon it from west and north, sending a flanking movement down two ravines to the west of Crook's hill to separate the main command from Royall's men.

This action changed the course of events. The General saw at once that the line on Crook's Hill must be reestablished. He directed Captain Munson to take six men, sharpshooters, to some rocky ground on the crest to drive back the Sioux movement. War cries rising above the noise of battle, the Sioux rolled on. But Munson held his position in the rocks with the aid of a dozen men of other companies and some twenty Indian allies.

By now, the Sioux were a compact mass of color that swept

along the crest and down the valley. Splendidly mounted on their ponies, they rode like Centaurs, singing their battle songs.

Lt. Bourke, his *Diary* for the moment forgotten, instantly sized-up the situation. The Sioux charge must be broken if the main command was to be saved. Personally assuming command of the Shoshones and the platoon of cavalry detailed to act with them, he commenced a counter-charge in his right flank in the vicinity of Crook's Hill, the Shoshones having lined up on the crest facing west. Colonel Randall rallied his Crows, who strung out along the valley south of the crest forming the left flank of the line. Before the Shoshones was a formidable yet brilliant figure. Washakie, stripped to the waist and wearing a gorgeous headdress of eagle feathers that swept the ground, reared his spirited pony into position.

"Medicine Crow, the Crow chief, looked like a devil in his war bonnet of feathers, furs and buffalo horns," Bourke recalled later.

With Bourke on the right flank, then, and Black Jack Randall on the left, the line charged westward. They took the Sioux in flank, driving, forcing, compelling them back, back. The bright June day became an inferno of rearing whirling ponies, thwarted wolfish yells, whizzing bullets, dust, dirt, fetid smells from naked, sweating bodies and wounded horseflesh. Bourke and Randall pushed on, driving them back westward along the crest, and up the valley.

Cornered in a little valley, the Sioux turned at bay. There was a mad, frenzied little skirmish, man against man, hand against hand. Rallying their allied forces, Black Jack Randall and Diarist Bourke charged again, this time driving the Sioux back to the rocky point at the head of Kollmar Creek, vacated by Captain Andrews, where they flew to the sanctuary of the trees on the ridge southwest. Behind, the little valley was strewn with the bodies of many Sioux and horses.

From his position (later to be known as Andrews' Point), Bourke caught a glimpse of Royall's predicament. Royall was besieged on the ridge south of Kollmar Creek, a mile west of Crook's Hill, by 500 Sioux and Cheyennes. Was it any wonder he had failed to comply with the General's order?

But Bourke had little time to note details. Though the Sioux charge was broken—they had been driven away from the main command—it was a futile victory. This far point he and Randall had gained was so alone, so exposed, that the Crows and Shoshones bolted from it simultaneously in consternation, without orders, and a retreat began.

In the confusion, Lt. Bourke and his bugler, Snow, were left alone on the hill. At the first signs of retreat, the hostiles, quick to seize every opportunity, had billowed out from the wooded ridge. Bourke barely escaped the charging Sioux. Later, when he had more time, he wrote in his *Diary:*

"My usual good fortune attended me, but poor Snow rode back to our lines badly shot through both arms near the elbows."[13]

The cavalry retreat continued back to the vicinity of Crook's Hill—the whole distance covered by the mounted charge being one mile. The following hostiles recommenced their long range fire from the conical mound to the northwest.

General Crook, whose awakening eye had followed the charge and countercharge, was now convinced that he could not take his full command down the canyon for the attack on Crazy Horse's village. He barked out an order that three companies of infantry were to form a skirmish line across the crest and down to the valleys on each side, to charge northwest and drive the Sioux from the conical mound.

This skirmish line was formed at 11:00 o'clock. Captain Munson stated in his official report that after his men had helped to repulse the charge of the Sioux, he was ordered to deploy his men on the right of this skirmish line.

Assuming that the men were defending Crook's Hill for about a half hour, it would seem that the Sioux charge occurred about 10:30, which would allow about a half hour for the charge and return of the friendly Indians.

The three infantry companies accordingly advanced, drove the Sioux from the conical mound, then occupied the crest nearby. The place on the main crest vacated by the three infantry companies was soon occupied by Van Vliet's two companies, who received orders to rejoin the main command at 11:00.[14]

Four hundred yards northwest of Crook's Hill was a rocky shelf—a strategic location for sharpshooters to pick off the gyrating Sioux. To this shelf, General Crook sent the twenty packers and a few Montana miners about 11:00, when the Crows and Shoshones had returned from Bourke's and Randall's charge. Armed with Sharp's Sporter rifles, these seasoned frontiersmen performed excellent sniping service.

At 10:30 during the Sioux charge, a band of them rode down the Rosebud between Royall's men and Van Vliet on the south bluffs, capturing a herd of horses at the campsite where the attack was first made. This herd had been left in charge of a small Shoshone boy, who was shot in the back and scalped on the banks of the spring where Crook had been playing cards not so many hours ago. The band attempted to return with the horses to their own forces when Van Vliet became suspicious that they were not "friendlies" and opened fire on them. The band abandoned them and fled to their comrades.

After the Sioux charge on the center of the line had been repulsed, General Crook had sent Captain Nickerson with word for Royall to rejoin him on the main crest preparatory to going down the canyon to attack the village of Crazy Horse.

Colonel Royall, struggling to drive off the Indian force which almost encircled his men, had attempted to follow this order by retreating southwest to the next ridge on the south side of Kollmar Creek. The led horses which Crazy Horse desperately wanted had been retired first. Down the hostiles had swarmed from their cover behind every little hill and ledge bent on capturing them. Valiantly returning their fire, Royall's men had beaten them off. The enemy had then taken a position on a rocky ledge, running from the west edge of the ridge southwesterly for 400 yards to a point where the ledge came in from the east forming an acute angle.

Now again, Crook sent a message for Royall to rejoin the main body. And again the led horses were withdrawn first. The hostiles occupying the ridge just vacated by Royall and those posted on the ledges on left and rear, poured a murderous fire on the retreating men. Making another reckless effort to get the horses, the hostiles charged the line as it retreated southeasterly along the ridge south of Kollmar Creek. Ravaged by the past two hours of devastating onslaught, Royall's tired men yet swung about and gave them measure for measure.

To make matters worse, the Sioux who had previously been on Mills' front—he had withdrawn his forces preparatory to going down the canyon—now came swirling in about the beleaguered battalion. But still the retreat continued with the line strung out along the ridge and just north of the crest for protection, until finally it reached a point south of Crook's Hill, one half mile from their commander.

But worse was to come. The time arrived when it was necessary to change directions and cross the defile of Kollmar Creek if Royall ever hoped to join the main command. The foeman following, and those moving parallel with it along the next ridge 400 yards southward, struck suddenly. Charging across the intervening hollow, they forced the soldiers to make a stand on the ridge. When this was beaten off, Crazy Horse's forces made a flank attack from the northwest, coming down the valley of Kollmar Creek, sensing that the isolated battalion was almost within their grasp—more, the coveted horses. Quickly the soldiers in Blue formed new lines to meet with this new charge. Was there never to be an end to the struggle?

Over on Crook's Hill, the General had found it difficult to war with these insurgents. As was his custom, he placed his troops in a long line in true Civil War style, expecting the hostile Indians to form a line opposite. But they had refused to play his game. They attacked first on one flank, then on the other as a highly mobile force. It was the strategy of Crazy Horse to divide the command by retreating before the charges until the soldiers were scattered and then attack at the weak points. The Oglala had been careful not to attack his massed battalions, to avoid the infantry on the crest which were fighting dismounted, because of its deadly accurate long range fire. Crazy Horse's warriors fought mounted at all times, while the soldiers fought dismounted except when making a charge. Always the Oglala retreated in the face of a cavalry charge.

Had he wanted, Crook could not call for reinforcements from Terry; he did not know where Terry was. He could not get through to Gibbon. Gibbon was being held at bay on the banks of the Rosebud near the Yellowstone. Meanwhile he had heard nothing from Mills on his mission to Crazy Horse's village.

Mills on his journey to the canyon was having troubles, too. Having left his position on Crook's Hill, Mills had gone southward to the valley, then east along the base of the bluffs (as shown in cover map) until he arrived near the east bend of the Rosebud. Here, he was confronted by hostiles holding the west side of the canyon bluff. The outcome of this encounter and his ultimate journey down the canyon in quest of the village will be told in Chapter 7.

There were other disturbing elements, also.

According to the old soldiers in the command, this was as desperate a struggle as any they had ever seen in the Civil War days. To help Royall with his withdrawal, the infantry companies of Burt and Burrowes were charging dismounted at double time southward from Crook's Hill. But Crook's Hill was a half mile away. They were to take position on a small ridge south of that hill 600 yards northeast of the embattled battalion.

Captain Guy V. Henry, near the left of Royall's line on the ridge, was watching Burt and Burrowes infantry take position on the ridge south of Crook's Hill, when he was shot across the face by the enfilading fire from the northwest. A .44 caliber bullet struck his left cheek which came out his right cheek, blinding him temporarily. Shocked from the impact, his senses reeling, Henry fell from his horse. Appalled at the sight, his men lost courage and gave ground.

In the meantime, Crook had sent the Shoshones, under Washakie and Luisant, and the Crows, to the aid of Royall. These loyal Indians, boldly riding south and a little west down the ravine from near Crook's Hill, came upon the tragic scene.

Henry's body had no more than touched the ground than the "coupminded" hostiles rushed to it, some of them actually riding over his body. Knowing what it entailed, the Crows and Shoshones raced to his defense. Beside Henry's prone figure lay the body of his orderly, also seriously wounded. Over these two injured men there was fierce hand to hand fighting. The "friendlies" saved the bodies, however; Tigee, lieutenant of Washakie, was credited with holding back the hostiles until the troops came up.[15]

In pitiable condition, Captain Henry was taken to the field hospital near the crest.

Royall's battalion by this time had suffered heavily in wounded. There was also other loss of manpower. It required at least two men to take one wounded back to the hospital; one man in four to hold the horses. From various causes the battalion had been reduced to only sixty or seventy men on the fighting line.

At the same time that the hostiles were driving Royall's men southeastward down Kollmar Creek, a band of Sioux swept on past and rode down to the Rosebud and over the bivouac of that morning, around the east bend and northward down the canyon, making a complete circuit of Crook's command, an appalling event to a commanding officer.

And in dire fulfillment of the vision of Sitting Bull, *many soldiers falling into camp upside down,* Crook was catapulted over his horse's head as the big black charger was shot from under him.

Still the battle continued. Back and forth the contestants rocketed; defense and offense. Trampled beneath the flying hoofs, the roses of the valley withered; stained a deeper hue. Blood. Sweat. A cyclone of dust. Snorting horses, red-eyed, terrified, stumbled over rocks sprawling troopers upon the rough ground. Soldiers in Blue charged back up the bluff, met, rebuffed, retreated. The men, running, walking, crawling, cut by boulders and bushes, struggled to hold positions. Reloading carbine and Long Tom went on incessantly. And still the Sioux came on and on. Hundreds of them. Painted horses, white-faced, red-streaked, black-lined. Painted naked savage bodies, brilliantly feathered, hideous, daring, thrusting, slashing, whipping. Tomahawk and lance and rifle, they swept from position to position.

There was one among them, devoid of all ornaments, bereft of paint or headdress. A simple loin cloth girdled his lithe, sinewy body. Long, long back hair plumed out behind him in the hot battle air above a billowing calfskin cape: A youngish man, light of skin and light of mount, moving as though he and the spotted pony were one. Everywhere he was, yet alone, a man apart, sullen, defiant, a little sad, but withal a man of purpose, directing, encouraging, fighting with a desperateness to preserve a race, a way of life alien to the white soldiers.

Off on the crest, the man of the battered hat, the braided beard, was more silent than ever amidst the darkening tumult. The twinkle had deadened in the good-humored eyes. Tough, weather-beaten campaigner that he was, he knew when the cards were against him. Royall was in desperate straits. Vroom had been cut to pieces. Henry was dangerously wounded, if not mortally so. Every available man was needed. Horses lay dead and dying wherever his eye fell. Twenty-five thousand rounds of ammunition had been used—it was precariously low, his rations, short. Drs. Patszki, Hartsuff and Stevens. his surgeons, were working frantically with the wounded. The movement down the canyon for the village—the village that he had wanted so desperately—had been a mistake.

Reluctantly, Crook gave the order to Nickerson to go after Mills and recall him to the field of battle.

Royall was now in increasing difficulties. After the third charge against his forces, his line gave way. He gave the order to retreat to the horses secreted in the ravine and rejoin the command on the crest to the north. But while the men attempted to mount in the ravine, a party of Sioux and Cheyenne whooped down the ravine of Kollmar Creek from the northwest, making a last devastating play for the horses. Against this new onslaught, the horses fell like rain and several men were wounded. Yet the battalion held together, withdrawing as a body eastward down the ravine 400 yards amid a fusillade of bullets and arrows.

Riding courageously northward up a side ravine, they gained the plateau. Passing to the south and then east of Burt and Burrowes, the brave little battalion finally made the crest and the comparative safety of the main command who had protected them by several volleys with their long range rifles against which the foe dare not come too close.

Royall's men were then placed in line on the crest and across the gap, probably about 1:00 o'clock.

Down in the Rosebud canyon, Mills' cavalry was overtaken by Nickerson, just at the point where the canyon narrows, three miles north of the bend. Defiling to the west, they led their horses up the steep slope to the plateau and made a wide circuit to the west to come in behind the Sioux north of Crook's Hill. Crazy Horse's forces at this point were forming a new attack behind a low ridge north of the crest. When they saw the cavalry in their rear, they were disconcerted. Abruptly, the Sioux broke off the battle and retreated to the northwest. Mills' cavalry followed them for several miles, then returned to the crest.

West Point trained to follow through on plans, Crook would not relinquish his original idea. Consequently, he assembled some of his cavalry and rode down the canyon in another attempt to locate Crazy Horse's village. But, when he reached the point where the canyon narrows, his Crow scouts refused to go farther, claiming the canyon was a death trap. The Sioux, they said, were waiting for them to go into it so that they could destroy the command where it would not have room to deploy.

Crook then returned to the crest and the rest of his command. The battle was over at 2:30, having lasted six hours,[16] when Mills returned from the canyon.

Disappointed at the surprising, exciting day, Crook yet had his wounded to think of. He ordered the command to the valley by the stream and camped where bivouac had been made that morning. The hospital was moved to a rough shelter on the banks of the Rosebud where he saw that the wounded were attended to and made as comfortable as possible. The men of each company were to bury their own dead near the banks of the stream, and that night the Shoshones buried the boy in the bed of the river.

General Crook reported nine men and one Indian scout killed, and twenty-one wounded. Thirteen of the hostile Indians were found dead on the field after the battle. It was believed that many more were killed but not found because of their practice of rescuing their dead and wounded under fire. Yet it would seem that there was an understatement of casualties in his report.

"The number of casualties of all kinds," Lt. Bourke stated in his *Diary*, "is fifty-seven (57) including ten (10) killed outright, (4) mortally wounded, and many of no significance."

T. B. MacMillan, one of the correspondents with the command, reported in the June 24, 1876, issue of *Inter Ocean* that "We lost 10 killed, 4 mortally wounded, 1 officer and 10 men dangerously wounded and about 30 slightly wounded. Lost 16 horses that were shot, and 7 carbines."

Lt. Daniel C. Pearson, who was later to give his account of Mills' trip down the canyon for the Sioux village, says, "Not to leave the dead of those troops behind, they were swung across saddles for their last ride." Yet in the official report of casualties there were no dead reported from these cavalry companies who went down the Rosebud canyon.

Captain Mills states in his account that General Crook told him that "We have lost about fifty killed and wounded," and also that the loss in killed and wounded of the 3rd Cavalry was "principally of Henry's and Van Vliet's squadron and Andrews' company of mine." In the official report however, there are no casualties at all listed for Van Vliet's squadron.

Gruard, head scout, who was a more impartial observer, says in his account, "To sum up the whole battle there were twenty-eight soldiers killed and fifty-six wounded."

Perhaps the strangest feature in the question of casualties is the fact that official reports are found on file in the National Archives for all company commanders in the Third Cavalry except Lt. Bainbridge Reynolds, Captain Peter D. Vroom, and Capt. Crawford, whose companies were said to have sustained the largest losses.

It seems *incredible* that all these men could have fought for six hours with only the small number killed as stated in the official report. The statement of Gruard would appear to be closer to the truth.

There are no accurate figures as to the casualties among the Crows and Shoshones, but they must have been very high. According to Finn Burnett, who was at their Agency when the Shoshones returned after the battle, "The Shoshones lost a tremendous number of their best warriors in the fight."[17] The Crows followed their usual practice of concealing their casualties, but Many Coups admitted 1 killed and 10 wounded. Chief Old Crow was shot through his kneecap on a little knoll north of the house on the Burt Young place at the west bend, and limped the rest of his life.[18] He made many trips to the field after the battle and was a familiar figure to early settlers in the area.

Crazy Horse is reported as saying that 36 Indians were killed and 63 wounded.[19] According to a newspaper dispatch dated 5th Cavalry Camp, July 19, 1876, about 100 Indians were wounded and it was acknowledged that 86 were killed in the Rosebud battle.[20] There is no way of knowing which, if either, of these statements is correct, but Crazy Horse's statement would seem more authoritative. The soldier accounts agree that the bodies of 13 hostile Indians were found on the field; so there must have been many more killed.

Elmer Kobold, an early settler, tells the story of a Crow Indian named "Blue Bead" who returned to the field every year on the anniversary of the battle and pointed out the very spot where he had killed and scalped a Sioux Indian in the valley south of the west bend. The skeleton of an Indian boy found in the rocks northeast of the Kobold house may have been that of the Sioux boy killed in a charge on the soldiers.

Charles Young, who settled here in 1894, found north of his house a skull with a bullet hole in the top, believed to be the skull of an Indian shot while lying down. When Mr. Young first came, there was the body of a Piegan Indian killed in the battle, on a scaffold propped between the branches of a tree with a split trunk on the west slope of the high bluff within the west bend, near the top. Lightning struck the tree and the bones tumbled down on the ground where they were visible for years. One of the homesteaders told Mr. Young that he had found many Indian skeletons "buried" in the rocks just west of the Burt Young house at the west bend, and that he hauled away a wagon load and buried them.

Horse-Runs-Ahead was in the Rosebud battle and was wounded in the heel, so that he did not fight in the Custer battle, although he was there.[21]

Little Wing died of his wounds and was found by Custer's men in the lone tepee in the forks of Reno Creek where the encampment had been.[22]

Thunder Hawk, a Sioux Indian of the Brule tribe, was wounded in the Rosebud battle.[23]

Chapter 7

WITH MILLS ON THE RIGHT FLANK

CAPTAIN Mills and his four companies of the 3rd Cavalry were those most actively engaged on the right flank of the battle. While Noyes had 5 companies of the 2nd Cavalry, they were held in reserve most of the time. The right flank covered roughly all territory north of and between the two bends, including the large ravine north of camp.

"The Indians Came in Flocks or Herds Like the Buffalo"

General Crook's lack of appreciation for the power of the Sioux, the tactician qualities of their war leader, Crazy Horse, seemed to be a source of never-ending disturbance to Captain Mills, loyal to his commander though he was. He wrote in *My Story:*

"General Crook had previously to do only with the semi-nomadic tribes and from conversations with him I felt he did not realize the prowess of the Sioux, though it was hard to think that he was not well informed by his numerous guides, scouts and especially the 250 friendly Indians . . ."

Perhaps the attack when it came then was not so surprising to him as it was to Crook. He gave a top level report of the action on the right flank and down the canyon,[1] from the commencement of the battle:

"Everything was quiet, the day was beautiful, clear and very warm. All had unbridled and were grazing for perhaps half to three quarters of an hour, when my colored servant observed he heard shouting, and knowing that his ears were better than mine, I advanced up the hill towards D (south) until I got to a high piece of ground, when looking north, I saw on the crest of the horizon about two miles distant, great numbers of moving objects, looking somewhat like distant crows silhouetted on the clear sky above the horizon. I soon came to the conclusion that they were Indians in great numbers.

"The friendly Indians were supposed to be in advance to find the enemy for us. General Crook and the troops on the left bank of the river were prevented from seeing anything to the north by the rising bluffs between them and the approaching Indians. I am satisfied that I was the first person to observe the coming hostiles. They were, when I first saw them, from two to three miles distant, coming at full speed towards us and cheering.

"I immediately sounded the alarm, directing some of my squadron to mount, and calling out to General Crook, who was playing cards with some of his officers, that the Sioux were rapidly approaching. He ordered me to report to him with my squadron at once. When I met him after crossing the stream, which was very boggy, I told him we were about to be attacked by a large force, and that the Indians were coming from due north. He told me to march rapidly and as soon as I got to higher ground to take the bluffs and hold them. I did so . . . In all of this fight I do not remember to have received a single order except from General Crook personally or his adjutant, Major Nickerson. I marched as rapidly as I could through the rough and broken rocks, and as soon as I got on smoother ground gave the command 'Front into line' and sounded the charge.

"There were two prominent rocky ridges, the first above a half mile from where I met General Crook, and the second probably about a half mile further on. When I reached the first ridge the leading (Sioux) Indians were there but gave way. There were large boulders at its foot, some large enough to cover the sets of four horses. I dismounted and directed the horse holders to protect them behind these rocks, advancing the men to the top of the ridge where the boulders were smaller, but of a size to protect one of two soldiers, and appeared to be just what we wanted to fight behind.

"We met the Indians at the foot of this ridge, and charged right in and through them, driving them back to the top of the ridge. These Indians were most hideous, every one being painted in most hideous colors and designs, stark naked, except their moccasins, breech clouts and head gear, the latter consisting of feathers and horns; some of the horses being also painted, and the Indians proved then and there that they were the best cavalry soldiers on earth. In charging up towards us they exposed little of their person, hanging on with one arm around the neck and one leg over the horse, firing and lancing from underneath the horses necks, so that there was no part of the Indian at which we could aim.

"Their shouting and personal appearance was so hideous that it terrified the horses more than our men and rendered them almost uncontrollable before we dismounted and placed them behind the rocks. The Indians came not in a line but in flocks or herds like the buffalo, and they piled in upon us until I think there must have been one thousand or fifteen hundred in our immediate front, but they refused to fight when they found us secured behind the rocks, and bore off to our left.

"I then charged the second ridge, and took it in the same manner and fortified myself with the horses protected behind the larger boulders and the men behind the smaller one. These Indians lived with their horses, were unsurfeited with food, shelter, raiment or equipment, then the best cavalry in the world; their like will never be seen again. Our friendlies were worthless against them; we would have been better off without them.[2]

"On our right we were absolutely protected by the jagged and rough places down to the Rosebud Canyon, so we were most fortunate in securing this position. On examining my front after taking the first ridge, I found that one of my troops, Captain Andrews', was missing, and learned that Colonel Royall had cut him off and directed that he report to him, as he was moving to the left with Captain Henry's squadron.

"We could see little of the left, as the ground depressed and the rough rocks obscured vision of what was going on by either the Indians or Henry's, Van Vliet's and Royall's commands. I observed about this time two troops which I afterwards learned were Van Vliet's, going to D on the south bluff, and later saw them proceed in a northwesterly direction towards where we could hear firing from Henry's and Royall's commands.[3]

"Soon after I took the first bluff the infantry took position to my left and Captain Noyes with his five troops arrived, and was placed in reserve by General Crook in our rear and left, and the infantry joined on the ground lying on my left. General Crook held his position near my squadron between my squadron and Noyes' during the entire battle, but I had little communication with him save when he came to me to give orders, and I knew little of what was going on until finally most of the Indians left my front.

"About 12:30 he (General Crook) ordered me to take my command of three troops and ordered Captain Noyes with his five troops to report to me, and proceed with the eight down the canyon and take the village, which he said he had been reliably informed was about six miles down the canyon.

Noyes, who was one of the best cavalry officers I ever knew, moved off as indicated on the map. This canyon was about six miles long. I was directed to follow it until I came to the village, and take it, and hold it until he came to my support with the rest of the command.

"I obeyed the order until I reached the vicinity of the village, when I heard a voice calling to me to halt, and Major Nickerson, the Adjutant General, directed me to return at once to General Crook. Some of the officers advised not.

"'We have the village,' they said, 'and can hold it.'

Nickerson then came across the stream. I asked him:

"'Are you sure he wants me to go back.'

"He replied he was. The canyon had opened here so I found I could climb the rocks and get out, as indicated on the map."

Knowing how much General Crook wanted Crazy Horse's village, Mills was at a loss to understand his commander. Why had he been recalled at the very moment of victory? Why? Why?

Loyal to duty and commander, he complied with the order, yet at the first opportunity he questioned Crook in his direct manner.

"I returned about 2:30," Mills continues in *My Story*, "and found General Crook in about the same position I had left him, and said:

"'General, why did you recall me? I had the village and could have held it.'

"I never saw a man more dejected. He replied:

"'Well, Colonel, I found it a more serious engagement than I thought. We have lost about fifty killed and wounded, and the doctors refused to remain with the wounded unless I left the infantry and one of the squadrons with them . . . I knew I could not keep my promise to support you with the remainder of the force.'

"The General had assembled the hospital around him and the infantry, also two battalions near him. In visiting my wounded, Captain Henry heard my voice and called me. I did not know until then that he had been wounded, and going to him, found his breast all covered with clotted blood, his eyes swollen so he could not see, and a ghastly wound through both cheeks under the eyes. I said:

" 'Henry, are you badly wounded,' and he replied:

" 'The doctors have just told me that I must die, but I will not.'

"And he did not, although nine out of ten under such circumstances would have died."

Captain Henry did not die but he lost permanently the sight of one eye. Eventually, he regained the use of the other.

The first charge Captain Mills described took his men to the crest of the ridge east of the gap. Here the Sioux made a brief stand behind rocks bordering the east slope of the gap, finally retreating westward a half mile along the crest to Crook's Hill, where they maintained a heavy fire upon the troops. Crook's Hill, a quarter mile in diameter, rises abruptly on the east and south slopes, jutting into the valley, the western rim being rocky 100 yards south.

The north part of the hill, part of the long crest, continues a mile and a quarter west to the head of Kollmar Creek.

In the second charge, Mills took Crook's Hill, the Sioux retreating along the crest west and a little north to the large conical mound 1200 yards away. West of Crook's Hill, leading down south from the crest, are a number of large rocky ravines, the heads of small tributaries leading into Kollmar Creek.

After the first Sioux charge had been rebuffed, four companies of the 2nd Cavalry were advanced dismounted in a skirmish line across and to the east of the gap. The 5th Company (Company A, under Captain Dewees and Lt. Pearson), was detailed to round up and saddle the battalion's horses. The cavalry companies on the south side of the stream caught their horses, saddled up and awaited orders. Captain Mills led his men across the stream and deployed them to the east. His line cleared and extended beyond the skirmish line of the 2nd Cavalry companies forming a column of companies, four lines deep, with a front between 200-300 yards.

Meanwhile, the Crows and Shoshones were holding back the Sioux on the plateau northwest of camp until the infantry arrived on that front. The skirmish line was holding them back north of camp. Now it was that Mills, charging northward, took the Sioux in flank as the crest runs southeast on that side of the gap. Two knobs on the crest—one each side of the gap—

are one mile from the stream, while the east end of the crest is but three-fourths of a mile from it.

The field over which the charge was made is extremely rough and rugged, with little conical hillocks, topped with pines, steep rocky bluffs, large boulders, deep rocky ravines, shelves and rimrocks. Unreal, fanciful, it is a perfect picture of Indian land.

The battalions of Mills and Noyes formed the right flank of the battleline which at first extended east and west along the crest. After Mills' second charge along the crest, his line faced west though still on the right. Now the infantry and 2nd Cavalry companies were in his rear, protected from the Sioux who kept swinging back to attack their front.

Noon came, and Mills, under order from his commanding general, started for the village of Crazy Horse to destroy it.

"We Went Like a Storm"

With Mills on his mission down the canyon were the dynamic and fluent Finerty and the gallant and equally fluent Bourke. Finerty, who was with Company E, under Captain Sutorius of Mills' battalion, gives a slightly different account. The command was resting, he says, when:

"At 8:30 without any warning we heard a few shots from behind the bluffs to the north.

" 'They are shooting buffalo over there,' said the Captain (Sutorius).

"Very soon we began to know, by the alternate rise and fall of the reports, that the shots were not all fired in one direction. Hardly had we reached this conclusion, when a score or two of our Indian scouts appeared up the northern crest, and rode down the slope with incredible speed.

" 'Saddle up, there, saddle up, there quick,' shouted Col. Mills, and immediately all the cavalry within sight, without waiting for formal orders, were mounted and ready for action.

"General Crook, who appreciated the situation, had already ordered the companies of the 4th and 9th Infantry, posted at the foot of the northern slopes, to deploy as skirmishers, leaving their mules with the holders. Hardly had this precaution been taken, when the flying Crow and Snake scouts utterly panic stricken, came into camp shouting at the top of their voices,

"'*Heap Sioux! Heap Sioux!*' gesticulating wildly in the direction of the bluffs which they had abandoned in such haste. All looked in that direction, and there, sure enough, were the Sioux in goodly numbers, and in loose, but formidable array. The singing of the bullets above our heads speedily convinced us that they had called on business.

"'Why the Devil don't they order us to charge?' asked the brave Von Leutwitz.

"'Here comes Lemly,[4] the regimental adjutant now,' answered Sutorius. 'How do you feel about it?' he inquired turning to me.

"'It is the anniversary of Bunker Hill,' was my answer. 'The day is of good omen.'

"'By Jove, I never thought of that,' cried Sutorius, and loud enough for the soldiers to hear, 'It is the anniversary of Bunker Hill, we're in luck.'

"The men waved their carbines, which were right shouldered, but true to the parade etiquette of the American Army, did not cheer, although they forgot all about etiquette later on. Up, meanwhile, bound on bound, his gallant horse covered with foam, came Lemly.

"'The commanding officer's compliments, Col. Mills,' he yelled. 'Your battalion will charge those bluffs on the center.'

"Mills immediately swung his fine battalion, consisting of Troops A, E, I and M, by the right into line, and rising in his stirrup, shouted, 'Charge.' Forward we went at our best pace, to reach the crest occupied by the enemy, who meanwhile, were not idle, for men and horses rolled over pretty rapidly...

"We went like a storm, and the Indians waited for us until we were within fifty paces. We were going too rapidly to use our carbines, but several of the men fired their revolvers . . . Our men broke into a mad cheer as the Sioux unable to face that impetuous line of warriors of the superior race, broke and fled . . . I remember how well our troops kept their formation, and how gallantly they sat their horses as they galloped fiercely up the rough ascent. We got to the heights, and were immediately dismounted and formed in open order, as skirmishers, along the rocky crest.

"While Mills' battalion was executing the movement described, General Crook ordered the 2nd battalion of the 3rd Cavalry, under Col. Henry, consisting of Troops B, D, F, and L, to charge the right of the Sioux array, which was hotly pressing our steady infantry. Henry executed the order with characteristic dash and promptitude, and the Indians were compelled to fall back in great confusion all along the line.

"General Crook kept the five troops of the 2nd Cavalry, under Noyes, in reserve, and ordered Troops C and G of the

3rd Cavalry, under Captain Van Vliet and Lt. Crawford, to
occupy the bluffs on our left rear . . .

"General Crook divined that the Indian force before him
was a strong body, not less perhaps than 2500 warriors, sent
out to make a rear guard fight, so as to cover the retreat of
their village, which was situated at the other end of the cañon.
He detached Troop I of the 3rd Cavalry, Capt. Andrews and
Lt. Foster, from Mills to Henry, after the former had taken
the first line of heights. He reinforced our line with the friendly
Indians, who seemed to be partially stampeded, and brought
up the whole of the 2nd Cavalry within supporting distance.

"The Sioux, having rallied on the second line of heights,
became bold and impudent again. They rode up and down
rapidly, sometimes wheeling in circles, slapping an indelicate
portion of their persons at us, and beckoning us to come on . . .

"Under Crook's orders, our whole line remounted, and after
another rapid charge, we became masters of the second crest.
When we got there, another just like it rose on the other side
of the valley. There, too, were the savages as fresh, apparently,
as ever. We dismounted accordingly, and the firing began
again. It was now evident that the weight of the fighting was
shifting from our front, of which Major Evans had general
command, to our left where Royall and Henry cheered on
their men. Still the enemy were thick enough on their crest,
and Col. Mills, who had active charge of our operations,
wished to dislodge them. The volume of fire, rapid and ever
increasing, came from our left. The wind freshened from the
west, and we could hear the uproar distinctly.

"Soon however, the restless foe came back upon us, apparently reinforced. He made a vigorous push for our center
down some rocky ravines, which gave him good cover. Just
then a tremendous yell arose behind us, and along through
the intervals of our battalions, came the tumultuous array of
the Crow and Shoshone Indians, rallied and led back to action,
by Major George Randall and Lt. Bourke of General Crook's
staff. Orderly Sergeant John Van Moll,[5] of Troop A, Mills'
battalion, a brave and gigantic soldier who was subsequently
basely murdered by a drunken mutineer of his company,
dashed forward on foot with them.

"The two bodies of savages, all stripped to the breech clout,
moccasins, and war bonnet, came together in the trough of
the valley, the Sioux having descended to meet our allies
with right good will.[6] All, except Sergt. Van Moll, were
mounted. Then began a most exciting encounter. The wild
foemen, covering themselves with their horses, while going at
full speed, blazed away rapidly. Our regulars did not fire
because it would have been sure death to some of the friendly

Indians, who were barely distinguishable by a red badge
which they carried. Horses fell dead by the score, they were
heaped there when the fight closed . . . .

"Finally the Sioux on the right, hearing the yelping and
firing of the rival tribes, came up in great numbers, and our
Indians, carefully picking up their wounded, and making their
uninjured horses carry double, began to draw off in good order.
Sergeant Van Moll was left alone on foot, a dozen Sioux
dashed at him. Major Randall and Lt. Bourke, who had probably not noticed him in the general melee, but who in the
crisis, recognized his stature and his danger, turned their
horses to rush to his rescue. They called on the Indians to
follow them. One small misshapen Crow warrior, mounted on
a fleet pony, outstripped all others. He dashed boldly in among
the Sioux, against whom Van Moll was dauntlessly defending
himself, seized the big Sergeant by the shoulder and motioned
him to jump up behind.

"The Sioux were too astonished to realize what had been
done until they saw the long-legged Sergeant, mounted behind
the little Crow, known as Humpy, dash toward our lines like
the wind. Then they opened fire, but we opened also, and
compelled them to seek higher ground. The whole line of our
battalion cheered Humpy and Van Moll as they passed us on
the home stretch . . .

"We were compelled to drive them (Sioux) from the third
ridge.[7] Our ground was more favorable for quick movements
than that occupied by Royall . . . ."

The trip down the canyon was soon to come. Finerty, after
Mills had given the order to retire and remount, tells of the
difficulty in getting into the canyon:

"Troops A, E, and M of Mills' battalion, having remounted,
guided by the scout Grouard, plunged immediately into what
is called, on what authority I know not, the Dead Cañon of
Rosebud Valley. It is a dark, narrow and winding defile, over
a dozen miles in length, and the main Indian village was supposed to be situated in the north end of it. Lt. Bourke, of
Crook's staff, accompanied the column.

"A body of Sioux, posted on a bluff which commanded the
west side of the mouth of the cañon, was brilliantly dislodged
by a bold charge of Troop E under Captain Sutorius and
Lt. Von Leutwitz.[8] After this our march began in earnest. The
bluffs, on both sides of the ravine, were thickly covered with
rocks and fir trees, thus affording ample protection to an enemy
and making it impossible for our cavalry to act as flankers.
Col. Mills ordered the section of the battalion moving on the

east side to cover their comrades on the west side, if fired upon, and vice versa. This was good advice, and good strategy in the position in which we were placed.

"We began to think our force rather weak for so venturous an enterprise, but Lt. Bourke informed the Colonel that the five troops of the 2nd Cavalry, under Major Noyes, were marching behind us . . . Nevertheless, some of the more thoughtful officers had their misgivings, because the cañon was certainly a most dangerous defile, where all the advantage would be on the side of the savages . . . .

"Noyes, marching his battalion rapidly, soon overtook our rear guard, and the whole column increased its pace. Fresh signs of Indians began to appear in all directions, and we began to feel that the sighting of their village would be only a question of a few miles further on. We came to a halt in a kind of cross cañon, which had an opening toward the west, and there tightened up our horse girths, and got ready for what we believed must be a desperate fight. The keen-eared Grouard pointed toward the occident, and said to Col. Mills, 'I hear firing in that direction, sir.'

"Just then there was a sound of fierce galloping behind us, and a horseman, dressed in buckskin, and wearing a long beard, originally black, but turned temporarily gray by the dust, shot by the halted command, and dashed up to where Col. Mills and the other officers were standing.

"It was Major A. H. Nickerson, of the General's staff . . . He had ridden with a single orderly, through the cañon to overtake us, at the imminent peril of his life.

"'Mills,' he said, 'Royall is hard pressed, and must be relieved. Henry is badly wounded, and Vroom's troop is all cut up. The General orders that you and Noyes defile by your left flank out of this cañon and fall on the rear of the Indians who are pressing Royall.'

"This, then was the firing that Grouard had heard.

"Crook's order was instantly obeyed, and we were fortunate enough to find a comparatively easy way out of the elongated trap . . . We were soon clear of Dead Cañon, although we had to lead our horses carefully over and among the boulders and fallen timber. The crest of the side of the ravine proved to be a sort of plateau, and there we could hear quite plainly the noise of the attack on Royall's front. We got out from among the loose rocks and scraggy trees that fringed the rim of the gulf, and found ourselves in quite an open country.

"'Prepare to mount,' shouted the officers, and we were again in the saddle. Then we urged our animals to their best pace, and speedily came in view of the contending parties. The Indians had their ponies, guarded mostly by mere boys, in rear of the low, rocky crest which they occupied. The position held by Royall rose somewhat higher, and both lines could be seen at a ·glance. There was heavy firing, and the Sioux were evidently preparing to make an attack in force, as they were riding in by the score, especially from the point abandoned by Mills' battalion in its movement down the cañon, and which was partially held thereafter by the friendly Indians, a few infantry and a body of sturdy mule packers, commanded by the brave Tom Moore, who fought on that day as if he had been a private soldier.

'Suddenly the Sioux lookouts observed our unexpected approach, and gave the alarm to their friends. We dashed forward at a wild gallop, cheering as we went, and I am sure we were all anxious at that moment to avenge our comrades of Henry's battalion. But the cunning savages did not wait for us. They picked up their wounded, all but thirteen of their dead, and broke away to the northwest on their fleet ponies, leaving us only the thirteen scalps, 150 dead horses and ponies, and a few old blankets and war bonnets as trophies of the fray . . .

"We had driven the Indians about five miles from the point where the fight began, and the General decided to return therein, in order that we might be nearer water. The troops had nearly used up their rations and had fired about 25,000 rounds of ammunition. It often takes an immense amount of lead to send even one Indian to the happy hunting grounds.

"The obstinacy, or timidity, of the Crow scouts in the morning spoiled General Crook's plans. It was originally his intent to fling his whole force on the Indian village, and win or lose all by a single blow. The fall of Guy V. Henry early in the fight on the left, had a bad effect upon the soldiers, and Captain Vroom's company became entangled so badly that a temporary success raised the spirits of the Indians and enabled them to keep our left wing in check sufficiently long to allow the savages to effect the safe retreat of their village to the valley of the Little Big Horn.

"Had Crook's original plan been carried out to the letter, our whole force, about 1100 men, would have been in the hostile village at noon, and in the light of after events, it is not improbable that all of us would have settled there permanently. Five thousand able-bodied warriors, well armed, would have given Crook all the trouble he wanted if he had struck their village."

Lt. John G. Bourke, in his *On The Border With Crook*, substantiates this opinion:

"In one word, the battle of the Rosebud was a trap, and Crazy Horse . . . was satisfied he was going to have everything his own way. He stated afterwards, when he had surrendered to General Crook at the agency, that he had no less than six thousand five hundred men in the fight, and that the first attack was made with fifteen hundred, the others being concealed behind the bluffs and hills.[9]

"His plan of battle was either to lead detachments in pursuit of his people, and turning quickly cut them to pieces in detail, or draw the whole of Crook's forces down into the canyon of the Rosebud, where escape would have been impossible, as it formed a veritable *cul-de-sac,* the vertical walls hemming in the sides, the front being closed by a dam and abatis of broken timber which gave a depth of ten feet of water and mud, the rear, of course, to be shut off by thousands of yelling, murderous Sioux . . . ."

Bourke, as staff officer to Crook, was a busy man that day, carrying orders for his commander and leading various detachments into battle. The charge of the Shoshones and Crows was one of the most interesting features of the battle. Of his part in the charge, Bourke wrote in his book:

"I went in with this charge, and was enabled to see how such things were conducted by the American savages, fighting according to their own notions. There was a headlong rush for about two hundred yards, which drove the enemy back in confusion; then was a sudden halt, and very many of the Shoshones jumped down from their ponies and began firing from the ground; the others who remained mounted threw themselves alongside of their horse's necks, so that there would be a few good marks presented to the aim of the enemy. Then, in response to some signal or cry which, of course, I did not understand, we were off again, this time for good, and right into the midst of the hostiles, who had been halted by a steep hill directly in their front. Why we did not kill more of them than we did was because they were dressed so like our own Crows that even our Shoshones were afraid of mistakes, and in the confusion many of the Sioux and Cheyennes made their way down the face of the bluffs unharmed.

"From this high point[10] there could be seen on Crook's right and rear, a force of cavalry, some mounted, others dismounted, apparently in the clutches of the enemy . . . . a body of hostiles were engaging attention in front and at the same time a large mass, numbering not less than five hundred, was getting ready to pounce upon the rear and flank of the unsuspecting Americans."

That evening, after the battle, Bourke sat down on the banks of the spring where he had played cards with General Crook in the morning—the very site where the Shoshone boy had been scalped while faithfully guarding the horses—to write in his *Diary*:

"I found myself on the summit of the ridge in a place commanding an excellent view of the whole field. From the immediate front of our little party the Sioux were flying in dismay to the number of fifty or thereabouts . . . Major Randall then came up to me and suggested a falling back from that point to one more sheltered in the rear. The Shoshones, as is their wont, executed the order at a gallop leaving Bugler Snow and the writer alone upon the ridge, unsuspicious of danger. Scarcely had I mounted my horse and mechanically loaded my carbine, when I called out to Bugler Snow to mount at once as Sioux were charging up the ravine on the left of the hill. Sure enough they came to the number of thirty (30) or more, poor Snow being still on the ground. I gave them the contents of my carbine at more than 30 yards, at the same time yelling to make them believe there were still many of us there . . . . they halted for one brief space, long enough however to let Snow and myself put spurs to our horses, and rush after our commands nearly 400 yards away."

Because some of the detachments had ventured out too far, the extended line was too weak to withstand a determined attack, Crook sent orders that all troops should fall back until the line was complete.

"Burt and Burrowes were set with their companies of the Ninth Infantry to drive back the force which was congregating in the rear of Royall's command, which was the body of troops seen from the hill crest almost surrounded by the foe.

"Tom Moore with his sharpshooters from the pack train, and several of the Montana miners . . . were ordered to get into a shelf of rocks four hundred yards out on our front and pick off as many of the hostile chiefs as possible and also to make the best impression upon the flanks of any charging parties which might attempt to pass on either side of that promontory. Moore worried the Indians so much that they tried to cut off him and his insignificant band. It was one of the ridiculous episodes of the day to watch those well meaning young warriors charging at full speed across the open space commanded by Moore's position . . .

". . . . beyond taking an extra chew of tobacco, I do not remember that any of the party did anything to show that he cared a continental whether the enemy came or stayed. When those deadly rifles, sighted by men who had no idea what the word 'nerves' meant, belched their storm of lead in among the braves and their ponies, it did not take more than seven seconds for the former to conclude that home, sweet home was a good enough place for them."

Andrews' point is the highest crest on the field and is located at the junction of the two long ridges several hundred yards west of the head of Kollmar Creek. From it one can look eastward along the ridge to Crook's Hill, and southeastward along the ridge south of Kollmar Creek.

Packers' Rocks mentioned by Bourke are a row of huge sandstone rocks forming a spur about a hundred yards long jutting northward from the north side of the crest 400 yards west of Crook's Hill. It is clear that Bourke and General Crook were standing on Crook's Hill facing the conical mound to the northwest to which the Indians had retreated, and needed sharpshooters to keep them from making individual forays upon the Hill. It is probable that the skirmish line thrown out by Mills when he first took the Hill was in the vicinity of the rocks, as soldiers' shells have been found near the area.

"No Conclusion Was So Apparent as Our Defeat"

Lt. Daniel C. Pearson was with Company A of the 2nd Cavalry, under Captain Dewees. This was the company which stayed in the valley to saddle up the horses for the other four companies of that regiment, an activity which took about an hour, when they took the led horses to the crest together with the wounded. In his article, "Military Notes, 1876," in the September, 1899, issue of the *U. S. Cavalry Journal,* he told of his experiences in the battle:

"In our 17th of June affair on the upper Rosebud, our Indian allies, of whom the Crows were in their familiar country, proved of great assistance. The evidences we had of their wonderful eyesight were constantly with us. The Second Cavalry squadron was first in contact with the Indians. I recall the strange and unaccustomed sensation of that target practice in which the bullets whizzed thick and close to my firing point . . .

"I recall, too, the fact that at one time more than my share of bullets, apparently, struck the ground near by, and that I afterward discovered that the motion of my horse had inverted my open cartridge box and pitched a large percentage of my cartridges upon the ground. Does it not rank high among comical events of this world to think of a soldier creating a battlefield all by himself, and being dismayed by the sound of his own bullets as he unconsciously fires them at the ground? . . . .

"One of the recruits handed an Indian his carbine in token of surrender. The Indian, acting with dispatch in such close proximity to our line, grasped the carbine, smashed the soldier's face with the stock, and then dashed away. For one on the ground, it was impossible to tell of the duration of that fight. Thoroughly convinced that our foes were in multitudes, although for the most part concealed from our sight-momentarily assured by Crow or Shoshone, who, with penetrating eye and gesticulating hand, indicated the hostiles, that never in the world were quite so many Indians assembled before—no conclusion was so apparent as our defeat.

Finally, orders came to move down the Rosebud to the supposed Indian village. Nine troops of cavalry were disengaged from the fight and started in that direction . . . .

"The nine troops had rapidly passed some seven miles into the cañon, whither our Indian allies refused to go. At this point, an aide overtook us with an order to retire from the cañon by the quickest route. The reason stated by the commanding general in his report for countermanding the order for us to go down the cañon, was that he desired to use us elsewhere. The very evident fact to us was that we certainly would never have been of use elsewhere, except for that countermanding order. If of any immediate subsequent use on that day it was not apparent.

"Turning short to the left hand in the cañon, our path was up a steep, thickly wooded declivity. My part at that time was to be messenger to communicate directions to succeeding troops; to overtake the head of the column, and to be bearer of messages to the rear again until, breathless and leg weary, as the ascent was too steep for riding, I was the last to clamber out of that cañon fully persuaded that the whole Sioux nation was at my heels.

"Upon reaching the high and level ground there were the balance of the command and the wounded. In aiding the wounded much skill was manifested by our Indians. The first thing that struck me was the sight of our wounded prone upon the ground, in the hot summer sun, without protection. At the same time, there were the wounded of our friendly Indians with hastily constructed tripod and shelter over them. In all their treatment of the wounded, they displayed a certain skill that was born of familiarity with life and death contests."

Louis Dog, one of the Cheyennes active in the battle, once told Elmer Kobold that the large ravine or gap which cuts through the ridge north of his house was the route used by Mills when he defiled out of the canyon. One of the main points of the field, it was also through this gap that Crazy Horse's forces which came up the Rosebud arrived at the field. It was these hostiles who, seeing the horses and mules grazing in the valley, poured down the ravine to capture them, but were met by the unexpected fire of the men of the 2nd Cavalry, concealed behind some small bluffs. Louis Dog showed with sweeping gestures how the Indians divided, half of them turning to the right and retreating to the crest along the slopes bordering the west side of the gap, the others turning left and returning by the slopes on the east side. These were the Indians who later contested the soldiers' advance to take the crest at this point.

The battle over, Crook ordered his command to the bivouac of the morning to take care of the wounded and bury the dead. "The officers," as Mills later wrote, "then mingled and talked over the fight."

The casualties on the right flank as reported by General Crook were: 2nd Cavalry, Sergeant Patrick O'Donnell, wounded in the right arm and Sergeant Thomas L. Meagher, a slight wound in his right forearm; 3rd Cavalry, Private Horace Harold, shot in the right shoulder while aiming his carbine, and his jaw broken; Bugler Elmer A. Snow, shot through both forearms.

Mills stated that "Though the 3rd Cavalry had less than one-half of the soldiers engaged, their loss in killed and wounded was about four-fifths, principally of Henry's and Van Vliet's squadrons, and Andrew's company of mine, that of Vroom's company being the greatest in proportion, this owing to their isolated expose on level ground where the Indians could pass through them."

Finerty had praise for his fellow writers. "I am bound to add, for the honor of the journalistic profession, that Mr. Mac-Millan, who accompanied our battalion, showed gallantry throughout the affair, which lasted from 8:00 in the morning until 2 in the afternoon, and the officers with the other commands spoke warmly that evening of the courage displayed by Messr. Strahorn, Wasson and Davenport."

Though Crook apparently said little of the suddenness or the severity of the attack, most of the officers, as Mills said, "realized for the first time that while we were lucky not to have been entirely vanquished, we had been most humiliatingly defeated."

Finerty says the day ended with General Crook's deciding to "retire to his base of supplies, the wagon train, with his wounded, in view of the fact that his rations were almost used up, and that his ammunition had run pretty low. He was also convinced that all chance of surprising the Sioux camp was over for the present, and perhaps he felt that even if it could be surprised, his small force would be unequal to the task of carrying it by storm. The Indians had shown themselves good fighters, and he shrewdly calculated that his men had been opposed to only a part of the well armed warriors actually in the field."

Much has been written about the Rosebud canyon's having been a death trap. General Crook in his reports of the battle gave the impression that the soldiers had scored an important victory in preventing the Indians from driving them into this canyon and slaughtering them. Some modern writers and ranchers living in the area claim that the physical aspects of the little valley do not sustain this conclusion.[11]

The Rosebud valley for three miles north of the east bend is about a quarter mile wide; but when it reaches the side ravine on the west where Mills defiled, it narrows to about 150 yards wide at the bottom. The slope on the east side is high, steep and rocky, but the slope on the west is more gradual. Early settlers in the area say that the narrow portion was covered by beaver dams, fallen trees and rocks in the early days, an ideal place for an ambush.

Elmer Kobold told the writer that when he first came to this country he saw Indian boys rolling rocks down the steep east slope. Lt. Bourke claimed that, in an interview after surrendering in 1877, Crazy Horse made the statement that he had most of his warriors lined up along the canyon walls waiting for the soldiers to enter the narrow portion.[12] However all of the Cheyennes and Sioux interviewed by Grinnell and Stanley Vestal deny that there was any trap set.

On the other hand, John Stands-In-Timber told the writer

that the warriors had told him that there were many of them
hiding behind the fallen trees, rocks, and beaver dams, waiting
for the soldiers to enter; but when Mills led the men out of
the canyon before entering the narrow part, the Indians simply
swarmed out from their hiding places.

When Mills left the canyon, he immediately led his men up
on the plateau on the north side of the ravine, and returned
to the field by a circuitous route towards the west in order
that they might come in behind the Indians still fighting with
the main command.

However, today, the canyon does not look very forbidding.
The fallen trees, rocks and beaver dams have been cleared out
and it is now used as pasture. The narrow part extends northward only about a half mile, so that the long line of eight
troops of cavalry could have been cut in two by the Indians
in ambush, and destroyed in detail.

Another reason for believing that the Canyon was used as
a trap is that the story told by Crook and his officers about
the ambush was never denied by any of those who were critical of his action. If there had been no ambush, Frank Gruard
and Ben Arnold would have been quick to say so.

It was generally believed that the village of Crazy Horse
was situated all the way from six to twenty miles north in the
canyon on the basis of reports given by the Crow scouts. The
latter had no conception of distance in terms of miles so had
no adequate means of conveying to the soldiers just how far
north they believed the village to be.

Actually, no village was seen by Mills down the canyon, or
by any of the soldiers at that time. Later, Crook's command
was to pass down the Rosebud canyon the following August,
at which time Finerty mentioned that they found the site "of
the mammoth Indian village, to protect which Sitting Bull
fought on the 17th of June." But the village that Crook vainly
sought he never found. John Stands-In-Timber says the Crazy
Horse village was not in the large encampment, but was situated in the valley where Thompson Creek joins the Rosebud,
seventeen miles north of the battlefield.

A tributary of the Rosebud called "Indian Creek," which flows
in from the west—four miles north of the battlefield—is sup-

posed to have acquired its name from the Indian village located in the valley where it joins the main stream. There is
no evidence to support this theory. Some accounts of the battle
claim that Mills defiled up the canyon of Indian Creek in his
return to the field. These are obviously incorrect for the reason
that Indian Creek is north of the narrow part of the canyon
and all the soldier accounts say Mills defiled just before the
canyon narrows.

Author's Note: There have been relics found all over this
area. A number of .45–70 Springfield copper cartridge cases
as used by the soldiers have been found on the bluff immediately north of the Penson house at the extreme east end of
the field where the stream turns to the north. These were undoubtedly used by Troop E of the 3rd Cavalry under Captain
Sutorius when it charged a band of Indians contesting the
advance of Mills down the canyon.

It has been claimed that picket pins as used by the cavalry
have been found in the valley southwest of the Penson house.
These could have been left by the advance guard, or pickets,
at the first attack northeast of camp, located on both sides
of the stream extending from a little east of Kobold's house
westward a half mile. The Kobold house, situated on the Rosebud's north bank midway between the two bends, is nearly a
mile and a half west of the Penson house. An officer's spur
and mess knife were found behind the Kobold house, while
on the south side of the stream have been found many soldiers'
unfired shells. These latter could have been dropped by the
soldiers while loading their carbines with nervous fingers similar to those of Lt. Pearson. I have been informed that about
fifteen empty soldiers' shells have been found at the foot of
one of the fantastic little knolls north of the Kobold house,
probably used in the repulse of the Sioux down the big ravine
at the beginning of the fight. Mr. Kobold and his son George
have found a number of soldiers' shells scattered along the
little ridges bordering the west side of the large ravine. I
found a few also on the little wooded ridge halfway to the crest.

On the large knob at the west edge of the ravine at the
crest are a number of tepee camp rings. Here I found a stone
skin scraper, a broken arrowhead, and several pieces of flint

which had been worked on. Shells have been found scattered along the crest east of Crook's Hill. The one I found on my first trip was the .50–70 Springfield on the crest a little east of Kobold's house. This was the area covered by Mills' sweeping cavalry charge, so that shells do not occur in large quantity at any one place but are scattered all around and are very hard to find.

Crook's Hill is the most prominent place on the field and has the appearance of a high rocky crest. It is the place where visitors to the field naturally go. From it is obtained a view for many miles in all directions. Early settlers found both fired and unfired shells on top of the hill. Along the west rim, which is very rocky, a breastworks of rocks was piled up against the forays of the Indians from the west and northwest, probably made by the packers and infantry who occupied the hill during Mills' trip down the canyon.

Today the rocks have fallen down the steep slope on the west, but the outline of the breastwork can still be seen. Mrs. Rose Kobold, who was a teacher in the little schoolhouse near the east bend years ago, tells about her children coming to school with hats full of shells, many still loaded, which they had found on the hill. This area is pretty well picked over, but I have found three arrow heads near the west rim together with one empty .50 caliber Model 1865 Spencer rimfire cartridge with "JG" base marking, manufactured by Jacob Goldmark, a private contractor who made ammunition for the Government during the Civil War.[13] An old-timer even at the time of the battle, it was probably fired by one of the hostile Indians, although the miners undoubtedly had some Spencer carbines.

Archie Storm of Sheridan, Wyoming, found three unusual types of empty shells on the north side of Crook's Hill, which I have now in my collection. One is a .50-70 Springfield, regulation outside primer centerfire, using a 3 hole Berdan primer with a brass case. It is a standard commercial loading, probably of Winchester make. The case at the end is shattered in several places indicating that the shell was reloaded several times. It could have been used by the packers or miners, or in the .50-70 Springfield carbines which some of the hostiles had.

Another is a .45-70 Springfield Model 1873, brass case, standard external centerfire primer, probably of Winchester manufacture. The Shoshones used the latest model .45 caliber carbines, but the soldiers would not use commercial ammunition as long as ammunition was furnished free by the army.

The third empty shell was the most interesting, a bottle necked .45-75-350 Winchester Centennial Model 1876. Since production was started early that year, it is possible that this shell was used in the battle, although this model rifle was not marketed until later. The shell was probably used by one of the officers, who obtained a rifle from the Winchester Company. I have not had time yet to go over the whole hilltop with a metal detector, but it can be assumed that many shells of all types could be found there. My main purpose has been to locate the unknown ridges which were important positions in the battle.

I found two soldiers' empty shells and one .50-70 Springfield shell on the south edge of the crest, three hundred yards west of Crook's Hill, behind a small rocky ledge. These could have been used by a soldier and a friendly Indian in the charge of the Crows and Shoshones.

It took me a long time to locate the rocks four hundred yards in front of the line where General Crook sent the packers and a few miners to act as sharpshooters. I had assumed that one of the rocky ravines on the south side of the crest was the place but was unable to find any relics in any of them. In the fall of 1954 I blundered on to the rocks, where they are now concealed somewhat by the terrain. They answer the descriptions perfectly. I was able to find only 7 soldiers' shells, 1 .50 caliber Spencer, 2 .50-70 Springfield shells, and 1 loaded .50-70-450 cartridge used in Government Springfield and Remington Rolling Block rifles and carbines, it being of either Winchester or U. S. Cartridge Company manufacture. The packers were armed with Sharp's Sporters. During the action they would use any shell that they could get into the guns, and most Sharps rifles were of .50 caliber.

Charles Young told me that in the early days he had found many of them, some unfired, all around the rocks. The area is covered with layers of rock and few shells were trampled into the ground, most of them washing away down the slope. Nearly all the shells found are disfigured, looking as if they had been stepped on by a man or horse and trampled into the soil. It was quite a thrill for me to sit behind these rocks held by the "horny handed" packers and visualize the young warriors charging from the conical hill a half mile off.

Several hundred yards east of Packers' Rocks and facing north on the northern edge of the crest, I found a little breast-works with some of the rocks still piled up. The relics I found here told their own story. Outside of the breastworks I found a broken arrowhead, while inside beneath the surface were six .45-70 soldiers' shells; four .50-70 Springfield shells; and one .45 caliber revolver bullet slightly flattened on the end.

Very few .44 Winchester shells, used by the Indians, have been found. Probably the reason for this is that the Indians were on horseback all the time, so that the small shells were not trampled into the soil but were washed away down the gullies, during the cloudbursts. It is very discouraging to swing a ten pound metal detector around in the hot sun for hours at a time without finding anything, but when something eventually turns up, enthusiasm is renewed until the next long dry spell. Yet if these points are not gone over, one will always wonder if possibly they could have been key points in the battle.

On the south slope of the east side of the gap, running southeasterly, is a wall of rimrock a hundred yards long and twenty feet high. It presents a smooth sandstone surface in which at equal intervals are carved drawings and symbols. So far as I know, this Indian writing has never been transcribed. Could it contain the Indians' story of the battle?

Chapter 8

WITH CROOK ON THE CENTER

WHILE up on the bluff to the north of the spring where he had been playing cards, at the very out-set of the attack, Crook had formulated plans of battle. When he returned, he found a battle already in progress. Taking his place with the infantry, he again assumed command of his men. With his aides, Bourke and Nickerson, he was to make his headquarters with the infantry for the rest of the battle. The infantry, which was very active in the fight, was therefore under Crook's personal direction. In fact, it had seen action before his return.

Major Alex Chambers, his "Mule Brigade" for the moment dismounted, tells in his official report what his men did after the first attack to stop the onrushing Sioux:

"I sent, as ordered, two companies, dismounted, to the edge of the bluffs to protect that point, posted as skirmishers. Shortly after the three (3) remaining companies formed a skirmish line on top of the ridge. After occupying this position for some time, I was ordered to have the battalion mounted, and marched to the crest of the ridge which was done, as soon as the companies on the skirmish line could be recalled for that purpose, one returning for their animals, and the mules of the other companies, the men and animals being concealed as much as possible. The left of the cavalry line retiring closely pressed by the Indians, Two (2) companies of the 9th Infantry, G and H, were sent as a skirmish line across the plateau to drive off a body of Indians, behind a conical hill, who kept up a constant fire. This was successfully accomplished."

Company G, 9th Infantry, under Captain Burrowes and Lt. William L. Carpenter,[1] and Company H, 9th Infantry, under Captain Burt and Lt. Edgar B. Robertson,[2] the two companies sent to the edge of bluffs, were stationed in a line just under the ridge forming the extreme east end of the crest north of camp. This position was taken for the purpose of forming a trap for the Sioux. Captain Burt reports the outcome of the maneuver in his report:

90

"My company with the rest of Infty Batt. fell in dismounted and occupied adjacent hills, expecting the Crows and Snake Indians to draw the Sioux by feigned retreat to this position. We were discovered and the plan frustrated."

That Crook's men failed is substantiated by White Elk[3] one of the attacking Indians. He believed that Crook's scouts tried to lead the pursuing Sioux down between the two groups of his soldiers, but in the confusion, went down the wrong ridge. Apparently, the plan was for the allies to lead the Indians down the next ravine west of them and then eastward along the plateau below the waiting men. The Crows and Shoshones led the Indians down the ridge immediately west of the soldiers so that the latter were discovered. These were the first soldiers seen by White Elk's band, who were surprised to find other soldiers farther west up the stream. Shortly afterwards the two companies, as Chambers reported, returned to camp for the mules.

Meanwhile, Company D, 4th Infantry, under Avery B. Cain and Lt. Henry Seton,[4] towards the left, Company F, 4th Infantry, under Captain Luhn, in the center, and Company C, 9th Infantry, under Captain Sam Munson and Lt. Thaddeus H. Capron,[5] on the right, advanced to the plateau northwest of camp to meet the main advance of the Sioux.

According to John Stands-In-Timber the main attack came from the northwest upon the plateau and in the gap north of camp. It was the strategy of Crazy Horse to try to drive the soldiers into the canyon at the east end where they would have been boxed in, unable to maneuver. However, as Cain and Luhn came up onto the plateau where the "friendlies" were so valiantly holding back the hostiles, Crazy Horse divided his forces, the Sioux coming around the allies, to attack the soldiers and stampede or capture the horses.

The left flank of the Sioux came down the ravine north of where the Kobold house now stands. The right flank attacked the infantry line, was repulsed by Royall's men when it veered to the left.

The first charge of Crook's men was into the gap and the rough terrain east of it where fighting was hand to hand. The second charge was towards the northwest where the soldiers occupied the hills bordering the east side of the gap on the plateau.

John Stands-In-Timber, the Cheyenne Recorder, claims that Crazy Horse's warriors, reinforced by the late arrivals, drove Crook's men back to the willows bordering the Creek, a claim substantiated by the friendly Crow subchief Many Coups. According to both accounts, the retreat was almost a rout. However, the cavalry and infantry were finally rallied to make a counter charge. John relates that the fighting was heavy around the camp site at this point. The fact remains that numerous discharged soldiers' shells have been found on both sides of the Rosebud here.

Now Crook's men commenced an advance all along the line. Crook's Hill was gained and the crest to the east. Part of this advance, the three infantry companies, drove the Sioux forces back towards the northwest, occupying a spur which jutted off to the southeast of the crest. This resulted in twenty minutes of heavy skirmishing between Cain's men and the hostiles on Crook's Hill until the crest was cleared by Mills' second charge.

Now the Hill and crest were occupied by the three companies of infantry and the 2nd Cavalry, farther east around the gap. Mills' battalion took over the fight.

It was this third charge of the soldiers which occupied Crook's Hill and the crest, according to John Stands-In-Timber. The Sioux retreated to the conical mound and over to Royall's line.

A breathing spell seemed to settle over the combatants, short, yet one in which much was accomplished. The mules were needed. Captain Munson was quickly dispatched for them. While in camp, Munson met Burt and Burrowes on a similar errand. Munson and Burrowes secured their mules, also those of Luhn's company, then hurried back to take their places in the line on the crest. Burt's company got their mules and those of Captain Cain's company and, taking along the wounded from camp, went back to the crest.

Now, at 10:00 o'clock, the Sioux came swarming back from their first attack on Royall's men, attacking Crook's Hill and the crest from west and north.

When the charge was observed, "the call was given for help," Captain Munson wrote in his report, "and I was directed to take six of my men, sharpshooters, to some rocks and broken ground on the crest of the hill, and drive back the Sioux who were then charging. This I did, and held the position with the aid of about a dozen men of other companies and about twenty friendly Indians. We were then ordered to fall back and rejoin our companies, who were then preparing to form a skirmish line."

After the Sioux were repulsed and the Crows and Shoshones had made their charge, Munson and his sharpshooters were ordered to rejoin their companies who were forming a skirmish line.

With the high conical mound as their objective, Munson, Cain and Luhn with their Infantry companies advanced their skirmish line facing west across the crest and valleys on each side. Captain Munson describes this action:

"When this (skirmish) line was formed, my company occupied the right,—my skirmishers taking up the ground between the top of the hill and valley below—we met no resistance on that side of the hill—the Sioux retiring—a few only showing themselves and at long distance. The action being over, we were ordered to the top of the hill which we occupied until dark."

Once the conical mound was taken, Crazy Horse's warriors concentrated their fury on Royall's men, rather than face the long rifles of the infantry.

It was now 10:30, Crook ordered the companies of Burt and Burrowes forward to help Royall who was already in trouble. This order was not carried out till around 12:30 when Mills was leaving for the canyon.

"Subsequently, while waiting on the hill in line," Captain Burt wrote in his report, "I received orders with Maj. Burrowes to 'stop those Indians and occupy that ridge.' The line referred to was across a ravine and toward the left of the general line, some several hundred yards away. The Indians were the Sioux pursuing a battalion of cavalry. We dismounted and moved forward at double time and on reaching the ridge stopped the Indians quickly and decisively without loss on our part, my company disabled two Indians and three ponies. I make this statement carefully believing greater damage was done the enemy."

What were Burt and Burrowes doing during this two hour period? Why did they not carry out the order promptly?

Crook gave the order at 10:30 when Royall was at his first position (see cover map) one mile to the left west. Perhaps as Burt and Burrowes with their companies were leaving to come to his aid, the onrushing Sioux charge—coming from that direction—made it impossible to carry out Crook's order. Perhaps they were needed to help repell the attack. Perhaps, at around 11:00 while the dismounted skirmishers of Munson, Cain and Luhn were taking the conical mound, Burt and Burrowes were aiding in holding the crest thus vacated by the three advancing companies. Manpower was certainly needed as Van Vliet's men had not arrived from the bluff south of camp and were not available.

Whatever the reason for the two-hour delay, the time element is verified by Captain Henry, who reported that he was wounded while watching Burt and Burrowes make their charge.

On the crest, the commander's black charger snorted impatiently. Crook jerked the bridle, his beard bristling and issued orders tersely. He was displeased with the situation. Royall had not complied with his order to join him on the crest. Burt and Burrowes had failed to go to Royall's aid. The command must be assembled all together to make a swift, sharp drive on the village down the canyon. Abruptly, he again sent word that Royall "come in."

Royall was not to come in for a long time, and in the interval, the battle waged.

After Crook's Hill had been taken, the 65 miners and 20 packers took position on the east side of a ridge about 300 yards southwest of the hill, most of them remaining there throughout the battle. At 10:00 they had done good service in holding the line against the attack by the Sioux down the valley from the west, part of the general advance. At 10:30 the packers and a few miners were withdrawn and thrown forward in Packers' Rocks north of the crest, 400 yards northwest of Crook's Hill, where they remained until Mills had gone down the canyon, at which time they were again withdrawn to defend Crook's Hill. Again, when the Sioux made their final charge from the southwest in pursuit of Royall's men, the packers and miners helped to hold them off by firing over the heads of the retreating soldiers.

Packer's Ridge formed a link in the chain of a rough line of defensive positions extending from Crook's Hill southward to Kollmar Creek. South and east of Packers' Ridge, about 400 yards south of Crook's Hill, was the next ridge, occupied by Burt and Burrowes in protecting Royall's retreat. Two hundred yards south was another ridge used by the friendly Indians. All of these positions were used to protect Royall's withdrawal and to repulse the general Indian attack at that time. During the earlier general attack only Crook's Hill and Packers' Ridge were used.

While the infantry was not engaged in heavy fighting, three men of Captain Cain's company were wounded by long range fire: Private James A. Devine, shot in the head; Private John H. Terry, a broken leg, and Private Richard Flynn, shot in the shoulder.

Meanwhile, over on the south side of the Rosebud, Captain Van Vliet was holding the bluff. In his official report he says he arrived on the bluff south of camp just ahead of a Sioux force who strove hard to get it. Little has been written of Van Vliet's part in the fight, and other than saying that he received orders from General Crook to withdraw at 11:00, he made no mention of his battle on the bluffs.

Captain Mills' map shows that Van Vliet occupied the bluff at a point immediately south of camp. It would seem that he made his stand here, facing the enemy riding onto the east end of the field. Foundations of a breastworks at this point still attest to his valiant though little known stand. Shells also have been found nearby. According to Lt. Morton's [6] map, one company went directly to the western point of the bluff, forming a line north and south. This was probably the company of Lt. Crawford which fired on the Cheyenne band who killed the Shoshone boy guarding the horses, during the Sioux charge. These two companies rejoined the main command on the crest when action shifted from Evans command to Royall's, arriving there about 11:15.

"The Hostiles Were Apparently Everywhere"

General Crook's reports of the battle did not contain much more detail than Van Vliet's. He was a man of few words, both oral and written. Years later in his autobiography* he briefly described the battle,[7] which shows his dissatisfaction at the turn of events.

"In a short time the hostiles were apparently everywhere. I ran up on a bluff, not far from where we halted, to take in the situation, intending to make my dispositions after learning the exact situation. Some of the infantry went up with me and took possession of this bluff, which commanded our camp, which was now the place on the creek where we had halted.

"When I returned to camp, Captain Nickerson had scattered the cavalry, sending two companies on a high hill on the opposite side of the creek, and about a half mile distant, while he sent the remainder, under Major Royall, to my left, which were just passing out of sight as I came into camp. The Indians pressed Major Royall so closely that he took up a position on the edge of some bluffs for self defense.

"My intention was to charge the Indians in my front, as there was a comparatively level mesa in front of the infantry. For this purpose I sent orders for Major Royall's command to join me with the least possible delay. With my repeated urging for him to join me, it was over two hours before he finally accomplished the movement. It was there where most of our loss occurred. Captain Guy V. Henry was very dangerously wounded. By the time this junction was formed, the Indians had withdrawn from my front. Only a few could be seen skulking around in the hills."

In his report Crook stated that all the troops and officers had acted in a commendable manner. However, after years of thinking it over he apparently was disposed to blame Captain Nickerson and Lt. Col. (not Major) Royall for the miscarriage. When he went up onto the bluff, Crook did not expect an immediate headlong attack by the Sioux. He assumed that he had plenty of time to observe the approaching force and formulate plans of battle. But while he was on the bluff, Colonel Evans made the disposition of the troops, and Captain Nickerson carried the orders to the various battalion commanders. Evans, also, sent the infantry companies into action to relieve the Shoshones and Crows during their fight on the plateau. Twenty minutes passed before the soldiers were able to meet

---

* Reprinted from *General George Crook: His Autobiography*, edited and annotated by Martin F. Schmitt. Copyright 1946, by the University of Oklahoma Press. Used by permission.

the enemy, according to Frank Gruard, chief scout. In the meantime, the Crows and Shoshones held back the Sioux. If true, Colonel Evans had justifiable reason to act so promptly, otherwise Crook's troops would not have been able to go into action that soon.

Mills said the Indian allies were of no value in the actual fighting. Evidence, however, indicates that they saved the soldiers during that first onslaught of the Sioux. In the controversy which later developed between Crook and Royall, Mills sided with Crook.

"The Crows Met the First Charge of the Indians"

Frank Gruard, General Crook's chief scout, was stationed with his chief on the center during most of the battle, and gave a highly critical account of the action.[8]

"It was not long before an Indian they called 'Humpy' a little hunch backed Sioux, came riding down over the hills as fast as his horse could carry him, hallooing 'Sioux' as he came into camp and he said the Sioux were charging on us and almost at the same time you could hear the Sioux war cry.

"Indians and the scouts jumped on their horses and just then the Sioux came charging down over the hills. But the troops were not ready to meet the attack so the Crows met the first charge of the Indians and I believe if it had not been for the Crows, the Sioux would have killed half of our command before the soldiers were in a position to meet the attack. It was a hand to hand fight for quite a while between the Crows and the Sioux. It was on a kind of plateau where they were fighting and the troops were down under the hills.

"I charged up the hill when the Shoshones and Crows started out, so that I could see everything that occurred. It was all of 20 minutes I think before the soldiers appeared over the hill. As soon as the soldiers came up and commenced fighting the Sioux fell back. The coming together of the Sioux, Crows and Shoshones, I think, was the prettiest sight in the way of fighting that I had ever seen. They were all mixed up and I could hardly distinguish our allies from the hostiles. After the fight became general with the troops, our Indians drew back.

"I passed where one Crow Indian was sitting on the ground and he didn't act as if he had been hurt a bit. He was watching the fight between the Indians and every once in a while he would yell like a madman. He was unable to get on his feet having been shot just above the knee and the bone was terribly shattered. His horse was lying dead by his side. He seemed to be so interested in the fight that he had entirely forgotten his wound.

"The soldiers could not tell one Indian from another but the Redskins knew each other all right. . . .

"After the troops came up they formed into line and commenced driving the Sioux back. Then the Shoshones, Crows and Sioux commenced separating. The friendly Indians came back and the Sioux went into the hills. The soldiers kept driving the hostiles back until they got them on the big flat beyond the first line of hills. Col. Henry with his battalion was stationed on the left and he was ordered up the river. Mills' battalion was down below on the right and the other battalions were in the center of the fight. The Crows and Snake Indians got scattered out but would keep in behind the troops out of harm's reach as much as possible.

"I was close to the position held by General Crook and he was in about the center of the field. The General ordered a battalion to charge the (Sioux) Indians and chase them back.

"In the charge that followed one poor fellow's horse ran away with him and the animal went right for the Indians. . . . Of course they began shooting at the horseman, and as his horse began to turn, both of his hands were shot off at the wrists. When he came past me both of his hands were dangling. . . . I rode up on the hill and the poor fellow was calling for someone to check his horse. . . .

"I tried to head off the horse but the animal got in ahead of me, started down the divide and went right through the troops. . . . The Indians were on that side of the flat fighting, and he went through the line or troops toward them and I went after him. I got up as close as I could to him. My horse was a fast one but I could not reach the runaway animal's bridle. . . . I got up as close as I could to the horse and hit it on the side of the head. The blow turned the horse some but not clear around and the wounded man threw himself off. The horse went right in among the Indians. . . . The wounded man picked himself up and ran down the hill. . . . The Indians were shooting at us all this time.[9]

"When I got back to the command the Indians were going down below us, and the General had sent all of his aides out with orders to the different commanders . . . so he told me to go down and tell Captain Mills to drive the Indians out of the Rosebud cañon. I went down and carried the order to Mills. . . ."

"The Crows Were Disgusted"

After Mills had returned to the field from the canyon and Crazy Horse had taken his forces off to the northwest, General Crook collected some of the cavalry together and once more started down the Rosebud canyon. The village of Crazy Horse was what he wanted and what he would have. However, at the place where the canyon narrows, his allies refused to go farther. The reason for their stubbornness was given later to E. S. Ricker by Big Bat, Crook's Crow interpreter.

E. S. Ricker, a Justice of the Peace, near Chadron, Nebraska, spent many years collecting material for a book on the Indian wars, but died before the book was written. Ricker interviewed many old Indians, interpreters and guides who lived near the Pine Ridge Agency just over the line in South Dakota. He wrote down on ordinary pencil tablets the words spoken to him. These old tablets, now in the custody of the Nebraska State Historical Society, cover one account of the Rosebud Battle, Baptiste Pourier's. Dated January 6 and 7, 1907, it appears in Tablet 15, pages 131-139:

"Passing on now to the Battle of the Rosebud, Bat says that when Crook arrived on the scene where the battle took place, the General ordered his cavalry to dismount. Little Mountain Sheep, one of the Crow scouts, told Bat to tell the General not to dismount his men, as the Sioux were charging on him.

"The Sioux were charging, and Bat says the General would have lost his horses, for they would have scared them off. Immediately, the Crows and Shoshones made a counter charge. . . . This charge on the Sioux gave the cavalry time to get ready for action. . . .

"After Col. Henry was wounded there were two of his men who were killed by Cheyennes. They were dismounted and their horses had got away from them. Two Cheyenne warriors charged on them. The Crow Indians started to charge on these Cheyennes and save the soldiers' lives, which they could easily have done, but General Crook told Bat to call them back. Bat did so. The Cheyennes rode on to the soldiers, who gave up their guns from their hands to the two Indians who instantly shot the two men with their own guns. The Crows were angry because Crook had called them back, and they inquired what was the use to fight if the General would let his men be killed that way right in sight and would not let the Crows go to save them. As soon as the Indians had shot the two soldiers they jumped from their horses and struck them with their knives.

"Where the infantry fought Bat had noticed that the men had left great numbers of cartridges on the ground. They would lie or kneel down to fire; in each case they drew from their belts a handful of cartridges and laid on the ground handy for use. When they advanced they did not think to take these cartridges, but left them.

"The Indians all fell back out of sight. This was a decoy. When the Crow scouts came to the Rosebud canyon they refused to go into it. One of the headmen named White Face was spokesman. He told the General they wanted to go back. The General asked them what for. He said they did not want to get killed, as they all would if they went into the canyon. The Crow, having in memory that the Crows had been called back from saving the two soldiers, asked why he had not let them fight back there when the two soldiers were killed.

"The General said he wanted to get to the Sioux village and fight them there. White Face answered and said that 'the force you have been fighting is only a little war party; if you go to the village you will find as many Indians as the grass. If you go down there you can never get out of the trap; you will all be killed,' and the knowing Indian rubbed the palms of his hands together in imitation of grinding stones which is the Indian sign of complete destruction. He added that he was going back; that he had a lot of wounded men. Bat had been interpreting all this. He now spoke to the General and told him what he had observed, and added that the Indians had told him that they had seen the same thing. So the General dispatched an orderly to the officers to inquire about the ammunition supply among the men, and word came back that it was very short. Then the General said there was not ammunition enough to advance and he would have to go back.

"The command was withdrawn to the camp where the battle began. The soldiers killed were buried on the field. The column remained at that camp till next morning, the wounded being attended to in the meantime; next morning he began his movement back to Goose Creek. It was this second morning that the Crows quit Crook and went home—the second morning after the battle. The reason the Crows wanted to return to their camp was that they saw a roan horse among the Sioux which they had left at home, and they were afraid that the Sioux had been at their villages and killed people and taken horses. But the real reason no doubt was that the Crows were disgusted with the way the fighting had been done that day, and they so told a certain infantry officer, Capt. Burk or Bourk."[10]

Disappointed, Crook returned to the battlefield. Stubborn, steel-willed, he would not see that which was apparent to Mills or others of his command. Crazy Horse had out-scouted, out-surprised, out-maneuvered him. He could not know the appalling consequences of this day.

"A Panoramic View of Barbaric Splendor"

In camp again, there was much to talk over among the men, different encounters, the exploits of the allies, the daring of Crazy Horse's warriors. Captain Azor H. Nickerson,[11] who had spent most of the day carrying orders to various commands through the thick of battle, gives a vivid description of the Indians on both sides.

"Sioux or Cheyenne warrior, in battle, wears very little except his decorations, his arms and cartridge belts. Of the latter, I have often seen a brave with as many as three filled with cartridges, strung across his body. The horse he rides on such occasions, is especially reserved for the purpose, it is somewhat smaller than the thoroughbred American horse, but wiry, fleet, and well adapted to his master's needs.

"In place of a saddle, a strong rope of raw hide is drawn tightly around the animal just back of the forequarters. When the warrior mounts, he takes a twist of this rope around either leg, and then he is securely fastened in his place as if he had been born there—a veritable Centaur. A rope, or twist of horsehair about eighteen or twenty feet long in length is fastened around the horse's neck, and the remainder, coiled up, is carried in the left hand. On his right wrist is fastened what one would take to be a policeman's club, from its resemblance to that weapon. It is about the same length and size, but has about a half-dozen leather thongs or lashes attached, and is used by the warrior as a whip for his horse, or as a weapon for his enemy, according to circumstances. In his right hand he carried his repeating rifle; while diagonally across his back, is a sort of quiver, what most persons would suppose to be a lance, from its resemblance to that weapon. It is not a lance, or a weapon at all, but is what is known as a Coup Stick. With this the warrior preempts whatever he claims, very much as boys touch each other when playing tag. It makes no difference who fires the fatal shot that kills the enemy or the buffalo; it is the Indian who first strikes the prostrate body with the Coup Stick, who is thus invested with the right to that body with all its belongings.

"The warriors dashed here, there, everywhere; up and down in ceaseless activity; their gaudy decorations, waving plumes and glittering arms, forming a panoramic view of barbaric splendor, once seen, never to be forgotten.

"Our efforts were directed toward closing in with the enemy

by a series of charges, and theirs to avoiding close contact until, by the nature of the ground, our forces began to get scattered, and then their tactics changed from the defensive to the offensive. Each separate detachment was made the objective of terrific onslaughts; the warriors charging up to them, careening on their horses, and firing from behind them, while exposing as little of their own persons as possible. All the time they were whooping and yelling, hoping thereby to strike terror into the hearts of their adversaries and, if possible, stampede them. And woe to the officer or soldier who, at such a moment, lost his presence of mind. Let him turn to seek safety in flight, even for an instant, and immediately a score of warriors would pounce upon him and the chances would be, ninety out of a hundred that, in less time than it takes to tell it, his bloody scalp would dangle at the belt of an exultant brave."

"They Repeatedly Courted Death"

Robert E. Strahorn, the correspondent for the *Rocky Mountain News*, was with Crook on the center. He published his account of the battle in the July 4, 1876, edition of that newspaper. The article was signed by his pen name "Alter Ego" and is valuable in describing the Indians, the various incidents and sidelights of the battle.

"The Sioux were all spendidly mounted, and so long as pressed did much of their firing on horseback. Some of the most reckless feats of equestrianism imaginable were performed by them within range of the broadsides of an entire company. In numerous instances one or two warriors dashed out from behind their cover of rocks, hugged close to the neck of the pony and half bounded, half tumbled down the nearly vertical banks after a bold Crow, Snake or white skirmisher, delivered a shot or two and like a flash disappeared in spite of volleys sent after them.

"Up hill or down, over rocks, through cañons and in every conceivable dangerous condition of affairs their breakneck devil-may-care riding was accomplished. One reckless brave got badly pressed by the cavalry, at a certain point in the field, and jerking out his bowie knife he slashed apart his saddle girt, slipped it with all of its trappings from under him while his pony was at full speed, and thus unencumbered made his escape. So closely did the Indians approach our skirmishers at times that they inflicted several wounds from battle-axes, lances and arrows, and in one or two instances they closed in upon a brave soldier and got his scalp before comrades could rush forward to the rescue. They repeatedly courted death by endeavoring to secure the bodies of their own dead . . . .

"The friendly Indians are blamed for not discovering the Sioux village the night before the battle, and thus losing to our column the grand opportunity of a surprise. They certainly manifested much carelessness and apathy previous to the fight, having their war dances and infernal noises around camp at night, and firing at buffalo and other game to a sufficient extent to alarm the country, in the day time. But a hostile volley once fired and they were different beings. They manifested the greatest delight at speedily meeting their old foes. They threw aside extra luggage, some even stripping to the simple breech-clout, and fairly flew to the hills occupied by the enemy, when Captain Randall, their leader, indicated the time to start. The Snakes were evidently the better Indians from the beginning to the close, exercising more judgment, displaying more real courage, and affecting as much as the Crows, or more, considering the disparity in numbers in favor of the latter . . .

"Our troops fired over ten thousand rounds of ammunition, and it is believed the Sioux discharged from a third to a half more. Behind a ledge of rocks from where a band of them fired for a little over half an hour, about a peck of cartridge shells were found, and other places of concealment were strewn with them almost as thickly. Many of these were the long, hardshooting Sharps, which show another decided advantage they have over our troops. But the marvel of it is how so much ammunition could be expended with so little loss of life to our forces. Dodging, and skulking, and scattering out, as the savages always do, we could not expect to hand them a very long mortality list, but not possessing that snakelike, weasel-like faculty of being where we are not, or not being just where we are supposed to be, it is hard to see why an average Indian marksman could not kill but once in a thousand shots.

ALTER EGO"

That the Indians were well armed and had plenty of ammunition was attested to by the Correspondent of the *Army & Navy Journal,* in the July 22, 1876, issue of the publication on page 802.

"They (the Sioux) are quick to seize positions, quick to give them up when necessary and seize better ones, are far better armed than our troops, and in fact, possess all possible elements necessary to make the best light cavalry troop in the world . . . .

"At several places where the Sioux fought, piles of shells were found; in one place five hundred representing four different calibers; in others boxes of ammunition had been brought up to their skirmish line."

Author's note: Packers' Ridge is a spur leading south from the crest and jutting out into the valley about 300 yards. It is separated from Crook's Hill by a wide ravine which forms the head of one of the small gullies leading down to Kollmar Creek a half mile away. This ridge is about 200 yards south of Crook's Hill and about 200 yards west. The crest west of Crook's Hill is over 100 yards north of the south part of the hill. I first found eight .50-70 Springfield shells in the spring of 1954, lying on the surface close together on the east side of the ridge, just below the crest. From that position they were facing west and southwest, overlooking the valley.

With my metal detector, I found a lot of various types of shells up to five inches deep, within an area of about fifty feet along the ridge by twenty feet wide. Apparently some of them had rolled down the slope. Since none were soldiers' shells, it was obvious that some of the packers and miners occupied this ridge. The miners had their own guns probably of every kind and description, while the packers used Sharps' Sporters mostly of .50 caliber taking .50-70 Springfield cartridges. Evidently, the Shoshones were not there, their rifles being mostly the latest model .45-70's. Only one shell found here could have been used in those guns. It is possible that the Crows were here, since they used .50-70's and may have had some Spencers.

As the ridge farthest south of this defense line had quite a few shells used by the Crows and Shoshones and Daly says in his account that the friendly Indians were next to the creek, I am of the opinion that at least some of the packers and miners were on the ridge and the allies were further south. I found no other shells along this ridge; and as there were 65 miners and 20 packers, some of them must have taken position elsewhere, probably with the infantry on the next hill. This is the list of shells I found on Packers' ridge:

Twenty-eight .50-70 Springfield, center fire inside primed with Martin 2 hole disc, copper case as produced at Frankfort

Arsenal in late 1860's to 1871, empty cartridge cases.

Four .50-70 Springfield, centerfire inside primed using experimental bar anvil primer as developed by Col. Benet of U. S. Ordinance Department, Frankfort Arsenal late 1860's to 1871.

One .45-70 Model 1873 Springfield brass case external center fire primer, made by U. S. Cartridge Co.

Three .56-52 Spencer rimfire copper case made by Winchester Company with a raised "H" on base.

Five .56-56 Spencer rimfire, copper case, Government Contract, probably manufactured by Frankfort Arsenal or private contract or U. S. Government.

One .50 caliber Spencer Carbine Blank rimfire copper 1865 period, made by Winchester Company with raised "H" on base.

The east slope of this ridge is steep; there must then have been heavy firing in order for so many shells to have remained all these years; it is probable that ninety-nine per cent of those used have been washed down the gully.

The next defensive position south was the one on which Burt and Burrowes made their stand in protecting the retreat of Royall's men from the ridge south of Kollmar Creek to the crest. This is another spur extending 400 yards south of Crook's Hill and jutting into the valley. At the south end on top I found 25 soldiers' shells in a line extending about fifty feet in a northwesterly direction. This was about the length of an infantry company line and was undoubtedly where Captain Burt's company was located, as on the New York *Graphic* map his company was north of Captain Burrowes' company. On the side of the slope, southeast, I found in a line following down the end of the ridge more soldiers' shells. This was probably where Captain Burrowes' company stood when it poured its fire into the Indians. At this same place there was a large variety of other shells indicating that some of the miners had reinforced the infantry companies. About halfway down this spur from Crook's Hill, I found a .45-70 lead bullet flattened out on the end, showing that it had passed through either a man or a horse and, as it was a soldiers' bullet, had probably gone through some part of an Indian or his horse, or both. On the west side of the spur at the top I found another .45-70 lead bullet from a soldier's gun, a groove out of one side indicating that the edge of the bullet had hit something solid.

The following is a description of the shells I found on the east slope of the ridge:

Ten .45-70 soldiers' shells.

Four .44 caliber Colt's Old Model black powder revolver, external center fire primer, unknown manufacture. This was not used by the soldiers as they were armed with the .45 Colts.

Seven .44 Winchester Model 1866. These were the same kind as used extensively by the Indians, but some of the friendly Indians or miners may have had one of them.

Two .56-56 Spencer copper rimfire.

One .50-70 Springfield outside primed with 3 hole Berdan primer of Winchester manufacture.

One .50-70 Springfield copper shell with bar anvil primer.

Ten .50-70 Springfield Martin 2 hole disc primer, Frankfort Arsenal late 1860's to 1871.

One .45-70 soldiers' Springfield cartridge still loaded.

Four .45-70 Springfield 1873 Model brass case centerfire outside primer manufactured by U. S. Cartridge Company. Two of these were shattered indicating that they had been reloaded several times. One of them had a part of the side gone as though poked out with a ramrod after having been stuck in the barrel.

Ramrods were not part of the soldier's equipment but some of the Indians had obsolete guns with ramrods. The shells might have been removed with these.

At the south end of this chain is a little ridge standing off by itself about 250 yards south of Burt and Burrowes' ridge and about the same distance from Kollmar Creek. From the type of shells found here I believe it was occupied by friendly Indians. These are the cartridges which I found on the east side just below the crest:

Thirteen .50-70 Springfield centerfire Martin 2 hole disc primer copper case Frankfort Arsenal late 1860's to 1871.

Five .45-70 Springfield Model 1865 to 1868, copper centerfire inside Martin type crimped in primer. (Soldiers' shells).

Three .50-70 Springfield outside primed 3 hole Berdan primer. Standard commercial loading of Winchester manufacture. They were brass and two of them were shattered, indicating that they had been reloaded.

Three .45-70 Springfield Model 1873 external centerfire

primer brass case manufactured by the U. S. Cartridge Company.

One .45-70 soldier's shell broken about halfway down it's length, with the lead bullet and wads still in place. This resulted in the defective extracting mechanism of the 1873 Springfield carbines used by the soldiers. After firing four or five shots rapidly, the extractor would not operate because the shells would stick in the chamber. The black powder used would cause the shells to stick. In this case the man could not even get his shell in the chamber all the way, and in trying to pull the shell out, broke it off in the middle leaving in the chamber the half with the bullet. This was pushed out some way. Custer's men had the same trouble with these carbines, and some of them became useless on account of parts of the shells sticking in the chambers.

One .45-70 soldier's shell still loaded.

One .44 short rimfire revolver cartridge of unknown make, a short cased type as used in early Bulldog type revolvers.

One .44 caliber rimfire Model 1866 Winchester, also known as the .44 Henry Flat rifle type.

The first time I went to the conical mound west of Crook's Hill was with John Stands-In-Timber and Elmer Kobold. As we drove towards the mound, John said:

"Heavy fighting here, almost hand to hand. Indians on north side of crest and soldiers and scouts on south side. Were only thirty or forty yards apart and both sides would crouch down so as to be hidden by the crest and then would jump up suddenly and fire and then crouch back down."

We walked over the south side of the crest, where I found two .50-70 shells right on the surface probably indicating where some of the Crow scouts had been. Then we moved over to the north of a little low rocky crest where all of us immediately found empty shells used by the Indians lying right on the surface. In fifteen minutes John found eight or nine of these; Kobold found about as many just with the naked eye. Using my metal detector, I found them as fast as I could dig them up, surprised to find that they extended quite a distance down the north slope.

The next day the weather changed to cold and windy and I was able to go over only the north side of the mound, for about two hours. Here I found shells thicker than any other place on the battlefield, and I hope to go back and cover this hill fully next summer. On the south side of the crest I found five .50-70 empty shells ordinary type, while on the north side I found the following:

Twenty-eight .44 caliber shells ordinarily used in a Bulldog type revolver of unknown make but having a very short case. I believe these shells were used in the Indians' 1866 Model Winchester indiscriminately with shells designed for that type of gun, for the reason that both types of shells bear the same pronged firing pin markings.

Twenty-one .44 caliber shells with raised H stamp on base of Winchester manufacture ordinarily designed for the model 1866 Winchester rifle.

Two .45-70 soldiers' shells, one of which had been fired in a .50 caliber gun and was swollen and split along one side. It was possible that an Indian ran out of shells for his .50 caliber gun and used the smaller caliber shell in it; but whoever did this foolish thing probably had his face burned from the exploding shell.

Five .44 caliber Colt's outside primed shells. Old Model black powder.

Five .50-70 centerfire Martin type primed shells. These were manufactured at Frankfort Arsenal from about 1867 to 1878. The peculiar feature about this type is that the primer is formed from one continuous piece of copper, as is the case itself. It was impossible to reload this type of cartridge which is readily distinguishable from the other shells of this caliber because there is a deep hollow about the outside primer.

Five .50-70 Springfield Winchester manufacture with outside primed brass shells.

One .50-70 Springfield brass one hole Berdan type primer probably of Union Metallic Cartridge Company make.

Two .50 caliber Spencer rimfire used in Spencer rifles and carbines. Either Government or contract manufacture and made in about 1865.

One .50 caliber Spencer carbine blank. Rimfire, copper case of approximately the 1865 period.

Two .56-56 Spencer rifle rimfire, copper case.

One .45-70 lead bullet out of a soldier's gun lying on the surface. It was not deformed in any way indicating that it did not strike anything, but was spent after having travelled a long distance.

One .50-70 lead bullet flattened at one end, indicating that it had struck and passed through some object. It is probable that this bullet passed through some portion of one of the Indians who had jumped up to fire just once too often.

I found all these shells and bullets on one small portion of the mound in two hours. It is probable that the hill is literally covered with them.

John Stands-In-Timber confirmed my timetable of the action to the extent that the charge of the Snakes, which extended as far as Andrews' Point, preceded the charge of the three infantry companies upon the conical mound. It was probable that these were withdrawn from the Mound before Mills went down the cañon, so that they could occupy the crest thus vacated by those men. This is borne out by Royall's statement in his official report that the advanced portions of the line were abandoned when the men went down the cañon and released many of the Indians to join in the attack upon his line. Thus the conical mound was probably abandoned about twelve o'clock or earlier.

At the time that Royall was being driven from his third position, the Indians made a general attack all along the line from the west, and the action was hot and heavy. They came down the hollow between the bluffs on the north and the ridge south of Kollmar Creek on the south and were flanking Royall from the bluffs from which he had been driven, on the south. The defensive line of Packer's Hill, Burt and Burrowes' Hill, and Crow Hill were heavily engaged; and the fact that some of the Indians rode over these positions might account for some of the .44 caliber shells found there.

Henry W. Daly, one of the packers occupying the ledge, told about this broad advance:

"Up the valley came the Sioux and the Northern Cheyennes— a solid phalanx from stream's edge to bluffs. There were no handsomer Indians and no better riders. The chiefs rode in front. From the forehead to the waistline each warrior was painted with stripes of black and red. Their gorgeous head-dresses fanned the breeze like the tails of a boy's kite. They chanted a war song in unison and in perfect time. They attacked with great fury and with the precision of trained cavalry. The Sioux under Crazy Horse struck to the right front of the ledge from which I was firing over the heads of our forces. The Cheyennes under Dull Knife struck our left column, which was on the river side. At first they shouted to our Indian allies, 'You go home! We want to kill only white men!' But the Shoshones and Crows were loyal, and they, with the supporting troops, were hotly engaged. Meantime the Sioux on the right attempted to dash between our cavalry and the bluffs and gain our rear.

"The shock of the first onrush sent both of our columns back. The ledge from which the miners and we packers were fighting was surrounded. The hostiles charged it. We fired point-blank, but on they came. Several reached the top of the ledge and one of them came at me with a tomahawk. A scar over my right eye, which is still visible, enables me to recall the incident the more distinctly.

"The attack was progressing satisfactorily for Crazy Horse. His Sioux were working around the right flank to our rear. Their object was to drive us forward into the cañon ahead, which would have been our death trap. But Crook, who did not underestimate Crazy Horse as a tactician, had anticipated this maneuver and had held five troops of cavalry and two companies of infantry in reserve. At the right moment these charged the Sioux, who, caught between two fires that were punishing in their intensity, were driven back in some disorder. This retreat exposed the flank of the Cheyennes, who also fell back."[12]

During this charge by the Indians some of them rode over to the Rosebud and down the valley over the bivouac of that morning, then back north around in front of Crook, thereby completely encircling his command.

After the attack on this broad front the Indians withdrew, and Royall's men retreated east of the defense line and took position on the crest, where they were soon engaged by the Indians forming a line to the north of them. While the Indians were gathering their forces in preparing to attack, Mills with his cavalry returned from the cañon and appeared in their rear, whereupon the Indians broke off the engagement and rode off to the northwest, being pursued by some of the cavalry for several miles.

The five infantry companies formed the backbone of Crook's defense; and had it not been for the companies of Burt and Burrowes, it is doubtful whether Royall's men would have escaped. It was true, then as now, that when the more glamorous branches of the service got into difficulty, it was the Walk-a-Heaps with their little rifles who were called to the rescue. Who was there who could laugh at the "Mule Brigade" now?

Chapter 9

WITH ROYALL ON THE LEFT FLANK

THE hardest fighting in the whole battle took place along the ridge south of Kollmar Creek where Colonel Royall with four companies of the Third Cavalry was outnumbered and surrounded by the hostile Indians, many of whom were Cheyennes. As a part of Mills' second charge, Royall detached the last three companies in the column of six companies, and, charging towards the southwest, crossed Kollmar Creek and cleared the Indians from the two ridges south of the creek, who threatened to enfilade the whole line. The Indians fled before this three pronged cavalry charge; and in the excitement of the chase, the two platoons of Captain Andrews' Company were soon occupying prominent points over a mile west of Crook's Hill, where Mills had terminated his charge and posted his men as skirmishers to the west of it.

Lt. Foster's platoon, which had ridden the full length of a rocky wooded ridge one half mile southwest of Andrews' Point, rejoined his company, which was then recalled to the ridge where the other four companies were being placed in line by Colonel Royall. This ridge formed a portion of the heights south of Kollmar Creek, and was almost exactly a mile west of Crook's Hill and separated from it by the wide valley of Kollmar Creek. Colonel Royall stated in his official report that he occupied this first position by instructions from an aide-de-camp of General Crook. When Captain Meinhold's company was sent to join the main command, the men remaining on the ridge simply took wider intervals to cover the area thus vacated.

According to Lt. Morton's map, three companies occupied this hill; Company D, then, under Captain Guy V. Henry and Lt. William W. Robinson Jr.,[1] must have been held in reserve. The three companies on the ridge were Company I,

111

under command of Captain Andrews and Lieutenants Albert D. King[2] and James E. H. Foster, which had been detached from Captain Mills battalion; Company F under command of Lt. Bainbridge Reynolds; and Company L under Captain Peter D. Vroom and Lt. Chase.

Colonel Royall and Captain Meinhold both said that this hill was a half mile from the advanced positions of the main command, although it was twice that far from Crook's Hill. It is possible that they meant the main crest in front which was occupied for a short time by the charge of the Snakes and Crows, or the conical hill which was taken by the troops some time after 11:00.

Colonel Royall referred in a general way to only one advanced position, that being the second one, so it is impossible to determine just how long the first hill was occupied. Because of its exposed position, being subjected to fire from the crest in front and a "plunging and enfilading fire" from the west where the Indians had lined a cross ridge about six hundred yards away, it was probable that Royall soon abandoned it and formed a more defensible line on the adjoining hill to the southeast separated from the first position by a deep ravine about a quarter of a mile wide. The Indians had congregated behind low ridges to the west and rear; and Lt. Bourke, when he surveyed the situation from Andrews' point during the charge of the Snakes, estimated that there were 500 of them.

This conclusion is confirmed by the actual fighting line as indicated by the empty soldiers' shells found along the ridge, which was about 300 yards long. None was found along the westerly half, but the line of them just below the crest on the south side commenced in about the center and continued to the east end where the line bent to the north. The shells were thickest at this point, showing that the men crowded to the east end of the ridge to escape the frontal fire from the north and the flanking fire from the west. For the same reason the led horses must have been kept behind the lines at the southeast corner of the position. The ridge was also vulnerable from the rear, as Indians could have occupied the adjoining hill to the southeast which later became the soldiers' second position.

When the troops fell back to the second position, the companies of Vroom and Andrews occupied the high hill facing north, while Captain Henry's two companies were extended southwestward to the left and rear down a rocky ledge to keep the Indians from taking them in flank and rear. Royall had about 200 men in the four companies; but every fourth man acted as a horseholder and was out of the fight, leaving only 150 men for the line. The men facing north on the hill must have had a fine view of the charge of the Snakes at about 10:30 and of the fight around the conical hill later. The first two positions were occupied by Royall for about two hours, and a fairly close estimate of the period would be from 9:30 to 11:30 or possibly a little later.

It is known that Captain Henry was shot in the 12:30-1:00 period at the third position, and it was probable that the retreat from the second position including the fight for the led horses and the last stand on the third bluff took about an hour. Colonel Royall claimed that before he received the order to retire, the advance points had been vacated by the troops and the Indians were free to concentrate on his men.

When he received the order to rejoin the command on the crest, Colonel Royall obeyed by gradually retiring his led horses under the protection of a line of skirmishers. This movement being perceived by the Indians, they began to close in upon him in large numbers; and the troops were subjected to a severe direct, flank and rear fire.

There was quite a struggle to protect the horses, which at that point were probably located near the southeast corner of the hill which would afford some protection for them from the north and west. Captain Henry's men retreated from the ledges on the west and south and, with the two companies on the hill remaining in position until the last, a movement described as a "left about wheel"[3] was executed, with the result that a new line was formed facing the south and west with the led horses leading the retreat, being protected by the line.

The Indians then took the hill just vacated and the rocky ledges and poured in their fire from the north, west, and south. Royall's men had to cross a low place or gap in the ridge for about a half mile, and the retreat was unprotected by the terrain across this flat stretch of ground. East of the gap was a high hill marking the resumption of the ridge south of Kollmar Creek, which extended for nearly a mile eastward and a little south, nearly to the Rosebud. The troops maintained their line well down the slope of the north side of the ridge, which protected them from Sioux forces following in a roughly parallel line to the south. In this manner the horses were led down Kollmar Creek to a point one half mile south of Crook's Hill, and for protection were placed in a ravine running into Kollmar Creek from the north.

It was at this point that Colonel Royall, now being the shortest distance from the main command, determined to cross the "last defile," the deep ravine of Kollmar Creek at the foot of the ridge, and the valley to the north. In his report Colonel Royall said:

"For protection in the passage I had directed Lieutenant Vroom and company to precede and line a crest which covered it; but by this time every Sioux in the engagement was surrounding this single battalion and the position assigned was too exposed to be even temporarily occupied."[4]

Vroom's company went to the crest of the bluff to try to hold back the Indians in order that the rest of the command might mount their horses and rejoin the main command. But when this single company appeared on the bluff, it was immediately surrounded and cut off by the Indians who had massed on the south side of the ridge. For better protection the men formed a circle on the crest and the rest of Royall's men rushed to the rescue. Captain Henry's company, which was in the lead, got there first and with the other forward companies drove the Indians back from the crest. In this brief period Vroom lost five men killed and three wounded, according to the official report. Ben Arnold was undoubtedly referring to Vroom's fight when he stated that one company was outflanked and lost thirteen men killed, while five Crows and seven or eight Shoshones were killed.[5]

The hostile Indians continued their attacks, and the whole command formed a line on the crest and parallel with the ridge about 325 yards long, the east end being immediately south of the led horse ravine. The Indians operated from behind the next parallel ridge to the south about three hundred yards away. The rocks behind their lines referred to in some of the accounts were those in rear of the Burt Young house, where so many of their skeletons were found "buried" in later years. There was also a cluster of large rocks on the south bank of Kollmar Creek north of the hill at the west end of the mile long ridge, which was behind their lines during a flank attack from the west. It was just south of these rocks that the Cheyenne warrior by the name of "Limpy" had his horse shot from under him, according to John Stands-In-Timber.

The fighting was hot and heavy, the hostiles attacking from the front and from both flanks and rear. It was during a flank attack from the west and rear that Captain Guy V. Henry was shot across the face by this enfilading fire, while he was on his horse watching Burt and Burrowes' men make their charge to their ridge to the northeast.

When he fell off his horse, the enemy saw the fallen leader, rallied and charged, while the soldiers retreated down the slope. Upon seeing this desperate situation, General Crook sent the Crows and Shoshones just in time to rescue Captain Henry. After a hand to hand struggle over the officer and his orderly, who was also wounded, the Sioux forces were compelled to retreat once more. During this interval the soldiers reformed their line on the crest, while Captain Henry was hurried to the field hospital.

The Crows and Shoshones were soon driven back by a counter-charge of the hostile Indians and rejoined the soldiers, occupying the crest to the east of them. After several more attacks the little band was forced to retreat to the horses in the ravine below, the Crows and Shoshones covering the retreat, where the command was mounted in an orderly manner.

Before the men rode off, some of the Indians attacked over the bluff and down the ravine of Kollmar Creek from the west; and although they were driven off, they managed to wound and kill a number of the cavalry horses by unaimed fire. Some of the wounded horses had to be shot, so that according to the map in the *New York Graphic* there were horse bones of eight horses in the ravine after the battle. When the command left the ravine and rode down the valley of Kollmar Creek, the Indians tried to surround them; the men then had to cut their way through for about three hundred yards, riding up on the plateau under the protection of the infantry of Burt and Burrowes, and the Crows on the ridge south of it. Their route was over the valley east, and during the retreat several men who had been dismounted were killed. Arriving at the crest the men were placed in line where they stayed until the battle was over.

When Royall's men retreated to their horses, it was a signal for a grand charge by all the hostiles on the field. Many who had been occupying positions in their rear charged eastward down the valley and attacked the packers and soldiers on their row of defensive ridges running southward from Crook's Hill. This was the climax of the battle. There was heavy action for a few minutes, but the fire power of the troops and their allies was so great that the Indians were compelled to retreat, although some of them continued on down to the Rosebud, down the canyon, and thence back to the field, completely encircling Crook's command.

There were several companies of cavalry and infantry on the main crest during this attack, some of whom aided in driving back the Indians. The action of Royall in crossing the valley is referred to in some accounts as the fighting in "Bloody Hollow," but this seems to be misleading, as nearly all the soldiers were killed on the heights south of Kollmar Creek.

After this repulse many of the Indians went to the north of Crook's Hill and the conical hill, where they prepared for another attack from a series of ridges. They broke off the fighting, however, on the appearance of Mills' and Noyes' men in their rear, returning from the canyon. There are statements to the effect that the Indians were pursued for three or four miles and that the fighting lasted until after dark, but there are no details available.

"Don't Go Back On the Old Third!"

The most comprehensive description of the fighting on the left is given by an unknown officer writing in the July 13, 1876, issue of *The New York Daily Graphic*. The article, signed by

"Z," is entitled, *A thrilling Description of General Crook's brave fight by an Officer of the Command—Wonderful Bravery of the Troops,* dated June 20, at Camp on Goose Creek. It is clear that he was with the troops on the left. With the article appear three maps, one showing all of the battle area, another showing a sketch of Royall's last position, and the third showing the operations of General Crook's column from Fort Fetterman to the Rosebud field, and the return to the summer camp near the Big Horn Mountains. There is one puzzling omission in the recital, and that is any reference to Vroom's fight on the bluff. The letters referring to various points on the field, as contained in the first map, are further identified in parentheses.

"Colonel Royall, with Mills' battalion, consisting of Mills', Sutorius', Andrews, and Lawson's troops of the Third, pushed into the valley between the ridges marked respectively "B" and "C," (B is the high crest to the north and C is the ridge south of Kollmar Creek), and going left front into the line at a gallop, ordered Andrews, with I Troop, to carry the ridge on the left, and Mills, with the remainder of his battalion to take the one on the right, both of them being held by a strong body of the enemy.

"The plateau was gained, and reforming, the charge was sounded and the crests cleared with a dash and spirit worthy of all praise, the officers riding gallantly in advance of the platoons, although the retreating enemy were all the time delivering a sharp fire on the advancing line. Mills pushed on to the point marked "B" (Crook's Hill) when he was ordered to halt and hold the ground won. This he did until ordered by General Crook to join him on the hill occupied by the infantry.

"Andrews, after detaching his subaltern, Lieutenant Foster, with the second platoon, to charge a body of the enemy further to the left, dashed on under a strong fire with the remainder of I Troop and carried the point marked "C" (Andrews' point) holding it until peremptory orders came to fall back and rest his left at the point marked "E" (Royall's first position). The point taken so gallantly by Andrews is a natural redoubt, commanding everything within range, and the enemy afterwards occupied it and annoyed Royall's first line terribly by an enfilading fire.

"In the meanwhile Foster, in accordance with his orders, lead his platoon, charging as foragers[6] over the valley to the left, and gaining the crest of the ridge marked "H" (the second ridge south of Kollmar Creek) drove a body of the enemy that held it pell-mell from their position. Continuing his charge, the next ridge was carried in the same style, when wheeling to the right in order to conform to the general direction of the main line, he swept along the plateau, the enemy, though superior in numbers, running before him, firing from their ponies as they gave way.

"The rocky knoll marked "I" was next charged for and taken and a sharp fire coming from a timberclad point of a ridge marked "K" (continues the *New York Daily Graphic* article by the unknown "Z") the plucky little party numbering less than twenty men, was placed under cover behind the knoll marked "I" from whence issued some of the best shots, fired on the enemy occupying the point "K," (the long wooded rocky ridge lying about a half mile southwest of Andrews' point). With an abiding faith in his men and horses Foster again advanced, charging and carrying the point "K" and following the retreating enemy along the crest of the ridge, both pursuers and pursued firing rapidly as the movement was executed. Occupying the end of the ridge "D" it was determined to halt and await the advance of the line, but finding that a body of the enemy were moving along the ridge on his right "L" with the evident intention of intercepting the party, the retreat was ordered.

"The moment this retreat began the Indians followed rapidly, delivering a heavy fire as they advanced, but they were kept at a respectful distance by the fire of the retreating platoon, who fell back deliberately and in perfect order to a point just south and east of "K" which position it was determined to hold. At this moment an orderly from Colonel Royall, and Private Weaver, of I Troop, from Captain Andrews, came up, after running the gauntlet of a sharp fire from the enemy, with peremptory orders to fall back at once and as rapidly as possible, as the Indians were trying to cut off the platoon.

"Starting at a trot down the hill, at the base of which ran the dry bed of a stream about eight feet wide and as many deep, with steep banks on either side, the platoon had gotten half way to the bottom when the advance of the pursuing Indians reached the crest just abandoned, and poured a scattering volley into the party. The order was given to take the charging gait and make for our own lines. A broad valley had to be crossed to reach the left of Royall's first position, and in doing so two men, Privates O'Brien and Stewart, and one horse were wounded. The platoon now joined their troop on the left about the point marked "E" (Royall's first position).

"In the meanwhile Henry's battalion, consisting of his own, Meinhold's, Vroom's and Reynold's troops of the Third, had occupied this line, but Meinhold being ordered back to report to General Crook, I Troop extended their line, and the ridge

was held as before. The left now suffered from a front fire
from the ridge "B" and a fire by the Indians that occupied "L"
and "C." At one time a number of men in this part of the
line started to go back. Being strongly appealed to by the
officer in charge, one of them turning about said:

"'All right, Lieutenant, if you say "stay," we'll stay.' They
went back and remained without a murmur until the positive
order came to abandon the position and fall back.

"This retrograde movement was made on foot, and the enemy,
occupying the position just abandoned, fired steadily and heavily
on our retreating line. Occupying the second line, the enemy
not only pressing us in front but getting on our flanks, Royall
refused the left of his line and held on stoutly against from
500 to 700 Indians, until again the order came to fall back
from the commanding general.

"The men and officers, not knowing the object of the withdrawal and knowing well that Royall's immediate command
was not whipped, naturally supposed that some disaster had
happened on the right. Again the retreat began. This time the
enemy, emboldened by our withdrawal a second time and
evidently reinforced, pressed on even harder than before, coming in on the left flank. The line was promptly halted, faced
about, and the braver of the savages who had pressed on in
advance of the others compelled to retire. The retreat was
then continued to the last position, which was destined to be
the scene of the fiercest encounter that has ever taken place
between Indians and United States troops.

"The officers, with the four companies under the immediate
command of Colonel Royall—Henry, Andrews, Vroom, Reynolds,
and Foster—remained mounted, and, although a conspicuous
mark for the enemy's rifles, were on the line with their men,
who were fighting on foot, during the whole engagement. First
Sergeant John Henry, of I Troop, Third, also remained mounted
in the line doing efficient service and displaying courage of
the highest order. He has been recommended to the consideration of the department commander.

"The affair now became serious, and the men were cautioned
to husband their ammunition and to fire only when they had
a fair assurance of hitting their man. A few minutes had only
elapsed when, with their wild yell, firing as they came, a vast
mass of savages dashed at the line. The men received them
steadily and, pouring in volley after volley, drove them back
in confusion to their cover in the rocks and ravines beyond
the slope. One warrior was left dead on the field within fifty
yards of the line, the others that were hit either holding on
to their ponies or being carried back by their companies.

"By this time the four companies, that had averaged about

forty men each at the opening of the fight, were so depleted
by casualties and details necessary to carry the wounded to
the hospital, as well as losing the services of every fourth man
who had been detailed in the morning to hold the led horses,
did not number in all more than sixty or seventy men, whilst
in their front, if the estimate of experienced officers who could
see the whole field from higher ground further back is to be
considered, there were upwards of 700 Sioux warriors.

"The Indians, who all the while had kept up a steady rolling
fire from the front, now extended their line down a ravine on
our right flank, rendering it necessary to refuse that portion of
our line, which was done promptly. Colonel Guy V. Henry, of
the Third Cavalry, was wounded by this enfilading fire, being
shot through the head immediately below the eyes, the ball striking the apex of the right cheek bone and coming out at apex
of the left cheek bone. The gallant fellow . . . would have
returned after having the wound dressed but that the surgeon
in charge positively refused to permit it. . . . The slanderous
assertions that were made in regard to the regiment for the
alleged acts of one of its companies at the affair of Powder
River, which assertions had been published in journals like
the *New York Tribune*, induced the line officers with Royall
to expose themselves unnecessarily—facing death with a laugh
and a passing joke, and with an utter recklessness that may be
charming to those who admire high courage and unquenchable
pluck, but that induced General Crook to say that he did not
desire that such officers should throw their lives away. He knew
the stuff they were made of and felt satisfied that they would
'stay put' wherever they might be ordered. . . .

"The firing was now terrific, the repeating rifles used by the
Indians enabling them to make it one continuous volley. Officers who were through the war and were there say that they
never in their experience saw anything hotter. Again the Sioux
advanced. With their 'Yip; Hip! Hi-yah! Hi-yah!' urging their
ponies to their utmost speed, they came in myriads from the
ravine on our right. Facing by the right flank and breaking to
the right and left in open order the men gallantly poured in
volley after volley, and again the pride of the Sioux nation
were dragged in the dust and drenched with their best blood.
Returning to their cover, they again endeavored to shake the
everlasting courage of the gallant little band by their scorch-
ing fire. Men, brave men and true, were falling every moment.
The wounded were carried back to the hospital by details
called from the line, which, growing thinner and thinner, seemed
to be dwindling so constantly that annihilation was apparently
but a question of time.

"'Better die right here than back in the ravine,' said one

officer to another. 'It's only a question of cartridges,' said a soldier to his comrade, who stood by him in the line.

"Royall sent Lt. Lemly, of his staff (who had already had a horse shot), at a gallop back to General Crook asking for help. Already the order had come to retire, but seeing no way to withdraw he asked for assistance to cover the retreat of his men to their horses. Morton, acting adjutant of the Third Cavalry, after carrying orders all day through the hottest of the fight, as calmly as though on a pleasure ride, now took charge of the headquarters escort and with them did good service.

"At last the supreme moment arrived. The Sioux, massing in all their strength, charged with a yell on the right flank and on the front. For an instant it looked as though Royall and his little band were doomed. The Indians never flinched under our fire, but pressed on, and the worn-out harrassed little battalion gave way. The officers with one accord dashed forward. Sergeant Henry's clear, ringing voice was heard high above the tumult shouting,

" 'Face them, men! — — them, face them!' whilst some officers, calling out, 'Great God, men! Don't go back on the old Third!' raised a cheer and the line faced about, fired into the enemy at such short range as to almost burn the noses of their ponies, and drove them back almost 200 yards over the slope on their front, the officers riding with and ahead of the charging line.

"A lull followed—a season of rest thankfully welcomed by the officers and men. Again it was broken by the enemy, who opened fire as before from the rocks and ravines on our front and right. The order was given to make for the horses and mount in the ravine below, and then fall back rapidly to the hill on which the field hospital had been established and that was now occupied by the infantry and C, G, and B, Troops, Third Cavalry. (Under Van Vliet, Crawford,[7] and Meinhold respectively).

"This movement was executed at once, Burt and Burrowes, of the Ninth Infantry, coming down from the hill and each firing a volley into the mass of savages that had again advanced when they saw our line withdraw. This aid, though late in coming, checked the main body who were rushing over the crest, but a party of Sioux that had started down the ravine killed and wounded a number of our men while mounting. . . .

"The ground in front and on the flanks of Royall's last stand was found to show unmistakable signs of the rough handling that the enemy had undergone. Clotted pools of blood back behind the rocks showed where their killed and wounded had been carried before final removal from the field. Sitting Bull evidently intended to have another Phil Kearny massacre; but the breechloading rifles and the pluck of the officers and men, who fought with such magnificent courage under Royall's able command, gave him a setback.

"Colonel Royall has highly commended the gallant conduct of the officers who were with his immediate command, and personally complimented Lieutenants Reynolds and Foster on the evening after the engagement. . . .

"A feeling of sadness seemed to spread over the companies whose ranks had been depleted of some gallant spirits. Especially were Allen, of I Troop, and Sergeant Marshall, of F, mourned by officers and men. Old soldiers—both of over twenty years service in the regiment—they were well known and respected by all. They died like true soldiers, facing the enemy gallantly, and their memories will long be green among the commissioned and enlisted of the Third Horse. . . .

"Farrier O'Grady, of F Troop, Third Cavalry, accompanied by a small party of that gallant command, displayed great courage in dashing back and bringing off the corpse of Sergeant Marshall in a shower of bullets from the then rapidly advancing enemy, thus saving from mutilation the remains of a gallant old soldier whose service in the regiment had extended over a period of twenty-five years.

"William W. Allen, of I Troop, Third, died as such a soldier might be expected to. His horse was shot twice and he was dismounted, and being hard pressed by the enemy he turned upon them, determined to sell his life as dearly as possible. Nobly the brave fellow fought, standing all the while and firing cooly with his carbine, until the Sioux, coming in on either side, shot him down. Allen then tried to draw his pistol, but one of the Sioux, clubbing his carbine, struck the poor fellow over the head, thus ending the unequal contest. Sergeant Groesch, who lay desperately wounded near by, witnessed this scene, and was saved from a similar fate by the timely arrival of the Crows and Shoshones, accompanied by a number of men of his own company, who took him back to the hospital.

"Private Herbert W. Weaver, of I Troop, displayed high courage in carrying the order for Lieutenant Foster to withdraw, as in doing so he had to pass over open ground commanded by the rifles of the enemy, thus running the gauntlet of their fire at the imminent risk of his life. . . .

"Private McMahon, of I Troop, also deserves special mention. He was in the charge made by the Second Platoon on the extreme left in the morning, and when the third and last charge was made, rode alongside the chief of the platoon, and was first on the ridge just abandoned by the enemy. McMahon was reprimanded for riding ahead of an officer whilst he was

leading a charge and complimented for his courage at the same
time.

Z"

There are a number of discrepancies between the summary
of this action at the beginning of this chapter and the account
just quoted as to details. The versions as related in the summary are believed to be correct, as most of them are based
upon the official reports of the men involved. For instance,
the unknown officer stated that the Indians attacked from the
right flank of the soldiers' line, which would be from the west,
but that Captain Henry was shot across the face from right
to left. This could not be correct, as the Captain was facing
northeast when he was shot by this enfilading fire, which would
mean that the bullet struck the left side of his face first and
came out on the right side. It will be noted that there are
similar discrepancies wherever the same incident is related by
different people, but this is only to be expected, as no two
people see the same thing in the same way.

"If One Indian Was Shot Five Were There to Take His Place"

Private Phineas Towne of Lt. Reynold's company in Captain
Henry's battalion was in the thickest of the fight. He was
severely wounded by a pistol bullet which remained in his
abdomen and years later received the Order of the Purple
Heart; but he did not mention his wound in the account he
gave to C. T. Brady[8], published in *Indian Fights and Fighters.**

"While our Indians were making their charge upon the Sioux,
General Crook gave orders to saddle up, for well he knew
that a battle was on hand. After we had saddled and formed
in line, my troop, F. Third Cavalry, was placed on the left flank
of the command, and it with two other troops were detailed as
skirmishers and were ordered to make a flank movement to our
left and gain the hills, where we dismounted, leaving each
fourth trooper to hold the horses. We then formed the skirmish
line on foot, which was commanded by Lt. Col. Royall. . . .

"After remaining on the skirmish line for perhaps two hours,
we were ordered to fall back and remount our horses to take
a new position, our horses were held in check in a ravine, as
it was impossible to hold our present position against such
overwhelming odds, I must say that I never saw so great a body
of Indians in one place as I saw at that time, and I have seen

* From *Indian Fights And Fighters,* by C. T. Brady. Copyright 1904
by Doubleday & Company, Inc.

a great many Indians in my time. It seemed that if one Indian was shot five were there to take his place. If we had remained in our first position we would have all been killed, and I consider that we retreated in the right time.

"I had not gone more than one third of the distance from our position to where the horses were when I overtook three other soldiers of my own troop carrying a sergeant by the name of Marshall, who had been shot through the face. I knew that time was precious and none to lose. I could not give them the cold shoulder by passing them without giving a helping hand. Glancing back I saw the hostiles coming over the hill. There I was down in that ravine, alone and in the midst of a lot of murderous savages. They captured one other comrade of mine by the name of Bennett of L Troop, Third Cavalry, and completely cut him in pieces. His remains were buried in a sack."

R. B. Davenport, the correspondent for the *New York Herald*, was with Colonel Royall throughout the fight, his account of the battle appearing in that newspaper on July 13, 1876. The *Daily Graphic* article was so complete and comprehensive that it would only be repetition to use the Davenport account here. It should be mentioned in passing, however, that General Crook was greatly angered by some of Mr. Davenport's statements. One of these was to the effect that if Colonel Royall had not been restrained by General Crook, he could have driven the Indians away from the heights around Andrews' Point. Crook referred to this criticism in his dispatch of July 23, 1876, from Camp on North Goose Creek, Wyoming, to General Sheridan in Chicago, as follows:

"I understand the *New York Herald* has published most villainous falsehoods from its correspondent with this command in regard to the Rosebud fight of the Seventeenth (17) ultimo. which is intended to do the command and myself great injustice. Of course the reason is obvious. There was a correct account forwarded from here to the *New York Herald Tribune*, but it never reached its destination, and it is supposed here that is was suppressed in the telegraph office at Fetterman."

(signed) George Crook, Brig. Gen'l."

It would seem that the criticism was unfounded, inasmuch as Colonel Royall was already too far from the main command. If he had extended his advance further, he would have had even more trouble in returning to the crest. One wonders why Colonel Royall sent only one company, Meinhold's, instead of moving his whole command so as to connect with the rest of the troops as Crook ordered. If his order had been complied with, Royall's men would not have been trapped on the ridges.

Printed with the Davenport article was the map of the battlefield as prepared by Lt. Charles Morton. All of the maps of the field made at that time were very inaccurate both as to terrain and positions occupied by the troops. This was only natural, as the country was very rough and rugged and the men were there only one day, during which time they were fully occupied with the hostile Indians. The map in the *Daily Graphic* is the most accurate as to terrain and as to the action on the left, but shows little of the fight elsewhere. While Lt. Morton's map is fairly accurate as to the terrain and action in the center and right, it is very much confused as to the left. Mills' map, which was prepared by C. T. Brady upon descriptions furnished by Mills, shows only the east half of the field, but is valuable as to the area in which Mills operated. The field was so large that no one person could become familiar with all of it in such a short time. Those who were in only one of the three separate battles could know accurately only about the terrain and various positions in that immediate area.

That evening after the battle, the troops went into camp in the valley along the banks of the stream on the site of the bivouac of that morning. The camp was in the form of a square with the horses and mules in the center. There is a hopeless conflict as to where the dead were buried; and, so far as is known, none of the graves has been located. Some say that each company buried its own dead, while others say that all the soldiers were buried in one long trench. Most of the soldiers said that they were buried on the banks of the Rosebud, but several claim that they were buried on the field.

Various Superintendents of the Custer Battlefield Cemetery have tried to locate the bodies, so that they might receive suitable burial in the Custer National Cemetery, but so far have been unsuccessful. General Godfrey of the Seventh Cavalry also did some investigating and digging near the Penson ranch house, but was unable to locate them. John Stands-In-Timber told the writer that the Cheyenne warriors who had been in the battle had told him that the soldier dead were buried near the Penson ranch house. Elmer Kobold says that years ago Frank Gruard showed Jim Gatchell, late of Buffalo, Wyoming, the place where five bodies had been buried; this was on the north bank of the stream ten feet west of the present garage near Kobold's house. Mr. Gatchell told this to Kobold years later during a visit to the field, and pointed out the spot. There was a sunken place about fifteen feet long at this point; but when some local residents dug down to a depth of five feet, in the summer of 1953, nothing was found, although the ground had been disturbed for a depth of several feet.

Charles Young tells about another place within a sharp U bend in the stream a mile west of Kobold's house where it is believed by some that the soldiers are buried. About a hundred yards to the southwest of the bend was located a large tree upon which the letters "U S" together with an arrow pointing to the U bend had been burned, presumably with a ramrod. The surface of the tree had been squared at that point so that the letters were on a flat surface. This tree was cut down years ago by an early settler below the burnt writing, and only the squared stump remains.

In the Hardin (Montana) *Tribune-Herald* for January 20, 1933, there appeared an article which throws some light on the question of where the men were buried. The article was the report of an interview by Dr. Thomas B. Marquis with James Forrestell, who was in Troop D of the Second Cavalry at the Rosebud battle, and was with Crook's column the following August when it went down the Rosebud in pursuit of Sitting Bull's encampment.

"Our nine dead men were buried at the base of a cut bank along the edge of Rosebud Creek. Then many horses were led back and forth over the grave in order to conceal the place of burial. With recruits and additional supplies we started out again in early August. We went over the same route to the scene of our Rosebud battle. We paused there long enough to make a change in the burial place of our dead comrades. We took the bodies from the side of the creek and made new graves for them on more suitable ground away from the stream."

No mention has been made of where the Crow scout was buried, nor of the four soldiers reported mortally wounded by Bourke and Wasson, nor of any of the other dead soldiers as claimed by Gruard and Ben Arnold. In all probability five of the soldiers were buried near Kobold's garage, as there is no reason to doubt Frank Gruard's story, and all the soldiers were reburied on some point of the bluffs overlooking the valley, since there is no reason to doubt Forrestell's story either.

All of the men reported killed in the battle were in the Third Cavalry who fought on the left under Colonel Royall. Sergeant David Marshall, Private Roe Gilbert of Lt. Reynold's company; Privates William W. Allen, Eugene Flynn of Captain Andrews' company; Sergeant Anton Newkirken, and Privates Richard Bennett, George Potts, Brooks Conners, and Allen J. Mitchell of Lt. Vroom's company were killed on the bluff where Royall made his last stand.

The only officer wounded in the engagement was Captain Guy V. Henry, and none was killed.

In Lt. Bainbridge Reynolds' company Private Otto Broderson was slightly wounded and not treated; Private William Featherly was shot in the left arm; and Private Phineas Towne was shot in the abdomen, where the bullet was allowed to remain. In Captain Meinhold's company Private Henry Steiner suffered a broken shoulder as the result of a gun shot wound while riding in the valley to join the main command.

In Lt. Vroom's company Sergeant Samuel Cook and Trumpeter William H. Edwards were both shot in the thigh, and Private John Kremer was shot in the shoulder. Most of the wounded were in Captain Andrews' company, where Sergeant Andrew Groesch was shot in the left arm and chest and had both arms broken; Corporal Carty had a slight wound not carried on sick report; Private Francis Smith suffered a broken leg; Private Charles W. Stuart was shot in the wrist and arm; Private James O'Brien was shot in the forearm; and Private John Loscibosky was shot in the right elbow. Captain Andrews also reported six horses of his company wounded.

After the battle it was estimated that 25,000 rounds of ammunition had been expended by the troops, and one of the newspaper correspondents reported that seven carbines were lost in the fight and that 16 horses were shot.[9]

Author's note. When I first started looking for Royall's positions in the battle, I went over the little bluffs and ridges immediately northwest of the bivouac, but did not find a trace of anything. It was difficult to visualize the large distances covered by the cavalry charges, so I next went over the series of ridges lying west of Crook's Hill but south of the crest, and extending toward the head of Kollmar Creek. Only one empty shell and one lance point were found in this large area. The lance point was of some kind of pink stone and John Stands-In-Timber pointed out that on one side there was scratched in the stone the figure of a man wearing a hat with the brim turned up in front like a soldier's. John would not say much about it, but I surmised that the figure was some kind of special "Medicine" of one of the hostile Indians.

The sketch of Royall's third position in the *Daily Graphic* showed the line facing northwest and extending from a ravine southwestward to the crest of the bluff, with a small hill immediately and precisely in rear of the line. I had looked for such a line and went all over the area with a metal detector wherever such a combination was found. There were many little hills beside ravines, and I did a lot of hard work going over them but finding nothing. I finally took pictures of all the surrounding terrain and, during the winter of 1954-1955, studied these with a view to finding the series of ridges occupied by Royall. In an enlightened moment I saw the large gap in the ridge near the head of Kollmar Creek and, checking on the aerial photo map of the field, saw what might be rocky formations extending to the southwest. Upon returning to the field the next June, I drove over a trail leading north of the Charles Young ranch house for about a mile and here found the whole field spread out before me as described. Parking my car on top of the second position, I could see the ridge forming the first position northwest across the large ravine, with Andrews' Point about six hundred yards beyond. To the southwest extended the rocky ledges for about four hundred yards, at which point another rocky ledge joined it from the east, forming an acute angle. Towards the east was a gap in the ridge about a half mile long with a high hill on the other side where the ridge was resumed.

Royall's first position was literally surrounded by small ridges and bluffs on the west and south, and one could understand why the men gravitated to the east end where they had the protection of the end of the ridge. The south slope was steep where the soldiers were; but we found twenty three .45-70 soldiers' shells which had been fired, one .45-70 shell unfired, and one .44 Bulldog revolver short-cased shell on the crest, which had undoubtedly been fired by one of the Indians at the retreating men. There is a fence running north and south cutting off the extreme east end of this ridge, which is the dividing line between the land of Charles Young on the east and the Crow Indian Reservation on the west. This means that this ridge, Andrews' Point, the rocky ledges extending southwest, and the ridge southwest of Andrews' Point which marked the farthest advance of Lt. Foster's men, are all on the Reservation.

The ridge in the second position is on the land of Charles Young. On the south slope here just below the crest we found fifteen .45-70 empty soldiers' shells, and three .50-70 Springfield empty cases of the type with the Martin Crimped-in primer. The latter could have been used either by the Indian allies or the hostile Indians when they took over the ridge. I went along the ledges with a metal detector, but did not find anything until I reached the acute angle, where I found three .45-70 soldiers' shells back from the ledge about fifty feet. It was probable that the men defending this line secured the protection of the ledges by standing back from them about this distance, which would have the effect of protecting their bodies from the Indians, with just their heads showing. The ledges do not rise above the level of the adjoining ground, but consist of large rocks which form a steep bluff dropping off abruptly. On the west side are caves and irregular formations in the walls of solid rock. It was apparent that this line had to be held by the soldiers to keep the Indians from firing at them from behind the ledges.

After exploring the two battle ridges, I moved farther east in search of the third position and had considerable difficulty in finding it. Going by the *Daily Graphic* sketch, I looked for the line facing northwest in front of a hill. As I thought that the high hill one half mile to the east might indicate this position, I went over the hill and ground to the northwest of it with a metal detector. To the west of the hill I found two spent bullets on top of the ground, one a .50-70 Springfield and the other a .45-70 Springfield. Upon and near the hill I found three .45-70 empty soldiers' shells, three .50-70 Springfield empty shells, one .44 Winchester empty shell with the raised H on the base, and one .44 Bulldog short-cased revolver shell which had probably been used in an Indian's Model 1866 Winchester. This area was in the line of retreat of the soldiers to their third position.

I found several broken arrowheads near the rocky formation north of the hill. From here I went along the ridge, but did not find anything until I decided to try the detector just west of the fence between the Kobold land and the Burt Young land south of Crook's Hill. Almost immediately I found a soldier's empty shell and others close to it, and soon decided that this was the ridge where Royall made his last stand. This place was different from the sketch, as the line extended along the crest of the ridge almost east and west and did not face northwest as shown in the sketch. There was a small hill to the northeast jutting out from the slope which, by a stretch of the imagination, could have been that intended in the map.

The crest varied in width from about twenty yards on the east end to about forty yards on the west end. I found shells in a line 325 yards long commencing on the east end about 25 yards east of Kobold's fence and extending westward. There was a little depression or swale leading down from the crest at a point about 25 yards west of the fence, and I believe the men retreated down this depression to the horses, as it afforded some protection from enfilading fire from the west. I also found some shells, both loaded and unloaded, farther north down this depression toward the led horse ravine.

It gave me a big thrill to find this position, as some of the heaviest fighting in American history occurred here. With a metal detector I found, in this line, one hundred and thirty-three .45-70 empty soldiers' shells; two .45-70 unfired soldiers' shells; one .50-70 Springfield, Winchester, brass case with external primer, which had been reloaded; one loaded 45 Colt and Remington Revolver cartridge, inside primed center fire as made at either Frankfort or Springfield Arsenal about 1871, with internal primer held in place by two crimps near the base; and one 50 Spencer of Winchester make with a raised H on the base. I also found one .50-70 bullet flattened on the end; indicating that it had passed through some object and another .50-70 bullet nearly cut in two lengthwise, showing that it had struck some hard object. These were probably Indian bullets which had killed or wounded two of the soldiers, as they were found in the midst of the soldiers' shells. The shells were very thick at the west end of the line, as the men here had to turn around and fire at the Indians when they made their flank attack from the west and from the rear. They were also thick about fifty yards west of the east end of the line, and I believe this was caused by the heavy fighting around Captain Henry after he was wounded.

When I went over the field with John Stands-In-Timber, he pointed out three large flat rocks on the crest at the south edge of the bluff about twenty-five yards west of the fence, which the Cheyennes had placed here to mark the spot where Captain Henry had been shot. According to the sketch in the *Daily Graphic* the place where he was shot was indicated as behind the soldiers' line, probably fifteen or twenty yards down the slope from where the rocks are; but the rocks are, I believe, in the right place because at this point he was in plain sight of the Indians to the south and west, and the accounts all say that the Indians saw him fall and were encouraged to make their charge. If he had been farther down the slope, he would not have been in plain view of the Indians.

John Stands-In-Timber led us about a quarter of a mile eastward along the ridge from where Captain Henry fell, and showed us a pile of rocks on the crest which we had passed by many times and wondered about. This was the marker placed by the Cheyennes indicating the spot where the fifteen year-old Sioux boy was pulled from his horse and killed after charging too close to the line of the scouts. This occurred after Royall's men had retreated to their horses and while the Crows and Shoshones were north of the crest out of sight. The Sioux boy and another Indian charged the crest which they thought was unoccupied. When they reached it, the other Indian got away, but the scouts caught the boy and killed him. This incident is related in several of the Indian accounts.

I looked for shells around this spot and found one .45-70 (R. B.) standard Berdan primer made at Frankfort Arsenal, with the .45-70 imprinted on the base. It was made in the early 1870's and was the only one of its kind which I have found. Mr. Medicus has expressed the opinion that the shell was in the battle. The other shells found near were one .45-70 unfired Springfield soldier's cartridge; one 44 Old Model Colt's revolver cartridge; and one .50-70 Springfield with the built-in external copper primer with the large deep groove around the primer, which could not be reloaded. Except for the unfired soldier's cartridge, the others were used by either the scouts or the Indians, and they could have been used in this same incident.

John Stands-In-Timber showed us another spot which had sufficient significance to the Cheyennes to become part of their history: that was the place where the Cheyenne warrior by the name of "Limpy" had his horse shot. Limpy was badly crippled, having one leg much shorter than the other one, but he and five other Cheyennes made a charge from the west upon the retreating soldier line when it was on the slope south of Kollmar Creek. Just south of the rock formation Limpy's horse was shot and killed, and he was afoot. The other five Cheyennes turned their horses and circled back out of range, while Young Two Moon came riding back in order to rescue Limpy, who was being fired at by the soldiers. Limpy tried to mount in back of Young Two Moon as he came riding by, but was unable to do so because of his deformity. Young Two Moon circled back to where Limpy was again and slowed down to the point where he was able to mount and escape unharmed. This spot is now unmarked, but is about ten yards south of the south edge of the rock formation.

Mr. Kobold told me that one of the early settlers said that he hauled several wagon loads of horse bones from Kollmar Creek and that the hooves had iron shoes on them. It is probable that these bones were originally in the led horse ravine and were washed down the slope of the ravine into the creek. I went over this ravine very carefully and, in addition to many horse bones, found two horses' skulls which were very old and had green moss on them. One was buried in the soil with just the top visible. After digging it up, I found a bullet hole in the side of the skull and the top of the skull missing. One might speculate that this horse was so badly wounded that the trooper blew its brains out. It was a five-year-old gelding and could have been one of Colonel Royall's sleek and well groomed cavalry horses.

Brigadier General George Crook, Commander of the Bighorn and Yellowstone Expedition, who, in quest of Crazy Horse's village, defied the Oglala chief's warning not to cross the Tongue River, and was intercepted on the banks of the Rosebud where a major battle occurred.—*Courtesy National Archives*

This rare old tintype of Crazy Horse, never before published, is believed by Jake Herman, 5th Member of the Oglala Sioux Tribal Council to be the only existing, authentic picture of the great Oglala chieftain who led the Sioux against Crook at the Battle of the Rosebud. —*Courtesy Oglala Sioux Tribal Council.*

Captain Alex Chambers, a former commander of Fort Fetterman, was the leader of the "Mule Brigade," backbone of Crook's defense at the Rosebud.—*Courtesy National Archives.*

A. H. Nickerson, Adjutant General of the expedition and Crook's aide-de-camp. With only one attendant, he carried Crook's countermanding order to Mills down the canyon, at the risk of his life.—*Courtesy National Archives.*

Captain Anson Mills, 3rd Cavalry, who was ordered by Crook at the height of battle to withdraw his men from Crook's Hill and move upon Crazy Horse's village believed by the scouts to be eight miles down the dark Rosebud canyon.

The beloved and gallant Captain Guy V. Henry, tragic victim of the furious Sioux charges against Royall's isolated battalion.—*Courtesy National Archives.*

Site of Camp Cloud Peak, General Crook's base, June 19, 1876, on Big Goose Creek, where Crook was joined by his scouts and Crow and Shoshone allies.

The narrow canyon of the Rosebud looking north from the point where Mills defiled, as it looks today.

The site of Royall's third position where heaviest fighting of battle occurred. Many empty shells were found in a rough circle, foreground, indicating this was the point where Vroom's company was surrounded.

Royall's first position. This picture, taken from Royall's second position, shows the "rocky point" to the northwest at head of Kollmar Creek, farthest advance of Captain Andrew.

South spur of Crook's Hill from the west.

Little breastworks east of Packers' Rocks, looking northwest.

Ridge south of Kollmar Creek seen from Crook's Hill. Led horse ravine is indicated by trees in middle distance, with Royall's third position beyond trees.

Col. Royall, while retreating across a wide hollow, was charged by Sioux forces. Major Randall immediately countercharged with the Crows and Shoshones while the infantry poured forth a volley from a small elevation in middle distance.—*Courtesy of the Library of Congress.*

In this painting by J. E. Taylor, Royall's men, seen charging out of the led horse ravine in an attempt to reach the crest, are almost surrounded by 500 Sioux and Northern Cheyenne.

Upper, left:
Medicine Crow, one of the leaders of the Crow allies.—*Courtesy of The Smithsonian Institute.*

Upper, right:
Washakie, Chief of the Shoshones at the Rosebud battle.—*Courtesy of National Archives.*

Lower, left:
Crazy Head (standing) and Spotted Wolf. The latter led the Cheyennes at the Rosebud.—*Courtesy of The Smithsonian Institute.*

Upper: This large stone, carved by Crook's scouts, was found on the Hillman Ranch on the banks of Little Goose Creek. —*Courtesy of Frank Sibrava.*

Center: This sketch by Stanley shows the killing of a Sioux warrior the morning after the Rosebud battle, June 18.—*Courtesy of the Library of Congress.*

Lower: John Stands-In-Timber, the Cheyenne Historian, standing at place in gap where Chief Comes-In-Sights was rescued by his sister.

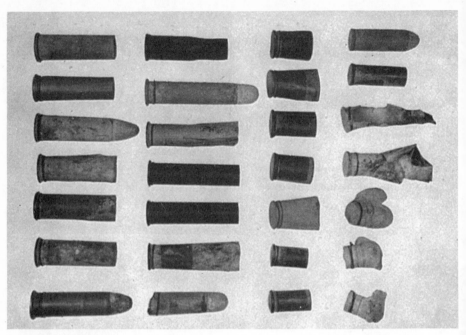

See opposite page for legend

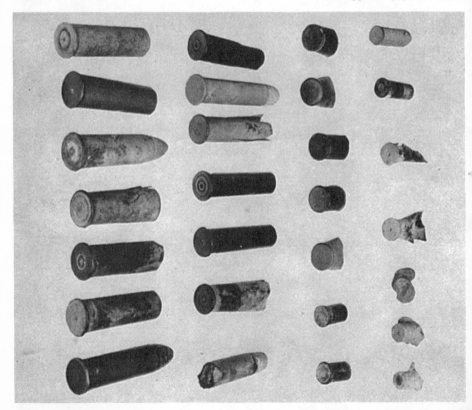

In the two views on the opposite page of the relics from the author's museum may be seen various types of shells and bullets found on the Rosebud battlefield.

Top row, left to right:

1. .50-70 centerfire Martin type primer made by Frankfort Arsenal. Primer is formed from one continuous piece of copper same as case, making it impossible to reload.
2. Bottlenecked .45-75-350 Winchester Centennial Model 1876 standard centerfire type using single flash hole Berdan primer. Production started early 1876.
3. .50 caliber Spencer carbine blank. Rimfire, copper base, made about 1865. Winchester make with raised H on base.
4. Loaded .45 Colt and Remington revolver cartridge, inside primed, centerfire as made at either Frankfort Arsenal or Springfield Armory about 1871. The primer is held in place by two crimps at the base. Found near spot where Captain Henry was wounded.

Second row, left to right:

1. .50-70 Springfield, centerfire, inside primed with experimental bar anvil Benet primer, made at Frankfort Arsenal, late 1860-1871 period.
2. Loaded .45-70 Springfield copper case used by soldiers.
3. .50 caliber Model 1865 Spencer repeating rifle and carbine rimfire cartridge, made by Jacob Goldmark as indicated by "JG" base marking. Goldmark was a private contractor who made ammunition for the Government during the Civil War.
4. .44 Colt Old Model black powder revolver cartridge with external centerfire primer.

Third row, left to right:

1. Loaded cartridge of .50-70-450 caliber used in Government Springfield and Remington Rolling Block Rifles, centerfire outside primed. Found behind Packers' Rocks.
2. .45-70 rifle ball made at Frankfort Arsenal early 1870 period, using Berdan type primer. It has "45 70" marked on base.
3. Caliber .56-52 Spencer rimfire, copper case made by Winchester with H head stamp.
4. .45-70 soldier shell forced from gun with ramrod which tore out side.

Fourth row, left to right:

1. .50-70 Springfield, outside primer, centerfire, 3-hole Berdan primer, brass case probably of Winchester make.
2. .45-70 Springfield rifle and carbine Model 1873, brass case, external centerfire primer, probably of Winchester make.
3. .56-56 Spencer rifle rimfire copper case.
4. .45-70 soldier shell which had been forced from gun with ramrod tearing out top.

Fifth row, left to right:

1. .50-70 Springfield, outside primer, centerfire, brass, made by U.M.C.
2. .45-70 rifle and carbine model 1865 to 1868 copper case inside primed made by Frankfort Arsenal, Martin crimped in primer.
3. .50 caliber Spencer rimfire used in Spencer rifles and carbines. Made about 1865.
4. .50 caliber lead bullet found on Royall's third position.

Sixth row, left to right:

1. Empty .50-70 Springfield, centerfire, inside primed with Martin 2-hole disc primer, copper case, Frankfort Arsenal.
2. .45-70 cartridge copper centerfire inside primed made by U. S. Cartridge Co.
3. .44 caliber short rimfire of unknown make as used in early bulldog revolvers. The hostile Indians probably used these in their 1866 Winchesters.
4. .50 caliber lead bullet found on Royall's third position.

Bottom row, left to right:

1. Loaded .50-70 Springfield, centerfire, inside primed with Martin 2-hole disc primer, copper case, Frankford Arsenal.
2. .45-70 Springfield copper case which has been pulled in two by ejector after cartridge had gotten stuck in gun. Bullet and wads still remain.
3. .44 caliber rimfire Model 1866 Winchester with raised H head stamp, commonly used by hostile Indians.
4. .45 caliber lead bullet, probably a .45-70, found near Infantry Hill.

133

Chapter 10

WITH CRAZY HORSE

THE last three chapters have been devoted to a detailed description of the battle from the viewpoint of the soldiers involved. They were, of course, acting under the orders of General Crook, who in turn was following the directions of army headquarters. The army was subject to the political powers in Washington, who were very sensitive to public opinion. Public opinion was bitterly opposed to any rights which the Indians might have had and clamored for their early extinction in the event they did not stay on their reservations and thus make way for the advance of white civilization, which was accelerated by the emigration to this country of the displaced peoples of Europe.

The Sioux had been yielding to this pressure for years, and some stayed on the reservations rather than go to war with the white man. But many of the Sioux and most of the Cheyennes had rallied under the banner of their leader, Sitting Bull, determined to fight for their land and the old carefree way of life whereby they roamed at will, depending upon the buffalo for the necessities of life. They were fighting for their form of civilization, for their women, children, and everything that they cherished.

The Indian wars were a conflict, then, between civilizations in which both sides were in the right from their individual points of view, but in which as Napoleon expressed it, God is on the side of the heaviest artillery. The Indians reached the zenith of their power at the Rosebud and Little Big Horn. After expending their supply of ammunition in these battles, they were strictly on the defensive and did not dare to meet the soldiers in open combat.

The Sioux and Cheyennes had learned from the battles of the Washita and Powder River what a soldier attack on their villages meant. This was the reason that they took the offensive against General Crook. Crook and his soldiers certainly found them worthy opponents.

Historians should be eternally grateful to a few people who had the foresight to interview and write down the battle experiences of some of the Indians when still alive. Mari Sandoz has written the life story of Crazy Horse, a valuable work which covers the history and battles of the Oglala tribe of Sioux during this period, from material obtained directly from his friends and relatives.

Stanley Vestal wrote down the story of the battle from the lips of White Bull, the Minniconjou Sioux warrior. The interview of four Cheyenne survivors of the battle by Jack Keenan, of the Billings, Montana *Gazette,* at the unveiling of the monument commemorating the action, June, 1934, is also a valuable contribution.

The Indians are pretty much in agreement as to the main facts. Many bands of them set out from all the camp circles the night before the battle. After riding all night, they stopped about daylight close to the field to rest their horses and to perform the complicated ritual necessary in preparing for battle. A large band of Oglalas undoubtedly came up the Rosebud from the Crazy Horse village, seventeen miles north of the field. Some of those from the large encampment rode up the south fork of Reno Creek and reached the field through Sioux Pass, three miles north and six miles west. Others crossed over the divide east to the Rosebud and came up the stream. Some of these latter stopped at Trail Creek, a little tributary of the Rosebud flowing in from the east, located fourteen miles north of the field.

Mr. Grinnell has definitely ascertained that Crook's Crow scouts and the advance scouts of the Sioux forces accidentally met on the high hill west of the stream on what was known later as the William Rowland ranch, located eleven miles north of the battlefield. This is confirmed by John Stands-In-Timber. There was a little skirmish here; and the main bodies of the Sioux and Cheyennes, hearing the firing, rode up and chased the Crow scouts back to camp, where they found the soldiers in bivouac. It was the advance guard of these pursuing Indians who made the impetuous charge towards the cavalry from the northeast.

Various bands of Indians kept coming in throughout the fight, the Hunkpapas being last to arrive. Some of the larger bands were commanded by the soldier societies, composed of professional Indian soldiers, in order to prevent the more impetuous from rushing ahead, thus giving warning of their approach. But all the accounts preclude the possibility of a trap's having been set by Indians lining up behind the bluffs around the canyon or by massing behind the high crest north of the bend, *before* the battle. This obviously could not have been done with the Crow Scouts far out ahead of Crook's command and the Shoshones posted on the north bluff.

It has been reported that Crazy Horse told reporters, in an interview after he surrendered in the spring of 1877, that he had most of his warriors lined up behind the canyon walls waiting for the troops to enter into the trap. Captain Nickerson also wrote that when General Crook and General Sherman visited the canyon a year after the battle, several of the hostiles who had served under Crazy Horse pointed out where the great body of them were lying in wait where the canyon narrows.

According to John Stands-In-Timber the first strategy of Crazy Horse was in instituting the main attack from the northwest in order to drive the soldiers into the narrow valley at the east bend; but when that failed, he lined the sides of the narrow canyon with warriors, intending to lead the soldiers there by feigned retreat. The soldiers were sent down there by General Crook but later recalled before they entered this portion of the canyon. After the soldiers had defiled to the plateau on the west, the Indians literally swarmed out of the canyon where they had been hiding behind every rock, fallen tree, and beaver dam.

While the Indian accounts disclose that there was little or no leadership among them in the military sense, yet under Crazy Horse they knew enough to avoid the mounted charges and the massed infantry companies, and to seek the weak places in the line. They were all on horseback, moving freely from one place to another, not attempting to form or hold lines. It was agreed by all of them that there were the three battles going on simultaneously: Royall's toward the west, Crook's on the crest with the main command, and Van Vliet's two companies on the bluff south of camp. At the last, all of the Cheyennes and some Sioux were concentrated on Royall's men, while the rest of the Crazy Horse's forces were lying in wait for Mills in the narrow canyon.

Author's note: According to the Indian code, it was an honor to attack the enemy and attract his fire during the charge. Of the Cheyennes there were a few who were continually making these forays. Among these were White Shield, Young Two Moon, Chief Comes-in-Sight, White Elk, Limpy, Scabby, and their war chief, Spotted Wolf, while most of the warriors were content to join only in the general attacks. Sometimes these charges were made by one Indian alone, while at other times two or more would make the attack.

When Chief Comes-in-Sight started to make his famous charge upon the soldiers, another Indian from the other end of the line started to charge in the direction opposite to that of the Chief, so that they passed each other. Immediately after this the Chief's horse was killed by the heavy fire of the soldiers and scouts. John Stands-In-Timber showed us the spot where the horse was killed early in the fight and described the various battle positions at that time. We stood in the center of the gap facing east and could see the little hillocks and ridges south of the crest from behind which the soldiers were advancing northward with the scouts in front.

North of the crest and fighting from behind little piles of rocks were the Indians who at this point were contesting the advance of the enemy along the east side of the gap. Chief Comes-in-Sight was on the crest west of the gap and charged southeastward towards the soldiers and scouts across the open stretch in the gap. His horse was killed near the east slope of the gap and a little south of the crest, probably about two hundred yards from the advanced line of scouts. Just as some of the scouts were charging on him, his sister, Buffalo Calf Road Woman, rode up from the north and paused long enough for him to mount behind her and escape. The Cheyennes always refer to the battle as "where the sister saved her brother."

From this point we went a short distance in a southwesterly direction to a small ridge running north and south. On the south end of this ridge was a pile of rocks which I had seen before and had wondered about. John explained that these rocks marked the place where a soldier had been killed. After the fighting in the gap many of the Indians retreated westward where they had taken position behind this bluff. While here one of the soldier's horses had run away with him; and as they reached this ridge, the Indians behind it shot and killed him. None of the soldiers' accounts mention such an incident, but it could have been one of the men of the Third Cavalry.

"It Was a Hot Little Fight"

The relatives and friends of Crazy Horse, many years after his death, told about his part in the battle to their friend Mari Sandoz; this narrative* from her book, *Crazy Horse*, is a composite of those stories:

"The night was thinning in the east when Crazy Horse stopped his Oglalas for a little resting. They were not far from the Rosebud now, and once a little wind brought a smell of water that stirred the tired horses and once the sweetness of the roses blooming so thick in that valley. But soon there was the soft owl hoot of another war party coming, so they rode in closer, for the soldiers must not escape them now. Daylight came upon the warriors behind the ridge north and west of the bend of the Rosebud. Stopping there they ate of their wasna and made ready for the fight. Crazy Horse loosened his long hair, tied on the calfskin cape, and threw dust over his spotted war horse while not far away the eighteen year old son of Red Cloud shook out a long tailed war bonnet and put it on as tho he were really a bonnet man of the Akicita, the other young men standing away from him, eve. the older ones silent, for this son of the agency could be told nothing at all.

"While the horses rested, the scouts were sent out to locate the soldiers and bring back word of them; but as they crossed the ridge they rode into the Crows coming up from the other side. There was shooting, a Lakota fell, two Crows were wounded, and all the warriors, forgetting about the resting horses whipped them to the ridge and stopped there in dark rows against the sky. Below him Crazy Horse saw the Crow scouts fleeing down the slope into the valley of the Rosebud, full of soldiers and Indians, so many they looked like a resting,

* From *Crazy Horse* by Mari Sandoz, courtesy Hastings House, Publishers.

cud-chewing herd of buffalo, the horses grazing, the men in dark little bunches. Beyond them was the willow lined creek, with more soldiers on the other side, and then the bluffs and the far ridge, so far that a horseman would look like one of the scattering of little trees. And between him and that place, as in the palm of a browning hand, were the soldiers, and once more Crazy Horse wished for guns, plenty of good rifles and warriors who would strike together in waves like flying hail. As the Crows fled howling back to the soldiers, they stirred into moving, running to catch their horses or lining up and then going off every way in little bunches, many horse and walking soldiers hurrying up towards the hostiles, coming in rows, a flag waving, a bugle sounding clear in the warm air. Behind them the Indian scouts were riding hard up and down, raising a great dust, making ready to fight too, now that the soldiers had gone ahead, shooting into the hostiles. Crazy Horse held his warriors together for a long time but there were so many soldiers and their rifle fire was so close among them that finally they fell back to the rocks of the second ridge, hoping to draw the whites along. And they came, off their horses now, crawling from rock to rock, and when they were well scattered, Crazy Horse led a charge. It was a hot little fight, many men going down, some even from arrows. Then more soldiers, followed by the Snakes, came galloping up from the side.[1] In the smoke and dust the Lakotas couldn't tell their friends from the scouts, so they withdrew awhile to rest their horses and to see how the fighting was going in other places. The Crows had been getting bolder too, and when young Red Cloud lost his horse and ran away without stopping to take off the war bridle to show that he was unafraid, they rode upon him and whipped him hard, grabbing his father's rifle[2] from him and jerking off the war bonnet, saying he was a boy, with no right to wear it. Crazy Horse and two others charged the Crows and got the young Bad Face back, not looking at him, shamed that they had seen one of their young men crying to his enemies for pity. By now the sun was high and the fighting had spread off to the opposite ridge, the charges going back and forth over miles of rough ground, with many brave things done, many afoot and wounded ones being carried off the field by warriors whose horses were so tired they could barely be whipped out of a walk. The Hunkpapas were helping strong now. They came late, their horses were fresher and their guns still loaded. Crazy Horse was with them awhile, shooting from the ground as always. When his spotted horse was played out, he got his bay and went to the bluffs where the Cheyennes seemed to be making a very good fight.[3]

"Once, when the smoke and dust lifted, Crazy Horse saw the sister of Chief Comes-in-Sight charge forward to where he was afoot and surrounded. With him on behind her she zigzagged back through the soldiers, bullets flying, the warriors making a great chanting for this brave thing done. Ahhh, the Cheyennes were indeed a strong people, Crazy Horse thought, but not the strongest heart and the longest arm, Lakota or Cheyenne, with only a bow was enough against these rifles. The warriors fought hard but always they were driven back. It was happening right now to his own Lakotas, his bravest men breaking into retreat before the bullets whistling hot around them, whipping hard to get away. Then suddenly they found Crazy Horse before them, his horse turned into their faces, crying out to them: 'Hold on, my friends. Be strong. Remember the helpless ones at home.' And with his Winchester held high as a lance he charged through them towards the coming soldiers. 'This is a good day to die,' he called back over his shoulder, the calfskin flying out like bat wings behind him. 'Hoka Hey. Hoka Hey,' the strong voice of Good Weasel answered him as he turned to follow, and then Bad Heart Bull, Black Bear, and Kicking Bear. 'Hoka Hey.' The warriors roared out together, thundering close behind them, charging back into the soldiers among the rocks, lifting their arrows to fall among the horses. When the frightened animals began to break from the holders the soldiers jumped back on and now even the youngest loafer could see that the whites were afraid and so pressed them harder, charging through them, shooting under the necks of the puffing horses, or from flat on their backs, until the Crows and Snakes fled from this wild charging, whipping, crying, towards the little bunch of soldier chiefs and traders sons down around Three Stars.

"Soon the whites were breaking as their scouts had, the Lakotas right among them, knocking the men from the saddles with their empty guns and the swinging war clubs, riding them down, never stopping except to pick up the dropped carbines, Crazy Horse ramming the stuck shells from them. So they drove the whole party like scattering antelope back into the valley, the warriors chasing after them. Here Crazy Horse saw many hurt ones, and many brave ones, too, particularly a little soldier chief sitting against a tree, his face all bloody still shooting with his revolver. Now there was a loud bawling of bugles and the soldiers fell back together and made a thick new line that would be hard to break. Besides, the sun was moving away and so Crazy Horse decided it was time to try something else. Turning, he led his warriors around over the creek and down the other side, letting their tired horses walk, making it seem they were giving up. As he hoped, a bunch of soldiers and some Crow scouts saw them go and followed down the other side, and once more Crazy Horse became the old thing he was so often, a decoy, making little stands behind the others, little charges towards the soldiers across the creek, as if to hold them back. So they came faster. As the Oglalas neared the bend of the Rosebud, signals were sent back, calling the others to come down to the narrow place in the valley, where it would be easier to fight with bows and tired horses. More and more hostiles began to string out down the creek behind the whites, who did not seem to notice these Lakota warriors coming.

"But before the soldiers got to the place for fighting, the Crows with them stopped, making the wild Crow howling, pointing ahead, refusing to go to where the ridge came towards the creek, with rocks and brush for the enemy to hide. And when a messenger from Three Stars came galloping after them, the soldiers swung far out around the Indians following them and hurried back in time to strike the rear of the warriors still fighting. So the Indians scattered. The shells were gone, even those they had got with the new guns, and the horses worn out. It had been a hard fight."

"One moring [after the battle as related by M. Sandoz] he [Crazy Horse] took a little party of Oglala boys over to the Rosebud to pick up the scattered ammunition, for it was well known that the soldiers often take handfulls from their belts, lay it down handy, and then move on with the fighting. The boys filled several unborn buffalo calf skin sacks and got very many empty shells to reload, some lead too, from bullets flattened against the rocks, and many arrow points and the shoes from the dead American horses. Nothing must be forgotten when iron is so scarce."

"The Enemies Kept Coming"

White Bull was a Minniconjou Sioux a nephew of Sitting Bull. Stanley Vestal includes his story of the battle in the book entitled Warpath*.

"White Bull put on a pair of dark blue woolen leggins decorated with broad stripes of blue and white beads, and beaded moccasins to match. Before and behind he hung a long red flannel breech cloth reaching to his ankles, tucked under his belt over his regular loin cloth. He put on a shirt, and over his right shoulder he hung the thong which supported the small rawhide loop, to which was attached four small leather pouches of medicine (earth of different kinds), a buffalo

---

* Quoted by permission from Warpath, The True Story of the Fighting Sioux, Told in a Biography of Chief White Bull by Stanley Vestal, Boston, 1934.

tail, and an eagle feather. This was his war charm. It hung under his left arm. Around his waist, like a kilt, he placed his folded black blanket and belted it there with his cartridge belt containing a hundred cartridges. He borrowed a fine war bonnet from his brother in law, Bad Lake. This bonnet had a long tail of eagle feathers reaching to the ground. The feathers began at the crown of the head and went straight down the back. There were no feathers around the head of this bonnet. All the way down the tail of this bonnet was colored red and white alternately, seven white feathers, then four red, and so on. These red feathers commemorated wounds received in battle. A man who wore such red feathers dared not tell a lie or he might be wounded.

"This bonnet had no protective power: White Bull wore it for its beauty. If he were to be killed, he wished to die in these fine war clothes. Otherwise those who saw him lying on the field might say: This was a poor man. He must not have been a good warrior. See how shabby he lies there. Besides, such fine war clothes made a man more courageous. White Bull took his seventeen shot repeating rifle, which he had purchased from an Agency Indian at Fort Bennett. Then he went out and saddled a fast horse. He tied an eagle feather in its forelock and tail and fastened an imitation scalp made of woman's hair to his bridle bit. Only horses which had been used to ride down an enemy could wear such a decoration. Then White Bull rode over to Sitting Bull's tent where the warriors were gathered. Almost a thousand warriors had assembled-Cheyenne, Oglala, Minniconjou, Sans Arc, Brule, and Hunkpapa. It was late at night when they set out. They rode until nearly daybreak, then stopped, unsaddled, and let their horses rest. At daybreak they saddled up and rode on until they came near a big hill. There they halted again and sent scouts forward to the top of this hill to look for the troops. When these scouts had travelled halfway to the hilltop, Indian government scouts appeared there, and firing was heard. The whole war party whipped up their horses and charged for the hill. There they found a Sioux wounded, and a horse killed. They rode over the hill and saw five government scouts dashing downhill to the troops. They charged these five men, shooting all the time, and wounded one of them. Still they pressed on, following the five scouts, close to the soldiers.

"The soldiers advanced, firing at the Indians. A Cheyenne had his horse shot under him. The Sioux who rode with him were all surrounded and killed. They got caught between two bodies of enemies. It was a hard fight. White Bull was not much given to singing war songs but as he advanced into that fight he was inspired to sing a song composed on the spot. There was a brave Cheyenne wearing a war bonnet and red leggins who led the attack. White Bull kept trying to get in front of this brave man, but could not; the Cheyenne had a better horse. But as the Government scouts and the soldiers came charging back, White Bull stood his ground and the Cheyenne retreated past him. White Bull was out in front at last. The enemies kept coming, and in the lead dashed a brave Shoshoni. He was riding a fast bald faced sorrel with white stockings. His horse's tail was tied up in red flannel and a red flannel strip was tied about its neck. This Shoshoni had a cartridge belt and a repeating rifle. He came straight for White Bull. On came the Shoshoni and White Bull sped to meet him. When he came near, the Shoshoni fired twice, but missed. White Bull pumped two bullets into the right foreshoulder of the sorrel horse and dropped it. He ran the Shoshoni down and lamed him in the right leg, then wheeled away to join his comrades in retreat. Afterward White Bull learned from the Crows that this Shoshoni was one of the bravest of their warriors. This Shoshoni was still living a few years ago; he may be alive today. This was considered one of the bravest of White Bull's many deeds, and when President Coolidge visited the Black Hills and White Bull was chosen to make the address of welcome for the Indians, the Chief was pointed out as the man who lamed the Shoshoni. It may be interesting to know White Bull's opinion of the various enemies he fought with: says he, 'the Crees are good fighters. The Flatheads fight well on foot with guns, but if you once get them to running, they sure do run. The Crows and the white soldiers are about the same at long range shooting, but in hand to hand combat the Crows are more dangerous. But of all the enemies I have fought, the Shoshones are the bravest and best warriors.' It was back and forth that day. All day long the Indians of both sides charged back and forth on horseback and not a few were killed on both sides. The troops lost nine men killed and twenty one wounded. Of White Bull's immediate friends, Little Crow, Black Bird, Sitting Bear, and Little Wolf perished.

There were many thrilling rescues. White Bull's brother, One Bull, saved Yells-at-Daybreak (Rooster). White Bull himself saved Haw Soldier after he was shot from his horse. He carried him back to his uncle. In another part of the fight a horse was shot and the Indian rider was pinned down. His leg was caught under the dead horse. White Bull ran forward and protected him until he could get his foot free and escape.

"There was a Cheyenne in this fight named Sunrise. He was painted a yellow all over and wore a stuffed water dog tied in his hair for a war charm. He was shot through the belly from behind and lay helpless. White Bull dismounted and ran forward under fire. He seized the Cheyenne by the wrists and dragged him back to safety. The Cheyennes still honor White Bull for saving this man. Sunrise died after they got him back to camp. Because of his war charm some of the Sioux remember him as Water-Dog. This was one of the hardest fights White Bull ever saw. It lasted all day, but when it was over Three Stars took his troops and hit the trail back to his base. The Sioux and Cheyennes rode home, leaving scouts behind to watch Three Stars movements. Two days later the Sioux returned to the battlefield. They found the body of a government scout there. Some say the Indians dug up the bodies of the white soldiers buried there, but White Bull knows nothing of this."

"We Fight Hard"

The only monument commemorating the Rosebud battle was erected by the Shining Mountain Chapter[4], National Society Daughters of American Revolution of Billings, Montana, in 1934 and is located just west of the present road from Decker to Busby on a little knoll near the east bend. It is constructed of stone and has a bronze plaque on which are inscribed the names of the nine soldiers reported to have been killed in the action. The monument was unveiled with considerable ceremony, with four old Cheyenne warriors who had been in the battle present. These gave their versions of the fight in an interview with Jack Keenan, a reporter for the Billings (Montana) *Gazette:* and these together with the complete description of the occasion appeared in the June 24, 1934, issue of that newspaper.

"Four wrinkled old men looked on last Sunday while Daughters of the American Revolution unveiled a monument of stone and bronze on a knoll in the pleasant little valley of southeastern Big Horn county. The marker was to commemorate the Battle of the Rosebud and the dedication had been purposely set for the fifty-eighth anniversary of the engagement which began the Indian campaign of 1876. To the ceremonies were invited these old men and one other whose age and blindness kept him in his lodge. Incredibly withered, the four who came braved sun and fatigue to again trod the valley. The five are, by common repute, the last of the Cheyennes who fought in the battles of the Rosebud and the Little Big Horn. Fierce warriors they were when Crook retreated from this peaceful valley and Custer died on the Little Big Horn, fierce with the courage of men fighting for their homes and families. Now they are old. Their arms are shrunken, their bodies emaciated. Their eyes are the eyes of men who have looked, helpless, while women and children were killed in their sight. For the tragedy of the Cheyennes only began with the Custer disaster. The gun, saber and the torch were the price they paid for that victory.

"Yet they came, Beaver Heart, Louis Dog, Charles Limpy and Wheezer [Weasel?] Bear, to pay their respects to the men they vanquished on that distant June day of 1876. In his lodge, near Busby, far down the Rosebud, Kills Night mourned because he could not see and be with the other survivors. They were in a talkative mood as they painted and dressed in war costumes for the ceremonies. Significantly, none would admit having counted coup against either Crook or Custer. The hostiles of 58 years ago have always borne a secret dread of further retribution and it was not until a few years ago that survivors would own up before strangers to their part in these battles. . . .

"Some distance to the west a scouting party went toward Sioux pass. The scouts intended to climb the highest butte and scan the Rosebud valley to the east, toward the big bend. Instead, they ran into a handful of Crook's Pawnees and Shoshones and the party was on. Crook was moving up instead of down the Rosebud.[5]

"The command, according to Grinnell, was scattered from the big bend to the pass.[6] The old warriors confirm this statement. While the scouts fought each other, and a small band of braves struck at an advance squad, Crazy Horse launched a charge on the main body of soldiers. In a few minutes three separate battles were in progress.

"Louis Dog and Wheezer Bear were with the scouts. Dressed in immaculate white shirt and blue trousers, moccasins and an agency hat, garments which he refused to doff for the old time breech clout, Louis Dog told of his experiences through an interpreter:

" 'We climb up peak. Shoshone scouts up there, too. They shoot. We shoot. They run. Then we see Crook's soldiers down below coming west. After while scouts and soldiers came toward us. We shoot and run. Then more Indians come and we make charge. Soldiers go back down valley.'

"Louis Dog waved his arms to indicate many men.

" 'Valley full. Three fights going on. We follow soldiers until they meet other soldiers. All go back to this place (indicating the amphitheater at the bend). Here we fight very long.'

"Charles Limpy takes up the story at this juncture. He is

crippled. One leg appears to have been broken and poorly set. From this injury comes his name. He is old, but his mind was alert as he sat, naked, in his tent, while his faithful squaw daubed him with red clay.

"'Three fights. My war chief is Little Hawk. We ambush soldiers between big bunch and scouts. They split up badly. We charge. They come together by and by and push us back to hills. Then we go downstream. Crook, he send one bunch to hill on south bank. Another bunch stays in valley. Big bunch goes up west hill toward the big bunch of Indians.

"'We fight hard. By and by Crook's soldiers chase us.' Limpy makes signs to indicate a running fight. 'Soldiers stop and we chase them. They come back to valley and all come together in one bunch. When it got dark Indians don't want to fight any more. They go away.'

"These narratives dovetail with the account of historian Grinnell, even to Limpy's story of his experiences. His horse was shot under him as his group rode out of ambush and down into the valley, some two and a half miles west of the bend. Limpy tumbled from his mount and immediately became the target for a volley from cavalry carbines. He scampered up the hill, crouched behind a rock and fought back with a six shooter.

"'Don't know whether killed soldiers,' he commented. 'He is very poor gun and sometimes no shoot.' Obviously Limpy bettered his fortunes before going into the Little Big Horn fight, for he recalled he had a carbine in that battle.

"Beaver Heart had little to do with the Rosebud affair.

"All the old warriors agreed that when the Indians left the Rosebud they went to their camp on Reno Creek. The village was on what is now the Jones Ranch. Crook made no attempt to follow, according to this gallant quartet."

It was long believed that the soldiers marched to the field over the present route of the Decker-Busby road which comes up from the south at the east bend, because many of the soldiers were marching west when some of the Indians arrived on the field. The soldiers marching west were Captain Henry's two companies on the south side of the creek, and several companies of cavalry under Colonel Royall. Prior to the action the direction of march had been straight east down the stream.

The action of the Sioux in withdrawing from the conflict at times variously stated from 2:30 in the afternoon to after dark, leaving the field in possession of the soldiers, has been a matter of some speculation by historians.

With this thought in mind I asked John Stands-In-Timber, "If Crazy Horse's forces were doing so well in the battle, why did they quit and go home in the middle of the afternoon?"

John's reply was, "They were tired and hungry, so they went home."

I was again reminded that we are dealing with flesh and blood human beings whose actions are more readily explained by the simple demands of the human body than by some obscure strategical reasons. The Sioux had ridden all night, fought nearly all day, and had exhausted their supply of food. They were tired and hungry, so they went home. It was as simple as that.

Chapter 11

RETURN TO GOOSE CREEK

BLUE twilight suddenly descended over the exhausted command on the banks of the Rosebud. Twilight had also temporarily eclipsed Crook's plans. His wounded needed attention. His rations were almost used up. His supply of ammunition was not sufficient for another encounter with the Indians led by the aggressive Oglala chief, who had shown themselves good fighters. All chance of surprising Crazy Horse and taking the village was lost. Reinforcements were needed. He could not make any extended movement until the five companies of infantry requested from General Sheridan in his telegram of June 19th arrived. His men had been roughly handled, even though casualties had not been excessive. The retreat of Royall's men while surrounded by hostiles had been a nightmare; the canyon of the Rosebud clearly an adroit ambush. There was nothing to do then, but retire on his wagon train at Goose Creek, his base.

Crazy Horse had displayed a superior system of tactics in dividing his troops by retreating his Indians and inducing the soldiers to follow, then turning upon them in savage strength and defeating his troops in detail. Cleverly maneuvered, it gave his soldiers a misleading sense of superiority to see the enemy retreat before every charge. For, when the troops, after being overextended, tried to return to their line, they were overwhelmed by hostiles emerging from every ridge and crevice.

The night passed without any further molestation by the Sioux, but early next morning, during the commencement of the retreat, there were several incidents which were reported by John F. Finerty:[1]

"During the night a melancholy wailing arose from the Snake camp down by the creek. They were 'waking' the young warrior killed by the Cheyennes that morning, and calling upon the

148

Great Spirit for vengeance. I never heard anything equal to the despairing cadence of that wail, so savage and so dismal. It annoyed some of the soldiers, but it had to be endured. The bodies of our slain were quietly buried within the limits of the camp, and every precaution was taken to obliterate the traces of sepulcher. The Sioux did not disturb us that night. There was no further need for precaution as to signals, and at 4 o'clock on the morning of Sunday, June 18th, the reveille sounded.

All were immediately under arms, except the Snake Indians, who had deferred the burial of their comrade until sunrise. All the relatives appeared in black paint, which gave them a diabolical aspect. I had been led to believe that Indians never yielded to the weakness of tears, but I can assure my readers that the experience of that morning convinced me of my error. The men of middle age alone restrained their grief, but the tears of the young men, and of the squaws, rolled down their cheeks as copiously as if the mourners had been of the Caucasian race. I afterward learned that the sorrow would not have been so intense if the boy had not been scalped. There is some superstition connected with that process. I think it had reference to the difficulty of the admission of the lad's spirit, under such circumstances, to the happy hunting-grounds.

"A grave was finally dug for the body in the bed of the stream, and at a point where the horses had crossed and re-crossed. After the remains were properly covered, a group of warriors on horseback rode over the site several times, thus making it impossible for the Sioux to find the body.

"This ceremony ended, our retreat began in earnest. Our battalion was, as nearly as I can remember, pretty well toward the head of the column. Between us and the 2d Cavalry came the wounded, on their travois, and behind them came the mounted infantry. Looking backward occasionally, we could see small parties of Sioux watching us from the bluffs, but they made no offensive movement. As I rode along with Sutorius and Von Leutwitz, I observed a crowd of Crow Indians dismounted and standing around some object which lay in the long grass some distance to our right. The lieutenant (Von Leutwitz) and I rode over there, and saw the body of a stalwart Sioux warrior, stiff in death, with the mark of a bullet wound in his broad bosom. The Crows set to work at once to dismember him. One scalped the remains. Another cut off the ears of the corpse and put them in his wallet. Von Leutwitz and I remonstrated, but the savages only laughed at us. After cutting off toes, fingers and nose, they proceeded to indecent mutilation, and this we could not stand. We protested vigorously, and the captain, seeing that something singular was in progress, rode up with a squad of men and put an end to the butchery." . . .

In returning to camp, General Crook chose the route which would avoid the numerous small tributaries of the Tongue River, because of the difficulty of getting the wounded on their travois over these streams bank full. The troops back-tracked for some distance over the route of the day before, but, instead of crossing the South Fork of the Rosebud, followed along north of it until they reached the top of the divide where the line of march was south and a little west. It is probable that they followed the site of the present trail leading south from the Charles Young ranch house to within several hundred yards of the south fork where the trail turns west and runs up onto the divide, roughly paralleling the south fork.

This line of march, substantiated by the map published in the *Daily Graphic,* had the advantage of level ground and being close to water. Crook probably then followed the present trail to what is now called Rosebud Gap, ten miles southwest of the field, whe... it runs between a large bluff on the east and the wooded conical hill on the west. Here Crook halted his command, waiting for the wounded on the travois to catch up. And here, on this little hill on the western edge of the divide, the Crows had their scalp dance in commemoration of an ancient victory over the Blackfeet.

"*June 18.* An immaculate sky this morning overhead and a heavy frost under foot," wrote Lt. Bourke in his *Diary,* "turned out of our beds at 3 o'clock. Made a hasty breakfast of coffee, hard tack and bacon. Surgeon Hartsuff informed me that the condition of the wounded was all that could be hoped for; all has passed a good night. Our jaded animals are much recuperated. God knows what they would have done had pasturage not been good and plenty and the weather pleasantly cool. A large ratio of them would have broken completely down.

" 'Travois' for the transportation of the severely wounded have been made of poles from the trees in the streams, bound together with thongs of hide and pieces of rope."

Once again, Crook put his mules to vital use, to help transport the wounded.

"Each sick man had six enlisted men detailed to attend his litter," described Bourke, "on steep grades the ends of the poles were carried by the attendants who performed their duty with alacrity and without a murmur, notwithstanding its onerous nature. Sergeant Warfield, Co. F, 3rd Cavalry, an old Arizona veteran, was charged with the superintendence of the detail. His discharge of his functions called forth warm eulogies from all observers. Tom Moore, our Chief Packer, and all his command were very efficient assistants in this delicate and important work.

"We struck out at first on our back-trail, following it nearly due south to the head of the Rosebud. This little stream has muddy bottom as far as I saw it, (that is to say from its extreme head to a point in the cañon, (7) seven miles below the point where the Sioux made their attack). It has but little timber except in the sandstone crags which lie near its current. Here quite a supply of good pine fuel can be obtained. Thick ledge grass and a variety almost identical with that known to the Mexicans as 'Cacaton' obstruct its channel. Striking closer to the mountains, this morning we entered a knolly country where the resources of pasturage are practically unlimited. The summit of the divide between the Rosebud and the 'Rotton Grass' (an affluent of the Little Big Horn) is marked by a small conical hill, studded with pine trees. This is the site of a sanguinary engagement of bygone times between the Crows and Blackfoot Sioux. . . .

"Looking down from the high point to the drainage of the Little Big Horn on the west and south, the passages of landscape were very fine. Long narrow ravines opened down into the valley of 'Rotton Grass' and framed in the scenery in a way at once beautiful and unusual. The high peaks of the Big Horn Mountains still snow capped, screened the horizon in our front, extending right and left as far as eye could reach. Intervening, the valley of the Little Big Horn and Rotten Grass filled all the middle ground, the ridge dividing them standing out dimly in the horizon. Elk, deer and buffalo sped at their approach as they moved along the deep cut buffalo trails beneath small bluffs, ledges of sandstone and grassy-sloped hills dotted with pines."

Crossing down the west side of the divide several miles south, Crook camped at the head of a small tributary of the Tongue River that night, his command having marched twenty-two miles. Here some of the command parted.

"The Crow Indians," wrote Bourke in his *Diary*, "left for their homes this evening as is the custom of all Indians after an engagement with an enemy. They promised they would be back within fifteen days. . . ."

During the night Crook's sleep was interrupted, as was the whole command's, not with the untimely, intense cold but with fear of another attack by Crazy Horse. In Bourke's entry for June 19th, he writes:

"An alarm for the pickets brought all to their feet about one o'clock but after careful examination it was found to be groundless. We broke into column at day break, striking across the hills to the forks of Goose Creek, or Tongue River. . . . No Indians made their appearance. . . .

"A total march of 25 miles brought us to Major Furey's corral 2½ miles above (South) the place where we left it. He reported no molestation from hostile Indians but had taken every possible precaution against surprise. His wagon train had been parked in a grassy bed of the stream, affording water on all sides and much protection through a heavy line of willow trees and underbrush. From wagon to wagon along the line of wheels, ropes were stretched and at every eligible spot, breastworks of earth and logs had been thrown up from behind which sharpshooters would have made it lively for any antagonist.

"General Crook pushed the command on to a new camp, 2¼ miles to secure green forage. Our pickets were at once posted in strength on bluffs commanding camp. Animals unsaddled and turned out to graze and drink. Details of men set to work putting up the hospital tent and our wounded kindly cared for. A few of the officers had lemons left in their satchels or valises—these were brought out—there were not half a dozen in all, but enough to make a pleasant glass of lemonade for each patient. The eagerness of their drinking was a most welcome token of their gratitude and their improving condition. This evening General Crook sent a courier in to Fort Fetterman with the following telegram to General Sheridan:

'12:30 P. M.
Camp on South of Tongue River, Wy, June 19th
   Ft Fetterman   June 23, 1876.

To Lt Gen Sheridan, Chicago Ills.

Returned to Camp today having marched as indicated in my last telegram when about forty miles from here on Rosebud creek Mont morning seventeenth inst Scouts report Indians in vicinity and within a few minutes we were attacked in force the fight lasting several hours we were near the mouth of a deep canyon through which the creek ran. The sides were very steep covered with pine and apparently impregnable the village supposed to be at the other end about eight miles off. They displayed strong force at all points occupying many and such covered places that it is impossible to correctly estimate their numbers the attack however showed that they anticipated that they were strong enough to thoroughly defeat the command during the engagement. I tried to throw a strong force through the canyon but I was obliged to use it elsewhere before it had gotten to the supposed location of the village the command finally drove the Indians back in great confusion following them several miles the Scouts killing a good many during the retreat, our casualties were nine men killed and fifteen wounded of third cavalry two (2) wounded second cavalry three men wounded fourth infantry and Capt Henry Third Cavalry severally wounded in the face it is impossible to correctly estimate the loss of the indians many being killed in the attacks others being gotten off before we got possession of that part of the field 13 (13) thirteen dead bodies being left we remained on the field that night and having nothing but what each man carried himself we were obliged to return to the train to properly care for our wounded who were transported here on mule litters and lie now comfortable all doing well I expect to find those indians in rough places all the time and so have ordered five (5) companies of infantry and shall not probably make any extended movement until they arrive officers and men behaved with marked gallantry during the engagement.

Crook Brig Genl.'

"*June 20th.* Under a bright genial sun, pushed up Tongue River seven miles and made our camp on the bank of the prattling brook, some 30 feet wide, 2 or 4 feet deep, current of great velocity and shady banks," continues Bourke's *Diary.* "Bottom of large boulders forming gloomy pools, under the alluvial bank. Every indication of a trout stream. After wounded comrades and tired animals had been cared for and camp laid out, great numbers of officers and men sought refreshment in the sparkling waters and when bathed, came back to camp to do what might be required of each for sending wagon train back to Fetterman for ammunition and supplies. The heat was very great throughout the day: at 3 P.M., the thermometer indicated 103° F in the shade. The result is that the grass about us is drying up rapidly and if we do not have rain within a few days our animals will suffer.

"*June 21st.* At 4 o'clock in the morning our wounded were placed in the wagons upon couches of fresh clean grass and moved off to Fetterman under the escort of Col Chambers who had under him Munson's and Luhn's companies of the 9th and 4th Infantry. The following officers accompanied him:
Captain Nickerson with his orderly Reynolds.

J. V. Furey, A. Q. M.
Captain W. S. Stanton, Engineer Officer with his draughtsman
McKoehlman and party.

Captain Guy V. Henry (wounded) and Captains Munson
and Luhn and Lieuts. Capron and Seton. Also MacMillen,
correspondent of the Chicago Inter-Ocean. I was very glad
to see poor Nickerson go away; his health has been wretched
upon the trip, and only his indomitable energy could have
sustained him. His gallantry and coolness during the engagement have been warmly eulogized by all who saw him . . . ."

Crook was to lose his Shoshones here, but like the Crows,
they promised to return when their scalp dance ceremonials
were ended. Promise of 300-400 more scouts, Crows, Shoshones,
Nez Perces, Utes, and Pawnees had been given him. Reinforcements also were expected within fifteen days; 5 additional
armed infantry companies, 1 company of cavalry, a body of
half-breed scouts, rations and supplies for 60 days and 300-400
rounds of ammunition. Terry and Gibbon would certainly be
in communication with him shortly and some definite plan to
break the power of Crazy Horse and his Sioux and Cheyenne
forces would be determined on.

Since all wagons but one had gone with Major Furey,
Crook's mules again did heavy duty, carrying the pack luggage,
subsistence and forage from camp to camp. Tents were rolled
and slung to the running gear of ambulances and wagons, which
carried the mess chests. Yet if the men were inconvenienced
by the packing, they were to enjoy other phases of the trip.
Daily temperatures soared bringing swarms of large green and
black flies, but the nights were refreshingly cool. Game
abounded for his men and the streams were filled with trout.

A bird fancier, General Crook was also an avid fisherman.
The entry in Bourke's *Diary* of June 22nd, states that, "General
Crook, Col. Van Vliet, Major Burt, and a small party started
up the mountains to hunt and fish. Colonel Royall left in
command of camp. Within the picket lines, squads of men
are devoting their leisure hours to bathing and trout catching.
Our breakfast composed some delicious fried trout—one of the
great luxuries imaginable.

June 23rd. Breakfast had hardly been finished when a courier
rode up in front of my tent with a packet of dispatches for
General Crook. He stated that he had started from Fetterman

with Lieut. Schuyler, ADC, and that the latter would be with us in a few moments. The dispatches embraced a telegram from Lieut. Gen. Sheridan at Red Cloud, giving notice that Lieut. Col. A. E. Carr with eight (8) Cos. of the 5th Cavalry had started out from that point with six weeks supplies to scout the country down the Little Powder, to about where Terry was supposed to be. This movement will help us somewhat, and if Gen. Crook will now order into the field Spalding's, Misc. and Wessell's Companies of the 2nd and 3rd Cavalrys, the Sioux will be crushed ere the summer solstice. The presence of these companies is not essential to the successful prosecution of the campaign, but very desirable that all the cavalry and most of the infantry of the Department of the Platte may have an opportunity to share in the glory of the good work.

"Schuyler was warmly greeted by old friends and new who pressed eagerly about him to extract the latest news. Hayes (of Ohio) and Wheeler (of NY) were the Republican nominees for President and Vice President. The former is a warm friend of General Crook—a man if not previously eminent as a politician, at least unsullied in his record as a soldier and public man. Wheeler is cousin to Lt. Foster of our command.

"General Emory had been retired, the promotions following being Merritt as Colonel 5th Cavalry, Dusby as Lt. Col. 1st Cav. and Sandford, Major 1st Cavalry. This puts Mason, 5th Cav. at head of list of Cav. captains. . . . A fight with Terry's command was reported at the agencies—one with heavy loss on both sides but indecisive in results. This is the Indian's story, very probably a lie out of whole cloth. It was rumored in camp that five Government Commissioners were coming out to treat with the Sioux Indians to learn the terms upon which they would agree to a peace. This is a stupid piece of tom-foolery. as stupid indeed as scarcely to deserve mention. Schuyler's little party of (3) three had made the ride from Fetterman in four days, travelling between suns and by dark. A very perilous proceeding which cannot be too severely condemned. On the other side of old Fort Reno they came upon suddenly the hour old trail of a small war party of Sioux and lay hid in the rocks all day. When night came they galloped forty five miles without halting. Our supply trains were met at the crossing of Clear Creek, thirty odd miles to the east of us. Nickerson examined the mail and conversed with the party which then recommenced the long ride of the night, terminating a few hours after sun rise in the camp of the expedition at this point. . . ."

Crook moved his camp three or four miles up Goose Creek the next day to a broad flat plain. With a rampart of the

Big Horn Mountains casting its glamour over the green, flowered site where Goose Creek flowed out from a deep shadowed canyon abounding in trout, the men found a fisherman's paradise.

"Lt. Lemly caught twenty," Bourke chronicled, "and Major Noyes, forty." And the following day, "Colonel Mills brought in this afternoon one hundred trout."

On June 26th, the anxiously awaited courier arrived bringing the men word from home, and newspapers and magazines for General Crook and his staff.

Author's note: In October, 1955, Elmer Kobold, Jesse Young, and I drove up on the divide to try to trace the line of retreat of Crook's men. While following the trail, we came upon the place where the blinded Sioux warrior was shot and dismembered by the Crows.

We drove on southward along the hilly divide which separates the Rosebud valley from the valley of the Little Big Horn, until we came to the Rosebud Gap, on the west of which was situated the wooded conical hill where the command halted and the Crows danced their scalp dance. While there are several other similar hills to the north, we were sure that this was the scalp dance hill. It was the only one with a small stream commencing near its base and running northwest into the valley of the Little Big Horn. The stream, now known as Owl Creek, in those days was the Rotten Grass. The hill is a perfect cone, its steep sides covered with pine trees. We climbed to the top of it and found an open space fifty yards in diameter where the Crows must have held their celebration.

The divide continues towards the south and is fairly level but the descent down the west slope is so abrupt that it would have been impossible to take the travois of wounded men down it. Jesse Young, who is familiar with this area, said that the command probably continued southward for several miles to a point where there was a more gradual slope leading westward down from the divide.

The place where the command camped the night of June 19th is about four miles west of Sheridan, Wyoming, on the banks of Big Goose Creek and immediately south of the present oiled highway. A picture of the site appeared in the original edition of *Life and Adventures of Frank Gruard,* by Joe DeBarthe.

Mr. M. D. Jenkins of Sheridan, who grew up on the ranch on this camp site, told the writer that in the early days there were numerous "chimneys" along the foot of the bluffs to the north—fireplaces made of rocks which Crook's troops had constructed to cook their meals. There are a number of other camp sites southwest of Sheridan, as Crook had to move his camp frequently in order to obtain forage for the animals, it being a very dry year. The main summer camp was established about fifteen miles southwest of the forks of Little and Big Goose Creeks, the present site of the Hillman Ranch, and the troops remained here and in this vicinity until August 3rd, when they again moved northward in the next expedition against the Sioux.

In clearing the land, the Hillmans, who were early settlers, found large quantities of scrap iron and debris which had been parts of wagons, several old type wagons with solid wooden wheels, and large quantities of beer and whiskey bottles. In recent years six truck loads of scrap iron were hauled away to provide reinforcement for one of the dams in the area.

Several years ago there was found on the Hillman Ranch near the creek a stone about two feet across and six inches thick, upon which were a number of inscriptions. One of these read:

"*June 23, 1876. Frank Gruard. Baptiste Pourrier, Louis Richaud. Camp Cloud Peak.*"

There has been considerable doubt expressed as to the validity of this stone, but it would seem that these carvings might be those of Crook's scouts. The command moved to this site on June 24th, and one would think that the scouts would go ahead and pick out the site the day before, on June 23rd. On the other side were carved the names of "Old Sebastian. Army Packer," and "Jim Bridger" with some earlier dates. The old Bozeman Road ran close by where this stone was turned up, and one might speculate that the three scouts, finding the stone beside the road, with the old carvings on it, proceeded to adorn the stone further, by carving their names.

While the troops were in camp waiting reinforcements, a wagon train arrived bringing a whiskey peddler and the irrepressible Calamity Jane. General Crook immediately put Calamity Jane under arrest to be sent back to Fort Fetterman with the first train. Many of the soldiers got drunk and the whiskey was seized.

"A Captain got intoxicated on duty," Finerty was to write, "neglected to place his pickets properly, was tried in the field, deprived of his command, and ordered, under arrest, to Fort Fetterman. This gallant but unfortunate soldier, for whom I entertained a sincere regard, was subsequently dismissed from the service, that being the finding of the field court martial."[2]

Finerty did not mention who the "gallant" captain was, but he had been closely associated with Captain Sutorius, the young Swiss, taking his mess with him. After this incident occurred, Finerty changed his mess to Lt. Lawson's. Captain Sutorius was never mentioned thereafter in Finerty's book, *Warpath and Bivouac*.

Lt. Bourke says that Sutorius was dismissed from the service after court martial proceedings.[3]

Four of Crook's men were to receive the Congressional Medal of Honor for bravery in the Rosebud Battle:

Michael A. McGann, 1st Sergeant, Company F, 3rd Cavalry, under command of Lt. Reynolds, for "Gallantry in action," issued August 9, 1880;

Trumpeter Elmer A. Snow, Company M, 3rd Cavalry, under command of Lt. Paul, for "Bravery in action; was wounded in both arms," issued October 16, 1877;

Joseph Robinson, 1st Sergeant, Company D, 3rd Cavalry, under command of Captain Guy V. Henry, for "Discharging his duties while in charge of the skirmish line under fire with judgment and great coolness and brought up the lead horses at a critical moment," issued January 23, 1880;

John Henry Shingle, 1st Sergeant of Troop I, 3rd Cavalry, under command of Captain Andrews, for "Gallantry in action," issued June 1, 1880.

The delay in Robinson's receiving the medal arose from an

effort's having been made to have the law amended so that a certificate of merit could be given to non-commissioned officers as well as to privates. The law was not changed, and Robinson had to be voluntarily reduced in rank to a private before he was eligible for the reward.

In *Deeds of Valor*, Vol. 2, p. 210, by W. F. Beyer and O. F. Keydal, Shingle's heroic action is described:

"In the attack upon the third bluff the troops suffered severely, especially Company L, of the Third Cavalry, under Captain Vroom, who had ventured too far forward. It was only the skill of Captain G. V. Henry of Company D, Third Cavalry, and Colonel Royall, who brought up reinforcements, which prevented the cutting off and, of course, consequent cutting up of this troop. In the melee Captain Henry was shot through the face. The gallant officer, with blood rushing from his mouth, kept on his horse, although for the time being completely blinded; finally he fell from the saddle fainting and exhausted. So close together were the contestants that a party of howling Sioux actually charged over the captain's prostrate body. But they were quickly repelled, as was the whole hostile line.[4]

"It was during this melee that First Sergeant J. H. Shingle, of Troop I, Third Cavalry, won his Medal of Honor. Shingle had been placed in command of the horses of a battalion of four dismounted troops, by Captain Henry. When the Indians swarmed around them, and Shingle saw some of the men waver, he left the horses in command of a sergeant, mounted his horse, rushed into the thickest of the fight and did exceedingly valuable service in rallying the breaking ranks, which finally enabled the hard-pressed battalion to keep the Indians at bay until the oncoming supports under Colonel Royall put the redskins to flight."[5]

Chapter 12

AFTERMATH OF THE BATTLE

CONTROVERSY swirled about Crook's head. Why had he failed to resume the offensive immediately after returning to his supply camp? Eight days after the Rosebud Battle, June 25, 1876, General Custer was overwhelmed by these same warriors under Crazy Horse—in addition to all the other warriors in the Sioux encampment—at the Little Big Horn.

It was contended that if General Crook had gone north shortly after his return to Goose Creek, he would have completed his part in the pincers movement and joined the forces of Custer and Terry and averted the disaster thirty miles northwest of the Rosebud's big bend.

In a scathing declaration against him in the Helena (Montana) *Daily Independent,* June 30th, an unknown correspondent writing of the battle from Fort Laramie, wrote that Crook had "sent to Fetterman and this post (Laramie) for infantry, which makes it pretty plain that the Indians are too many for him. It is reported here that General Sheridan, to whom a report of the battle has been made, has refused the reinforcements and ordered Gen. Crook to advance.

"The officers of the post speak in terms of unmeasured condemnation of Gen. Crook's behavior, and denounce his retreat in the face of the savage enemy as *cowardly.*

"It is also reported that the Crows refused to stay with Crook any longer, and have gone off in a body to Gibbon on the Yellowstone. They call Crook the 'Squaw Chief' and say he's afraid to fight.

"The news of the battle brought consternation to the military here, and as the details of the affair become known, it is looked upon as humiliating and disgraceful to the last degree.

"The idea of two regiments of American cavalry being stampeded by savages and having to *rally behind* friendly Indians is regarded as incredibly revolting to the pride and honor of the army."

160

There was also in the same edition of the *Daily Independent*
an editorial heaping coals of fire on Crook's head for the failure
of the campaign.

"It is now clearly evident that General Crook was not the
man to be intrusted with the conduct of the military expeditions in the Powder River country. His disastrous defeat at the
hands of Crazy Horse last winter, although variously reported
at the time and toned down as much as possible left the
general impression upon the country that a want of proper
management was at the bottom of the result.

"The *Independent* claimed at the time and has repeatedly
urged since that the expedition should have been instituted
from the banks of the Yellowstone, and not from the frontiers
of Wyoming. It should have been intrusted to General Gibbon,
and not General Crook. Events now transpiring clearly demonstrate that we were right. His recent battle with the Sioux on
the Rosebud, even if he obtained the victory he claims, is
nothing more than a practical defeat, since his retreat leaves
the country in the possession of the Indians and all of his work
will have to be done over again. But this is not the worst. The
driving the Indians into the Bad Lands gives them possession
of fastnesses in which they are the most secure and in which
the most protracted resistance can be made. The war, if possible, should have been prosecuted on the plains instead of in
the hills.

"If Gibbon and Custer had been permitted to acquire possession of the Powder river country early in the spring, and advancing in the direction in which General Crook has come
have taken the savages in front and rear at the same time, the
war would long since have been over. But instead of this the
plan of the campaign has been botched from the beginning.
Crook has delayed for months after the others were ready,
and in his eager desire to monopolize the honors of the campaign has suffered two defeats, both of which have been more
or less disastrous.

"The result of these engagements is to embolden the Indians
to more depredations and to render the whole stretch of
country between the Yellowstone and the Platte river un-
tenantable by white men. It is not two to one that Crook,
despairing of success when he has encountered two defeats,
will withdraw from the Rosebud with the same precipitation
that he did last winter from the mountains, and surrender the
country he was sent to render peaceful and safe to the murderous discipline of the scalping knife of the Sioux. The retreat
ordered after the battle on the Rosebud justifies this im-

pression. With three days rations in the knapsacks and supply trains within fifty miles he falls back for provisions. Attacked by the Indians, he maintains his ground just long enough to demonstrate his readiness to retreat. He may out-General the indolent Apache, but he is no match for the daring and aggressive Sioux."

Stubborn in the face of bitter condemnation, Crook would not admit defeat. And if the country rocked with censure against him, there were those who rose to his defense. Friends of the General claimed that he had displayed great generalship in avoiding the fate of General Custer. Defenders said that he had followed the prudent course in not endangering his command until he was sure of success.

Shortly after the editorial in the *Daily Independent,* the officers at Fort Laramie passed a Resolution in which they expressed their approval of General Crook's conduct in falling back to Goose Creek.

T. B. MacMillen, correspondent of the Chicago *Inter-Ocean,* who had been compelled to return to Fort Fetterman shortly after the battle on account of bad health, was a staunch defender of Crook. In the July 12, 1876, edition of his newspaper he replied to the *Daily Independent's* charges and similar criticism in the Salt Lake *Herald.*

"The death of General Custer has developed a discussion which will we believe be productive of great benefit to the entire country. And to none can it be of more service than those who have misconceived views as to the character and strength of the Sioux, and also as showing the peculiar difficulties and dangers which the military in the field against Sitting Bull have to encounter. It is easy to sit in our offices and parlors and club rooms and wonder why one soldier is not a match for two Indians, but . . . . a warrior, as well dressed and mounted as a trooper, with a thorough knowledge of every foot of his own hunting grounds, and a veteran in the line of bushwhacking warfare, is a match for any two average soldiers unused to that sort of fighting . . . ."

In order to clarify the matter, E. A. Brininstool wrote to Robert E. Strahorn, who was with Crook on the Center, a correspondent for the Denver (Colorado) *Rocky Mountain News.* Mr. Strahorn replied:

"Your question as to why Crook, with his 1100 men retreated to Goose Creek after the Rosebud fight, and called for
reinforcements, is easily answered. After some hours of pretty
close fighting with a body of Indians estimated all the way
from 2000 to 3000 to 4000 and incidentally, their retreat down
through a narrow gorge (canyon of the Rosebud) toward
their main command on the Little Big Horn, we happened to
be riding with Gen. Crook and his staff at the head of the
column in pursuit. Suddenly halting, and raising his hand as
a signal for that, he turned square back through the ravine—
of course facing the column all the way back and with a
disappointed look. I made bold to ask him why this move.
He said that with all those wounded on our hands, and with
an ambuscade clearly in sight, he would not take his men down
into that hole.

"So we returned to the battlefield, camped there for the
night, and buried our dead, which we had been carrying, and
made campfires over their graves, to mislead the Indians, if
possible, (who would naturally have dug them up to gratify
their usual appetite for plunder).

"That night Crook took the necessary steps to discover just
the situation down that canyon and below, assigning this duty
to Frank Grouard, and, I think, one other scout. Upon their
return they reported all sorts of preparations on the sides of
the canyon and in the *cul-de-sac* at the bottom, for a massacre
if we had gone down a little bit further.

"Crook thus took the only course open, and rode back to
his wagon train and sent for reinforcements. He had felt the
Indians out very effectively, much to his credit following the
safe course. He was on the offensive throughout the fight,
took his time to return to his base—and wasn't whipped.

"I was with Crook in every foray or movement throughout
the Sioux war, and am sure that his undoubted courage, ab-
solute devotion to duty, and unequalled experience in Indian
warfare, would have led him to persist in his march to a
junction with Terry on the Yellowstone, except for the needless
sacrifice of troops involved in certain further encounters with
the savages, whose overwhelming numbers were absolutely
unknown until then. Remember, that with every fourth man
taking care of the horses in a fight, (because you can't fight
Indians mounted); also providing adequate protection of the
wounded and pack train, and exhaustion of half his ammunition, Crook was actually in nearly as poor shape to advance
as was Custer when he rode to his doom, a week later.

"Doubtless, the Indians he engaged there would have returned with much larger forces, had Crook continued north-

ward; and while I think he was too adroit a campaigner to have duplicated the Custer fiasco, there is no telling how great a loss of men might have been suffered, but for his return to his base."

General Crook's decision to remain in camp was cited with approval by General W. T. Sherman[1] and Lt. General P. H. Sheridan[2] in their annual reports for 1876. Several months after the battle, President Grant said in a newspaper interview:

"General Crook is the best, wiliest Indian fighter in this country. He has had vast experience in Indian fighting. His campaign against the Idahos and many other tribes shows his brilliant talent as an Indian fighter. He is as wily as Sitting Bull in this respect, that when he finds himself outnumbered and taken at a disadvantage he prudently retreats. In Custer's case Sitting Bull had ten men to every one of Custer's."[3]

In his annual report for 1876 General Crook came to his own defense.

"At the fight on the Rosebud, June 17th, the number of our troops was less than one thousand, and within eight days after that the same Indians we there fought, met and defeated a column of troops nearly the same size as ours, killing and wounding over three hundred, including the gallant commander General Custer himself. I invite attention to the fact that in this engagement my troops beat these Indians on a field of their own choosing, and drove them in utter route from it as far as the proper care of my wounded and prudence would justify. Subsequent events proved beyond dispute what might have been the fate of my command, had the pursuit been continued beyond what judgment dictated."[4]

Fin G. Burnett was associated with the Shoshone Agency from 1871 to 1924 and had heard all about the campaign from the recitals of the Shoshones returning after the battle. His opinion justifies General Crook in not renewing the attack immediately, claiming it would have been like throwing his men into their graves.[5]

In Crook's favor too, was the fact that right after the Custer battle, the column from the north under Gibbon and Terry did not even consider following the retreating Indians, but headed right back north to their base to await reinforcements. They did not pause long enough at the Custer field to give the dead decent burial.

Had General Crook resumed the offensive shortly after returning to Goose Creek, he would have encountered all the
warriors in the Sioux encampment—as Custer did—who would
have annihilated his command. But if Crook could have met
and combined with Custer first, then the disaster at the Little
Big Horn would have been averted. However, Crook could
not reach Terry, and Terry could not advise Custer, and Custer
therefore rode on to his doom.

Crook always maintained that, since his command occupied
the field after the battle, he was not defeated at the Rosebud,
and that if the battle had gone according to *his* orders, it would
have resulted in a real triumph for his men. This view was also
held by his superiors, although they called it a "barren victory." His part in the campaign was to form a junction with
the other advancing columns, combining with them in returning the infractious Sioux to their reservations. His immediate
purpose was to find and destroy the village of Crazy Horse.
He accomplished none of these objectives. Instead he retired
from the scene, permitting the forces of Crazy Horse to concentrate their strength against the troops to the north.

If there was ever any question about General Crook's having been defeated at the Rosebud, it is certainly dispelled by
the frank account of Captain Mills when General Crook and
his officers received word of Custer's massacre.

"He (General Crook) read the dispatch, and while all of us
were horrified and oppressed with mortification and sympathy
for the dead and wounded, there was with all, particularly in
General Crook's expression, a feeling that the country would
realize that there were others who had underrated the valor
and numbers of the Sioux. While General Crook was a cold,
gray-eyed and somewhat cold-blooded warrior, treating his men
perhaps too practically in war time, there yet ran through us
a feeling of profound sympathy for his great misfortune, while
at the same time we had a still more profound sympathy for
the other gallant and more sympathetic Custer—at least, most
of us. There were some there, I regret to say, who had ranked
him and over whom he was promoted, that would insinuate,
'I told you so,' and for these sentiments the majority of us
had no respect."[6]

As to the responsibility for the loss of the battle, one can
sense a certain hostility between General Crook and Colonel

Royall in reading the official reports of those officers, and from the account of R. B. Davenport, who was with Royall on the left flank.

This ill feeling came to a head in 1886, when Colonel Royall was quoted in an interview with the reporters of two Omaha newspapers as saying that the defeat at the Rosebud was the result of faulty generalship on the part of General Crook. Crook resented Royall's reported statements, and there was a controversy between the two at the home of General Crook concerning the responsibility for the loss of the battle. Second Lieutenant Lyman W. V. Kennon, 6th Infantry, who was present, reported this incident in his Diary, now in the custody of the Army War College, Carlisle Barracks, Pennsylvania.

"Aug. 7, 1886—At Genl. Crook's house from 7 P.M. until 10 P.M. At about 8:30 to 9—Col. Royall started to go—At Genl. Crook's request I went with him to front steps where gathered Genl. Crook, Col. Royall, 4th Cavalry, Maj. Guy V. Henry 9th Cavalry, Capt. Roberts, 17th Infy., 2nd Lt. L. W. V. Kennon 6th Inf. . . . .

"Col. Royall said as we sat down 'These are all your friends I suppose.'

"Col. Henry said 'I am Genl. Crook's friend, but no more than I am your friend Col. Royall.'

"Genl. Crook said 'It has come to my knowledge from Washington and elsewhere, Col. Royall, that you have been going around the country making remarks and statements of a nature disparaging to me. This does not seem to me to be generous or in good taste. For ten years I have suffered silently the obloquy of having made a bad fight at Rosebud when the fault was in yourself and Nickerson. There was a good chance to make a charge, but it couldn't be done because of the condition of the cavalry. I sent word to you to 'come in' (?) and waited 2 hours—nearer three (3) before you obeyed. I sent Nickerson three (3) times at least. Couriers passed constantly between the points where we were respectively. I had the choice of assuming the responsibility myself for the failure of my plans or of court-martialing you and Nickerson. I chose to bear the responsibility myself. The failure of my plan was due to your conduct.'

"Col. Royall said 'I have never had any reason to think my conduct at the Rosebud was bad. Nickerson came to me but once and then I moved as soon as I received the order. Did I not move as soon as I could after Nickerson came Col. Henry?"

"Col. Henry said, 'Yes I believe you did.'

"Col. Royall said, 'I was with the leading battalion with Col. Henry. It was the leading battalion—I went with it where the enemy was thickest. I was not responsible for the scattered condition of the cavalry. As to what I said in the interview with the reporter I did not mention your name. I have the interview in my pocket (produced a slip of paper folded looking like a cutting from newspaper; then returning it to his pocket). The account given in the *World* was correct. (Col. R. here mentioned an interview with the Editor of the *World,* as if he had seen and talked with him). The account of the interview given in the *Bee* was garbled and incorrect.'"

It is possible that there could have been a misunderstanding of the orders to explain why Colonel Royall did not move to join the main command sooner. He stated in his report that he occupied the farthest ridge by order of the aide-de-camp of the Brigadier General Commanding, and that immediately subsequent to the delivery of those instructions he was directed "through an orderly, to extend my right and connect with the left of the main body occupying a remote portion of the highest crest." The wording "to extend my right" would seem to imply that his left should remain where it was. However, regardless of the exact wording of the command, the intention should have been obvious that Colonel Royall was to withdraw from the exposed position and take his place in the line, connecting with the left of the main command. The dispatching of Captain Meinhold's company could not be regarded as a compliance with either construction of the order.

In considering General Crook's conduct of the engagement, there are some self evident facts which cannot be ignored:

His ordering the command into bivouac with the horses and mules unsaddled and grazing in the valley, while he played cards with his officers, knowing the hostile Indians were in the vicinity, appears to indicate a careless attitude on his part.

From all accounts, including his own, Crook stayed so long on the bluff when the Indians first attacked, observing the enemy in true Civil War style, that he lost control of the situation.

He did not expect the headlong charge upon the troops which came immediately. However, troop dispositions had to be made immediately to meet the attack. Major Evans and

Captain Nickerson had to assume command as long as he was not present. Their orders were not in accordance with the plans which he had formulated while on the bluff, and upon his return to camp he found the men "scattered."

After the Indians had been driven back by the three-pronged cavalry charge, he was still so intent upon his original idea of going down the canyon to find and destroy Crazy Horse's village that he did not try to fight the battle at hand. Crook was occupied in trying to extricate the troops from the various parts of the field so that they would all be available for the attack on the village.

It was only after he had sent the eight troops of cavalry down the canyon, that he discovered that he was actually in a battle, and recalled them just in time to save the eight troops from ambush and to prevent the Indians from making another attack upon the harassed command.

This defeat rankled in General Crook's memory as long as he lived.

Like Custer, General Crook, had a contempt for the fighting qualities of the Indians. Both men had been very successful cavalry leaders in the Civil War and in the Indian wars following. They had acquired a supreme confidence in their commands and in their own abilities. This over-confidence was the undoing of them both. Before he started on his last march up the Rosebud, General Custer refused the offer of additional troops of cavalry and a battery of three Gatling guns, which could have spelled the difference between victory and defeat at the Little Big Horn. General Crook had been warned repeatedly of the warlike and ferocious propensities of the Indians, but he reckoned without the "prowess of the Sioux."

One could spend a lifetime in the study of the Rosebud battle and still not cover all of the various angles and details. There was fighting all over the 4 mile area, while the various accounts cover only the main movements of the combatants. The timetable of the battle is believed to be fairly accurate, although much of it is based on estimates. As in the case of other historic events there will be new material come to light from time to time in the future which will supplement our knowledge of the campaign.

One wonders how many serious reverses were suffered by the troops during the engagement and omitted from the "brief reports" of the battle officers. Many Coups and John Stands-In-Timber are the only sources for the information that the soldiers were driven back to the banks of the Rosebud at an early stage in the battle. One also wonders about the reports relating that one hundred cavalry horses (or mules) were stampeded and captured by the Indians. One question which will probably never be satisfactorily answered is the number of soldiers actually killed in the battle. Perhaps some day their final resting places will be found.

General Crook has been described as a self-effacing man who seldom wore his uniform, but perhaps his character is best revealed by an incident which occurred during one of his Indian campaigns.

The San Francisco *Chronicle* relates the following anecdote of General Crook:

"A soldier, one evening, after camp had been made, being detailed to bring in wood, found the General sitting on a log some distance from camp. The soldier approached, and thinking the General was a trooper or some camp follower (he dresses very plainly and seldom wears a uniform), sat down beside him and commenced as follows: 'I am awful tired and worn out with our fearful long march today. Ain't you?'

"'Yes; but I am resting now.'

"'If we would only kill some Indians once in a while, it would be some satisfaction, but this . . . marching up hill and down over burning sands and in the cold of the mountains, wearing men out for nothing—I don't believe we will ever see an Indian; do you?'

"'It looks that way. Still, we may find them.'

"'I don't go much on Crook. He's got a . . . of a reputation for fighting Indians, but I think it's all on paper—newspaper talk—don't you?'

"'I shouldn't wonder.'

"Here an officer approached, saluted, and prefacing his verbal message by calling Crook 'General,' the soldier realized his predicament, dropped his few sticks of wood, and broke for camp, worse frightened than if he had been suddenly surrounded by yelling Apaches. "[7]

It has been interesting to become briefly acquainted with Crook and some of his command. In the years that followed the campaign, there were men who remembered those exciting days.

In the July, 1924, issue of *Winners of the West,* the monthly newspaper of the National Indian War Veterans, appeared a letter to the Editor from W. E. Helvie, Pendleton, Oregon, who had served in Company F, Fourth Infantry, in Crook's Rosebud campaign. It was the rather pathetic appeal of a lonely old man whose comrades had gone to their "Long Home."

"Is there any of the boys living who waded Tongue River 18 or 20 times in one day. Is there any of the boys, I wonder, who remember Cap. (Black Jack) Randall, who was on Gen. Crook's staff, or Major Burt or Frank Gruard and Humpy, the hunchback Shoshone Indian that came tearing into our camp June 17, 1876, at Rosebud River battle after our all night hike from Goose Creek?"

Perhaps the most pathetic case was that of Lt. James E. H. Foster who so brilliantly led the cavalry charge of his small platoon on the extreme left at the Rosebud. Though still young, he was retired from the Army in 1881 because of tuberculosis. In his dying days he composed a poem, *Retired—To the Regiment,* extracts of which follow:

Never again in the saddle to wear the buff and blue;
Never again in the saddle to march with the troop in review,
Never again to hear with joy the boom of the morning gun,
As it sends its salutation to the rising of the sun.

Broken, worn out, and useless,
No longer to play in life's game,
'Tis hard, yet alive, to be buried;
To me it means just the same.

Never again to follow on the savage enemy's path,
Never again to meet the foe and face his hellish wrath;
Never again to lead the troop with its thundering hoof's behind,
With pistols out, and charging shout, and guidons flying to the
    wind.

Never again on the prairie, to see the sunset's glow,
O'er the sober brown of the heather, a bloodlike crimson throw;
Never again in the mountains, to see the lordly pine,
Or the flashing gleam of the crystal stream as it leaps and
    foams like wine.

My hope is beyond the sunset;
When the stream of life runs dry;
Oh, Comrades! Its harder retiring;
Better, far better, to die.

The Second and Third Cavalry regiments and the Fourth and Ninth Infantry regiments occupied the most remote army outposts for many years after the Sioux wars, the officers spending much of their time attending court martial proceedings. In these small posts the officers and their families were of necessity thrown into constant contact with each other which gave rise to many real and fancied difficulties which were often the subject of military court proceedings. Some of the officers at the Rosebud were victims of these petty personality conflicts which resulted in the termination of their military careers. Others died a few years after the battle as victims of disease incurred from the rigorous hardships of many Indian campaigns. A few of them, like Captain Henry, Colonel Royall, Captain Mills, Lt. Charles Morton, and Lt. Lemly, enjoyed long, successful careers in their country's service. Crook went on to lead his men in many brilliant victories, forcing the surrender of Crazy Horse and the Sioux, in 1877, and later Geronimo and his Apaches, in 1886.

It was a gallant company, indeed, which looked upon the bright face of danger on that Saturday in June many years ago.

NOTES

Chapter 1

1. "Then the battle of the Rosebud on the 17th, General Crook, defeating the united forces of the Sioux, which one week later, defeated and almost destroyed General Custer's command on the Little Big Horn, which latter sad event struck the country with such awe as to smother all consideration of the former, though it was probably the greatest Indian battle in our history—some 1400 soldiers and friendly Indians against some 5000 hostiles." *Journal of the Military Service Institution,* Vol. 15, p. 1316; Capt. Morton 3rd Cavalry, served in the Rosebud battle as Acting Adjutant for the Third Cavalry.

2. Mills, *My Story,* p. 167.

3. Ibid, p. 166.

4. Major Andrew W. Evans, 3rd Cavalry, had been a classmate of General Crook, graduating from West Point in 1852. He served all through the Civil War and was brevetted for gallant and meritorious services in the battle of Valverde, New Mexico; cavalry action at Appomattox Court House, Virginia; and for services resulting in capture and destruction of Comanche Indian Village at western base of Wichita Mountains, Dec. 25, 1868. *Annual Association of West Point Graduates for 1906.*

Captain Thomas B. Dewees, 2nd Cavalry, is quoted as saying that Evans was "one of the queerest men I ever met in the army. He was brave as a lion, but slow and generally peculiar. He was more fitted to be a professor in a college than a major in command of rough soldiers. He never associated with his brother officers. In fact he seemed to shrink from their society. He devoted himself mostly to books, and was well read on almost every subject under the sun." Finerty, *Warpath and Bivouac.*

5. Major Evans had with him Captain Azor H. Nickerson, Major Furey, Captain Randall, Captain Stanton, Dr. Patzki (a), and the following companies:

Company B, 3rd Cavalry, under Captain Meinhold and Lieutenant Simpson (b);

Company G, 3rd Cavalry, under Captain Crawford;

Company C, 3rd Cavalry, under Captain Van Vliet and Lt. Von Leutwitz;

Company I, 3rd Cavalry, under Captain Andrews and Lieutenant Foster;

Company L, 3rd Cavalry, under Captain Vroom and Lieutenant Chase (c);

Company I, 2nd Cavalry, under Captain Swigert and Lt. Huntington (d);

Company D, 4th Infantry, under Captain Cain and Lieutenant Seton (e);

This detachment made camp in the valley north of the fort, and had to be ferried across the river.

(a) Julius H. Patzki was born in Prussia and was appointed to the army from Pennsylvania. He served as a surgeon in the Civil War.

(b) 2nd Lt. James F. Simpson was appointed to the army from Connecticut and served with Connecticut infantry during the Civil War. He was brevetted for services in the battle of the Wilderness, Virginia; and Ream's Station, Virginia. *Army and Navy Journals*, Vol. 21, pages 235, 265, 304, and 976.

(c) Lt. George F. Chase was from Illinois and graduated from West Point in the class of 1871. He died December 13, 1925, at Washington, D.C., at the age of 77 years.

(d) Lt. Henry D. Huntington was from Vermont and graduated from the Military Academy in the class of 1875. He served in Wyoming, Montana and California. In 1878 he was in the campaign against the Bannock Indians.

(e) Lt. Henry Seton was appointed to the army from New York.

6. This ferry boat was propelled by the force of the current of the river striking against its sides. In moving to the south bank the boat was held in position by ropes so that it faced southwest and the current would force the boat along the cable to the south. In moving to the north the boat was faced to the northwest and the river would move it northward.

The ferry was located north of Fort Fetterman and a few feet east of the present bridge. "My father was a freighter to and from Fetterman in the seventies and according to my memory he told me the old ferry was just below (east) the bridge which I believe was at the same location as the present bridge." Letter of L. C. Bishop dated August 11, 1954.

7. "Captain Meinhold in attempting to swim his horse across, lost, by their becoming frightened, 100. They were subsequently recovered, with the exception of a few who, if governed by the usual good sense of a horse, are still running." Correspondent, *Army and Navy Journal*, (July 1, 1876), p. 758.

Captain Meinhold stated in his bi-monthly report in the company muster roll that one horse died of injuries in the stampede and four were lost.

8. Colonel William B. Royall, 3rd Cavalry, next in command to General Crook in this campaign, was in command of the fifteen companies of cavalry, which consisted of 10 companies of the 3rd Cavalry under Major Evans, and 5 companies of the 2nd Cavalry under Captain Henry E. Noyes. Royall had been appointed to the army from Missouri and served all through the Civil War and was brevetted for gallant and meritorious services in the battle of Hanover Court House, Virginia, and in the cavalry action at Old Church, Virginia. The latter action was described by Lt. Eben Swift, 5th Cavalry: "At Old Church, Virginia, in 1861, Captain, now Colonel W. B. Royall, armed with a revolver, with two troops of the Fifth Cavalry, charged General Stuart's advance under Captain Latane, who was armed with a saber. Royall and Latane met in the headlong charge. Latane was killed but Royall was able to charge through the enemy and rejoined his command with six saber wounds." *U. S. Cavalry Journal*, Vol. 5, p. 47.

After the Civil War Col. Royall served in the 5th Cavalry under General Carr and had extensive experience fighting Indians. In the "Record of Indian Engagements" published serially in the 1903 and 1904 issues of the *U. S. Cavalry Journal*, Col. Royall was mentioned twice.

Finerty described Col. Royall as "a tall, handsome Virginian of about fifty with a full gray mustache, dark eyebrows, overhanging a pair of bright blue eyes and a high forehead, on the apex of which, through the cropped hair, appeared one of several scars inflicted by a rebel saber in front of Richmond during the Civil War." Op. Cit., p. 50.

9. Coutant Notes of Western History and Archives Department, University of Wyoming, *Annals of Wyoming*, Vol. 4, No. 3, p. 358.

10. There are two accounts of the battle which have not been located. One is a detailed account written shortly after the battle by Lt. Henry R. Lemly which is mentioned by Captain Anson Mills in his speech to the Order of Indian Wars, March 2, 1917. The other account is referred to in the Baptiste Pourrier (Big Bat) narrative, Tablet 15, page 75, *Ricker Interviews:* "Bat says that a prospector was along who took down all this talk and wrote an account of the battle; his name was something like Toneburg; he was a tall man; he had a store afterwards in Deadwood where Colonel George lives, and Col. G. can give his whereabouts. He sold his store and went east."

Ricker Interviews are now in the custody of the Nebraska State Historical Society, Lincoln, Nebraska.

11. General Crook was brevetted (promoted) for gallant and meritorious services in the following Civil War battles: Lewisburg, Virginia; Antietam, Maryland; Farmington, Tennessee; campaign of 1864 in West Virginia; Fisher's Hill; and "for gallant and distinguished services in West Virginia." As a result of this brilliant record he was appointed Brigadier General in the regular army after the close of the Civil War. *Army and Navy Journal*, (April 10, 1880), p. 730.

It is interesting to note that although General Crook fought in the Civil War on the side of the Union, his daughter married the Confederate Cavalry leader, General J. E. B. Stuart, who was killed at the battle of Yellow Tavern. His widow was appointed an instructor in a Seminary for girls at Staunton, Virginia, after the war. *Army and Navy Journal*, (July 7, 1877.)

All biographical data on General Crook and his officers throughout this work was obtained from the *Army and Navy Register* for 1875 and subsequent years, the *Army and Navy Journal*, and *Annual Association of West Point Graduates*.

12. Report of General Sherman, *Army and Navy Journal*, (Dec. 2, 1876), p. 262.

13. Bourke, *Diary*, p. 401.

"The fight (Rosebud) appears to have developed the great steadiness, promptness to execute orders and elan of the soldiers, altho many were recruits very recently from the Depots." Editorial, *Army and Navy Journal*, (July 1, 1876), p. 757.

Chapter 2

1. Major Alexander Chambers, 4th Infantry, was an old friend of General Crook's. The two had been in West Point together where Chambers was in the class of 1853. He served with the infantry all through the Civil War and was brevetted for gallant and meritorious services in the battles

of Shiloh, Tennessee; Iuka, Mississippi, siege of Vicksburg, Mississippi; Champion Hills, Mississippi, February 4, 1864; and Meridian, Mississippi, February 14, 1864. He was commanding officer at Fort Fetterman from 1869 to 1871, and again in 1878.

2. Captain Henry E. Noyes, 2nd Cavalry, a West Pointer, class of 1861, served all through the Civil War. He was brevetted for gallant and meritorious services in the battle of Brandy Station, Virginia, and the capture of Selma, Alabama. After the Indian Wars he continued his services with the 2nd Cavalry and was in the Spanish American War. In 1899 he was appointed Colonel of the 2nd Cavalry Regiment.

3. Captain George M. Randall, 23rd Infantry, was appointed from Pennsylvania. Starting as a private in the Civil War, he rose through the ranks to Captain in the 23rd Infantry. He was brevetted for gallant and meritorious services in the battle of Antietam, Maryland; Petersburg, Virginia; in attack on Fort Steadman, Virginia. Indians called him "Captain-with-the-big-mustache-which-he-always-pulls," while the soldiers called him "Blackjack."

4. Captain William S. Stanton, appointed to West Point from New York, was in the class of 1865. In the Rosebud campaign he carried map making equipment but it is not known if he made any maps of the area. A search of the National Archives and Office of Chief Engineer of the U. S. Army has failed to disclose an official report or map filed by Stanton relating to Rosebud campaign. He built the iron bridge at Ft. Laramie in 1875 over which Royall's detachment crossed on their way to Ft. Fetterman.

5. Captain John V. Furey, Quartermaster's Corps, appointed to the army from New York, served all through the Civil War in Quartermaster Department. Starting as a private, he worked his way up through the ranks. He was brevetted for meritorious services in this Department during the Civil War.

6. Lt. John W. Bubb, Commissary of Subsistence, was appointed from the Army. He served with the infantry during the Civil War, starting in as a private.

7. Assistant Surgeon Albert Hartsuff, appointed from Michigan, served as surgeon all through the Civil War; was brevetted for "faithful and meritorious services during the war; during outbreak and continuance of Cholera in New Orleans, Louisiana."

8. Louis Richaud was the Sioux interpreter for General Crook. At the Council of War on June 14th he transposed Crook's words into Sioux which was understood by Old Crow, one of the Crow leaders, who in turn transposed them into Crow and Shoshone language.

9. Baptiste Pourrier (Big Bat) Crook's Crow interpreter, was a professional scout and frontiersman, and had spent his whole life among the Plains Indians. Several years before he had been one of a small band of 19 men who held off several thousand Sioux in the famous Hayfield Fight near Fort C. F. Smith. A few weeks after the Rosebud battle he was with Lt. Sibley when he made his scout towards the Big Horn Mountains where he had been sent by General Crook to ascertain the location of the hostiles. Big Bat was regarded by Crook as one of his most trustworthy scouts. He was called Big Bat to distinguish him from another famous Indian scout, Baptiste Garnier, who was called "Little Bat." See *Fighting Indian Warriors*, by E. A. Brininstool, The Stackpole Co.

Big Bat was a half brother of Mitch Bouyer, the famous scout and interpreter who died with Custer. They had the same father and the name "Bouyer" could have been the same name as "Pourrier", they being pronounced the same.

10. Finerty states that Joseph Wasson had had extensive experience in many Indian campaigns. Op. cit., p. 61.

11. "At the Sage Creek camp, I was introduced by General Crook to Mr. Robert A. Strahorn, a distinguished Western newspaper correspondent, who had made a reputation over the *non de plume* of 'Alter Ego,' and who in every situation proved himself as fearless as he was talented," Finerty, Op. cit., p. 61.

12. T. B. MacMillan was in poor health and was compelled to go back with the wounded to Fort Fetterman several days after the Rosebud battle. Finerty mentions his "eternal coughing" during the campaign.

13. "Mr. Davenport was entirely unused to frontier life, and some of the young officers and his brother correspondents used to banter him a good deal with regards to the horrors of Indian warfare. He took it all in good part, at the time, but he found means, before the campaign closed, to get more than even with some of the jokers. As a rule all of the correspondents got along well together, but one or two of them did not succeed in making themselves liked by several of the officers. Of all earthly experiences none so tests the strength and weakness of human nature as an Indian campaign, especially when attended by hardship and hunger." Finerty, Op. cit., p. 61.

14. Captain Charles Meinhold, Troop B., 3rd Cav. was a "very fine looking German officer with a romantic history." Finerty, op. cit., p. 70. He was an old campaigner and was mentioned in the "record of Indian Engagements," *U. S. Cavalry Journal*, (1903-1904) as follows: "Captain C. Meinhold, attacked a war party of Indians on South Fork of Loup River, Nebraska, killing 3 Indians."

15. Captain Frederick Van Vliet, Troop C, 3rd Cav., was appointed to the army from New York and served all through the Civil War. He was brevetted for gallant and meritorious services in the late campaign from Rapidan to Petersburg, and in the siege of Mobile, Alabama. "He was tall, thin and good looking." Finerty, op. cit., p. 75.

16. *Army and Navy Journal*, April 10, 1880, p. 730.

17. "On that day, (June 4th) for the first time, I saw an Indian 'grave.' It was situated on a little bluff above the creek. After dismounting I went up to observe it. The Sioux never put their dead under ground. This 'grave' was a buffalo hide supported by willow slips and leather thongs, strapped upon four cottonwood poles, about six feet high. The corpse had been removed either by the Indians themselves or by the miners who had passed through a few days before. Around lay two blue blankets, with red trimmings, a piece of jacket all covered with beads, a moccasin, a fragment of Highland tartan, a brilliant shawl and a quantity of horse hair. Scarcely had I noted these objects when a squad of young fellows from the 9th Infantry walked up the hill after firewood . . . 'Hello, Sam, hello Sam, what in h—— is that?' 'That—oh, that is the lay-out of some d—d dead Indian. Let's pull it up by the roots.' They did tear it up by the roots, and within ten minutes the Indian tomb was helping to boil the dinners of the 9th Infantry." Finerty, op. cit., p. 83.

18. "On May 29th our advance guard of two companies, already noted as having been sent out to meet the Crow scouts, encamped on the Dry Fork of Powder River. Scattered over the ground selected for their camp were numerous lately burned bivouac fires, and on several pieces of bark and board were found messages indicating who the recent visitors had been. They were a party of sixty-five Montana miners, under the leadership of Captain St. John, and had left that point two days before for the Whitewood district, Black Hills, via Pumpkin Buttes. The following was one of the messages, and is a fair sample of the spirit in which they were all written: 'Dry Fork of Powder River, May 27, 1876—Tony Pastor's opera troupe of emigrants from Montana, on their way east, camped here. Don't know how far it is to where they can get water, so have filled nose-bags and gum boots, and ride on singing, *There's Room Enough in Paradise*'." Robert A. Strahorn, *Rocky Mountain News*, (June 27, 1876), p. 4.

19. Captain Guy V. Henry, Troop D, 3rd Cav., was born at Fort Smith, Indian Territory, on March 9, 1838, and was the son of Major William Seaton Henry, 3rd U. S. Infantry. He graduated from West Point, class of 1861, and was assigned as second lieutenant to the 1st U. S. Artillery. Made Colonel of the 40th Massachusetts Infantry in the fall of 1863, he continued throughout the war with that command; was brevetted for gallant and meritorious services in action near Pocotaligo River, S. Carolina, battle of Olustee, Florida, and Petersburg, Virginia. He was transferred to the 3rd Cav., in 1870. Since the Civil War he was engaged with different Indian tribes in Arizona, Wyoming, Utah, Nebraska, and Dakota. In the Black Hills expedition, winter of 1874-75, he was badly frozen as were many men under his command. In Rosebud Battle he was severely wounded through face, losing use of left eye. Being broken in health, he was granted leave of absence and made an extended tour through Europe, returning to take part in the White River Expedition, fall of 1879. See article "Colonel Guy V. Henry," *United Service*, (February, 1892) p. 213.

Meeting him in Cheyenne before the campaign, Finerty describes him as, "a very fine-looking, although slight and somewhat pale, officer, and, what was still better, he was well up in all things concerning the projected Indian campaign." Finerty, op, cit., p. 32. Colonel Henry died October 27, 1899.

20. Finerty, op. cit., p. 91.

21. "In this skirmish Sergeant Warfield, F, 3rd Cav. received a slight wound in the right arm, and Private Emil Renner, D. 2nd Cav., a flesh wound in the left thigh, both from spent balls." Correspondent, *Army and Navy Journal*, (June 21, 1876), p. 741.

22. "One of the horses wounded and afterwards killed was the personal property of Captain Burt, 9th Infantry, who prized him very highly . . . Lieut. Robertson's horse was also shot." Bourke, *Diary*, Vol. 2, p. 370.

"June 9th, an attack was made on our camp, resulting in the slight wounding of 3 men and 3 horses, the latter having legs broken, were shot." Correspondent, *Army & Navy Journal*, (July 1, 1876), p. 758.

23. Capt. Samuel Munson, Co. C, 9th Infantry, was appointed to the army from Maine and had served with Maine troops all through the Civil War. Captain Munson was a seasoned Indian fighter and is men-

tioned as exercising an independent command against the Indians in the far west as early as 1868. "A small remnant of the Nevada Indians went north, and was met by a force under command of Captain Samuel Munson, of the Ninth Infantry, in Warner Valley, Oregon, on the 1st day of May, 1868. In this fight the guide, Mr. Hoag, was killed, and Lieutenant Hayden de Laney, was wounded, the latter receiving a brevet for gallant and meritorious service on that occasion. In the affair, the Indians evinced unwonted bravery, and, being well fortified behind rocks, a good deal of work was necessary to dislodge them, but the soldiers accomplished it." Col. A. G. Brackett, "Fighting in the Sierras," *United Service*, (October, 1891), p. 327.

24. Capt. Thomas B. Burrowes, Co G., 9th Infantry, was appointed to the army from Pennsylvania and served all through the Civil War with infantry troops. He was brevetted for service in the battle of Jonesboro, Georgia, and was retired in 1879, for disability from wounds.

25. "Colonel Chambers was instructed to send out three companies of the 9th Infantry, Burrowes, Burt, and Munson's to occupy the heights on the right." Bourke, *Diary*, Vol. 2, p. 369.

26. Captain William H. Andrews, Troop I, 3rd Cavalry, was appointed to the army from New York and served with New York Infantry during the Civil War. "Captain Wm. H. Andrews, retired, died at Washington, Monday last (June 21, 1880). He commenced his service in the 10th New York Volunteers, in 1862 as captain. At the close of the war he was transferred to the Veteran Volunteers, and afterwards to the 12th Infantry, and again to the 30th Infantry. He was unassigned in 1869, and assigned as 1st Lieutenant to the 3rd Cavalry in 1870. Captain Andrews had been for years a great sufferer from inflammatory rheumatism, but the immediate cause of his death was pneumonia, with which he was attacked but a few days since." *Army & Navy Journal*, (June 26, 1880), p. 963. Captain Andrews was one of the older officers who did not live long after the campaign.

27. Lt. Joseph Lawson, Troop A, 3rd Cavalry, was born in Ireland and was appointed to the army from Kentucky. He served with the 11th Kentucky Cavalry all through the Civil War, and died in 1881 at Fort Steele, which was located several miles east of the present site of Rawlins, Wyoming.

We are permitted a slight glimpse of his personality from the following tribute by Finerty: "At this time I changed my mess to Troop A, 3rd Cavalry, then commanded by First Lieutenant Joseph Lawson, an Irish Kentuckian, and as gallant an old gentleman as ever drew a sword. He was an original in every way, and joined the Union Army, on principle, at a time when nearly all his neighbors of fighting age were donning the rebel gray. Lawson was absolutely without fear, but his many peculiarities induced his brother officers to quiz him when they had nothing else to do. He bore it all with supreme good nature, and, on the day of battle, showed the whole brigade that an officer need not always hail from West Point in order to gain that place in the affections of his soldiers which dauntless courage alone can win." Finerty, op. cit., p. 200.

28. "The infantry on the right behind the trees stood well up to the work, and answered volley for volley with their 'long Toms.' During the progress of the fight one chief, 'The man with the Tin Hat,' made a

practice of charging backwards and forwards on the hill, a mark for the infantry below. While this performance was going on, another entertainment was on the boards along the river's edge. Several of the teamsters and packers had been watching 'Tin Hat' and suddenly they broke forth in a chorus of comic yells, using such expressions as these— 'Head him off,' 'Nosebag him,' 'Hobble him,' at the same time running and jumping and tumbling around there under the heavy fire. The boys said they 'had to have their fun out of that Indian.'" Correspondent, *Frank Leslie's Illustrated Newspaper*, (August 12, 1876) p. 373.

29. Captain Alexander Sutorius, Troop E, 3rd Cavalry, was appointed 2nd Lieutenant from the Army on April 22, 1863, and served through the Civil War. He was born in Switzerland. Like many of his brother officers he was very unfortunate and was court martialled and dismissed from the service in the fall of 1876. When the wagon train brought supplies to Crook's summer camp in July, 1876, there was a whiskey peddler along and Captain Sutorius overindulged and failed to place the pickets properly about the camp. General Crook was a stern disciplinarian and put Captain Sutorius under arrest and instituted the court martial proceedings.

30. Lt. James E. H. Foster, Troop I, 3rd Cavalry, was appointed to the army from Western Pennsylvania and served all through the Civil War with Pennsylvania troops. Lt. Foster was also something of an artist and some of his sketches are printed herein. "Lieut. Foster, 3rd Cav. has made a series of creditable rough pencil sketches of points of interest along the route; it is his intention to send them to *Harper's Weekly* for publication." Bourke, *Diary*, Vol. 2, p. 376.

Lt. Foster contracted tuberculosis as a result of many Indian campaigns and went to his home in Pittsburgh, Pennsylvania, in 1881, where he died on May 8, 1883. He was very unhappy during his enforced retirement and yearned for active life in the saddle.

31. Lt. Augustus C. Paul, Troop M, 3rd Cavalry, was appointed to the army from Missouri and served in the Civil War with Kentucky Infantry. Finerty mentioned Lt. Paul and Capt. Vroom as the two literary men of the outfit, "and their small, paper-covered circulating library found the rounds of the encampment, greatly to the detriment of the volumes." Finerty, op. cit., p. 143. Lt. Paul resigned from the service in April, 1881, after a court martial hearing, but the charges and proceedings were not published. He went to Denver with his family after which he disappeared from public life.

32. Lt. Frederick Schwatka, Troop M, 3rd Cavalry, was appointed to West Point from Illinois and graduated in the class of 1871. He headed a scientific expedition to the North Pole a few years after the Rosebud campaign, where he recovered the bones of Sir John Franklin and his party who had perished in the snow and ice on a previous polar expedition. Schwatka spent about a year and a half in the frozen north without any mishaps but as soon as he returned to this country he slipped on some ice in the street and broke his leg. After retiring to private life Schwatka was elected to Congress from Illinois.

33. "The pickets on every side were strengthened and the herd secured in anticipation of any attempt by the Indians to capture it. Half a mile up the river a band of Sioux tried to cross, but were driven back by the pickets. Indians were seen at the same time on the south side of

the camp but they remained distant. . . . One of the party of Indians, on attempting to cross the river, was shot, and was lifted from his seat by his companions. Those on the bluff led off the riderless pony. It was supposed that two Indians were wounded or killed, at least." Helena (Montana) *Independent,* (June 28, 1876), p. 1.

34. Captain William C. Rawolle, Troop B, Second Cavalry, was born in Prussia and was appointed to the army from New York. He served all through the Civil War and was brevetted for gallant and meritorious services in the Army of the Potomac from Aug., 1862, to Jan. 1863, including the battles of Second Bull Run, South Mountain, Antietam, Warrenton, Sulphur Springs, and Fredericksburg; for services in the west, including the cavalry campaign in east Tennessee, and expeditions into northern Mississippi, and for gallant, daring and good conduct in the battle of Brice's Cross Roads, Mississippi. He was wounded March 17, 1876, in the Powder River Fight. See "Record of Indian Engagements," *Cavalry Journal,* (1903-1904).

35. "Interested friends at the different forts, upon our leaving, usually said, 'Oh, you will have a holiday trip this summer. So different from our last winter's campaign, you know; nice warm days and pleasant nights. Really, I wouldn't mind going along myself.' " Strahorn, *Rocky Mountain News,* (June 27, 1876), p. 4.

"On the 6th Inst. by the upsetting of an ambulance, Sergeant O'Leary, Co. C. 9th Infantry, had an arm broken and side considerably bruised. He will doubtless be rendered unfit for service during the entire campaign, although his injuries are not of a dangerous nature. These are thus far the only casualties of the campaign, but the command is quite unfortunate in having a comparatively large number of men on the sick roll. Most of these are afflicted with aggravated attacks of the 'mumps', while digestive derangments and 'general biliousness' are claiming a number as temporary victims. The packers, who do the yelling for the entire command, furnish a majority of the cases of mumps and other throat diseases." Robert A. Strahorn, "Dispatch dated June 8, 1876, Big Horn Expedition, Camp on Tongue River, Montana," *Rocky Mountain News,* (June 27, 1876), p. 4.

Chapter 3

1. Big Goose Creek now flows in from the southwest while Little Goose Creek flows north into the east edge of the city and then turns west and empties into the larger stream. The course of Little Goose was changed years ago by the railroad: in 1876 it ran in a northwesterly course, west of its present location, and joined Big Goose about 200 yards south of the present junction. The camp site covered most of the present Sheridan business district, and all of the residential district between the forks and southward as far as the bluffs now occupied by the Courthouse and Cemetery.

2. As to the location of the camp on Goose Creek at the time June 11th to June 15th, Bourke uses the following expressions: "flows with the swiftness of a mill race through the channels on each side of us," and "The two little mountain brooks joining below our camp are lined," etc., *Diary* Vol. 2, pages 370-374.

3. "When Frank and Louis crossed Tongue River near our old camp, much discontent was manifested by the Indians because they misunderstood our march back to a new camp for grass as an indication of the abandonment of the campaign. They forgot that 1800 or 1900 mules and horses consume immense quantities of grass daily and need a frequent renewal of pasturage. Under this misapprehension, the great majority declined to follow further, so Frank and Louis pushed ahead bringing with them one chief, leaving 'Big Bat' to come along more leisurely with 15 or 16 of the Crows who remained." John G. Bourke, *Diary*, Vol. 2, p. 381.

4. Major Andrew S. Burt was appointed to the army from Ohio and served during the Civil War with Ohio Infantry. He was brevetted for gallant and meritorious services in the battle of Mill Springs, Kentucky; during the Atlanta Campaign, and in the battle of Jonesboro, Georgia.

In later years while stationed in Chicago Major Burt wrote a number of plays and light opera sketches which were successful and well received. He enjoyed a long and successful army career.

5. Letter of F. H. Sinclair of Sheridan, Wyoming, dated October 30, 1953.

6. Letter of Lt. Colonel E. S. Luce, 7th Cavalry, U. S. Army, retired, dated March 27, 1954.

7. *Army & Navy Journal*, (Aug. 5, 1876), p. 837.

8. Captain Nickerson was born in Ohio and was appointed to the army from that state. He served all through the Civil War with the 8th Ohio Volunteers and after that war served a few years with the 14th Infantry. He was appointed Captain in the 23rd Infantry on July 8, 1868. He possessed a droll sense of humor and after the Rosebud Battle one of his facetious remarks came to the attention of the *Army & Navy Journal:* "We advise the Winchester Arms Company to act upon the suggestion offered them by Captain Nickerson of General Crook's Staff, and prosecute the Indians for infringement of their patent. The Captain testifies, with others, that Winchester rifles are plentiful among them; the agency people and the traders solemnly affirm that they don't furnish them, so it can only be inferred that the Indians manufacture them themselves. If Gov. Winchester could get out a preliminary injunction, restraining the Indians from the use of his rifle, it might be a signal service to our troops in the next engagement." (July 22, 1876), p. 805.

Shortly after the Rosebud Battle, Captain Nickerson's health became so poor as a result of years of hardships and exposure that he was appointed to a position in the Adjutant General's Department. The *Army & Navy Journal* paid him this tribute in an editorial: "Even the unsuccessful aspirants for the vacant position in the Adjutant General's Department will commend the appointment of Captain Nickerson. He is an able officer, has a most excellent war record, and will do himself credit in any position. He entered the military service in 1861 as 2nd lieutenant of the 8th Ohio Volunteers, and was appointed in 1866 to the regular army as 2nd lieutenant 15th Infantry. Senator Gordon of Georgia was an earnest advocate of Captain Nickerson's appointment. He was in front of the position occupied by the skirmish line commanded by Captain Nickerson at the battle of Antietam, the two officers being not over two hundred yards apart when both were terribly wounded.

Captain Nickerson was also wounded at Chancellorsville, and again at Gettysburg, where a shot passed through one arm and another through both lungs. He was Adjutant General and Chief of Staff to Gen. Crook in the twelve years Indian campaign of that officer." (June 22, 1878), p. 745.

9. "No means of transportation were taken except riding horses and mules, and two sumpter mules to carry hospital necessities and pioneer tools." Correspondent, *Army & Navy Journal* (July 1, 1876), p. 754.

10. "We were told by Crook that our rations would be replenished on reaching Terry, who had supplies on the Yellowstone, thus exploding an unnecessary criticism, in the Washington *Chronicle,* that Crook did not desire to cooperate with Terry." Correspondent, *Army & Navy Journal* (July 8, 1876), p. 802.

11. Bourke's *Diary.*

Chapter 4

1. Captain Gerhard L. Luhn, Company F, 4th Infantry, was born in Germany and served all through the Civil War and was appointed from the ranks. He was brevetted for gallant and meritorious services in front of Petersburg, Virginia. Shortly after the Rosebud campaign his infant child died and was buried in the cemetery at Fort Sanders where he was then stationed.

2. "When night fell, 175 mounted riflemen were ready for the field." Bourke, *Diary* (June 15, 1876).

3. "This island is no longer in existence, as the creek beds were diverted some years ago. However there are elderly men who were born here and who recall the island very well as they had a swimming hole near it many years ago. The spot is about where the Sheridan Brewery Company has their plant today." Letter of F. H. Sinclair dated October 30, 1953.

When General Crook returned after the battle he found that the wagons had been moved 2½ miles west up the stream.

4. In those days all of the stream north of the forks of Big and Little Goose Creek, to its mouth, was called the "Tongue River."

"Sibley camped on south fork of Goose Creek about a mile above the junction of the north and south forks. Where they unite is beginning of Tongue River. They form Tongue River. Tongue River has 3 parts. 2 are called Goose Creek." Baptiste Pourier (Big Bat), *Ricker Interviews,* Tablet 15, p. 22.

Nowadays the stream which runs in a winding northerly direction from the forks at Sheridan is called "Goose Creek," while the stream which comes in from the west into which it empties is called "Tongue River."

5. "In like manner, Tom Moore, our chief of pack trains, organized from among his packers a small force of (20) Twenty wiry, hardy, horny handed veterans, every one a fine rider and as near being a dead shot as men get to be on the frontier." Bourke, *Diary* (June 15, 1876).

6. In this compilation Bourke's statement that there were 175 mounted infantrymen is accepted as probably more accurate than Finerty's esti-

mate of 200. Bourke, being a staff officer, was more apt to have been correctly informed than the correspondent, Finerty.

7. The breakdown of the six companies, as taken from the muster rolls filed by company commanders, dated June 30, 1876, is as follows:

Co. B, 3rd Cavalry, Captain Charles Meinhold 65
Co. C, 3rd Cavalry, Captain Van Vliet 59
Co. D, 3rd Cavalry, Captain Guy V. Henry 46
Co. F, 3rd Cavalry, Lt. Bainbridge Reynolds 51
Co. G, 3rd Cavalry, Lt. Emmitt Crawford 56
Co. L, 3rd Cavalry, Captain Peter D. Vroom 50

Total 327

8. Finerty, *Warpath and Bivouac.*
9. Finerty, *Warpath and Bivouac.*
10. Finerty, *Warpath and Bivouac.*
11. "On June 16 at dusk camp was made on the Rosebud after a march of about forty miles, and at a point where that stream runs nearly east." T. B. MacMillan, *The Daily Inter-Ocean* (July 12, 1876).

"They made a forced march yesterday of Forty Miles and camped in the fork of the Rosebud last night." T. B. MacMillan, *The Daily Inter-Ocean*, (June 24, 1876), p. 5.

12. Finerty, *Warpath and Bivouac.*

Chapter 5

1. Sitting Bull, who was 42 years of age at the time of the Rosebud battle, was the great medicine man of the Sioux nation. He was considered too old to fight and was not expected actually to lead the warriors in battle. He was a controversial figure all through his life. Historians are divided as to his qualities of leadership, some claiming that he was a physical coward and a rabble-rouser, others that he exercised high qualities of leadership and was the outstanding statesman of the Sioux nation. All through his life he had a bitter hatred of the white race and fomented hatred and discontent among the younger Indians. At this period he had an immense following and was the acknowledged leader of those Indians who were in open revolt against the government. The Sioux, together with some of the Northern Cheyennes, who had left the Agencies, flocked to his standard, and there were so many of them that a fraction of their number was able to defeat General Crook at the Rosebud, and their whole command was able to overwhelm General Custer's men at the Little Big Horn one week later.

While in Bismarck, North Dakota, in 1881, he was described by the Correspondent for the *Army and Navy Journal:* "He is below the medium height, stolid, and stoical-looking, and the thinness of his lips and a few wrinkles in his face give him the appearance of being older than 50 years, which Scout Allison says is his correct age. He was dressed in the traditional blue blanketing, sewed in the form of half civilized trousers, with great gaping places where the pockets should be, and when he walked often displayed a brawny leg. Over this he wore what was once a finely made and nicely laundered white shirt, but which had become greasy and dirty from long wear. The shoulders of the shirt and the sleeves had three long streaks of red war paint, with which the warrior's neck, entire face, and scalp at the parting of the hair was covered.

His hair is black, and reaches below his shoulders, hanging in three braids, one at each side and one pendent from the back, and braided from the crown of his broad head. The two braids hanging over the shoulders were thickly wound with a flannel, and the only ornaments worn were two brass rings, one on the little and one on the second finger of the left hand, and a lady's cheap bracelet of black gutta percha on the left wrist. This lack of ornament, in comparison with his better looking and more gaudily adorned chief advisers, is for the purpose of impressing the sentimental white man with his poverty. His moccasins were the most common pattern, dotted with a few beads here and there.

The manners of the Indians at the table were closely watched. They dined slowly, and handled knife and fork as gracefully as most white people. When ice cream was served Sitting Bull dipped his spoon into it, tasted it, and rose to his feet. He sat down again immediately, and remarked to Scout Allison, the interpreter that he 'could not see how such stuff could be frozen in hot weather.' While on the boat a greater portion of the time, Sitting Bull wore a pair of goggles which he sold here to some relic hunter for $5. He also sold his pipe for $100. He seems to have overcome all his shyness, as reported from Buford, and stands the observations of the crowd without any perceptible agitation, shaking hands with those who offer to do so, and writing his autograph, for which he charges from $2 to $5. The whole party are now at Standing Rock, with the other Indians. On Sitting Bull's arrival, with 190 other Indians, at Standing Rock, he was warmly greeted." Vol. 19 (August 6, 1881) p. 7.

2. Dr. T. Woodridge, Agency Physician for the Fort Peck Agency, sent a description of a Sun Dance he had witnessed to the Interior Department. "I have just witnessed the great Indian festival of the 'Sun Dance' or worship of the sun. Great preparations had been made for it and everything was on the grandest scale. The city of lodges was moved and the Indians encamped on a beautiful plain enclosing a hollow square large enough for the movements of thousands of horsemen.

In the centre the great pavilion or medicine lodge was erected, 150 feet in diameter, the outside formed of small posts of green poplar and willow thickly interwoven with green branches. Resting on this and on a rude framework within, all around for about twenty feet the space was covered with buffalo skins, forming the 'dress circle,' with places assigned to the musiciains and actors or dancers. In the centre was the great medicine pole, fifty feet high. The diameter of the central space—about one hundred feet—was open to broad sunlight. Only the men occupied the deep circle, where they were feasted during the performance of twenty-eight continuous hours, during which time about forty dogs were immolated and eaten, besides large quantities of buffalo meat, wild turnip heads and hot cauldrons of other eatables that are nameless.

The audience was composed of about five thousand Indians, but as only the men occupied the circle within, the common people, women and boys, had to be satisfied by viewing the performances through the wide entrance or through the interstices in the leafy barriers. All had on their holiday attire, the dresses of some of the chiefs and those acting as directors or priests were gorgeous.

"When all was prepared, amid the waving of banners, music and the loud applauding of the assembled throng, over fifty braves, entered, each an Apollo, painted and naked to the waist, except a profusion of ornaments, with headdresses of beautiful feathers, their black, glossy hair reaching down to their lower garments which were most beautifully and artistically arranged. Each carried in his hand an ornamental whistle, made from the bone of an eagle's wing, which was blown shrilly during the dancing. Each carried also a bouquet composed mostly of the wild sage. Their appearance and reception were grand and imposing.

The first afternoon's performance would have been called wonderful for display of heroism and power to endure and suffer. Many had from fifty to two hundred pieces cut out of the living flesh from their arms and back. The dance was kept up all night with unabated fervor, every performance having something new and startling. But in the morning torture reigned supreme, men dancing with two, three and four buffalo heads suspended from holes cut in their flesh. One Indian dragged on the ground eight buffalo heads fastened to the flesh of his back, and in the stooping posture he was forced to assume they had lacerated or torn the cuts in his back to the extent of three inches. Others were held by four different cords, two in the breast and two in the back, fastened to four stakes; and still others were fastened to the centre pole with ropes which were fastened to the breast and back. Some, in addition to being fastened by the flesh of their breasts, had buffalo heads suspended from the back, and they would be seized by the hanging heads and jerked till one would think their life would be forfeited. Others made frantic efforts to break loose, and I often noticed the integument to be stretched three or four inches from the body. Some fell faint and exhausted, and, with wild shouts, the din of music and weird songs, made of it a perfect pandemonium.

The dancers neither took food, sleep nor water during the festival. Their dancing, their invocations and their prayers were fervent. They laid their faces on the buffalo heads while praying for success in hunting, and the priest wept and asked the Great Spirit to give them success in the chase and let them have food for their wives and children; also to give them plenty of horses, to prosper them and help them to subdue their enemies. The sod was carefully removed in a spot four feet square, and within a white spot was made. This is all they knew, and with no teacher but nature we must judge them charitably. 'Count not impossible that which seems unlikely.' Their liberality was unbounded. Over two hundred horses were given away, besides great quantities of other articles." *Army and Navy Journal*, Vol. 16 (July 12, 1879), p. 887.

3. In 1878 a newspaper correspondent in company with some soldiers and former braves of Sitting Bull, retraced Custer's trail beside the little stream to the Custer field. "This part of the trail had never been traced since the battle. In going down the creek valley we passed the spot where Custer first heard the Indians were located, and saw the lodge poles of the large village which had moved two days before he came down to the other side of the Little Horn River. Here I picked up the skull of Little Wing, an Uncapapa Sioux Indian, who had been killed

in a fight with General Crook a few days previous to the Custer fight. He was known to the Indians who guided us, and his death was described by them." *Army and Navy Journal*, Sept. 21, 1878, p. 101. This was probably the dead warrior found in the burning tepee described in the Custer accounts.

4. "In the Custer massacre, the attack by Reno had at first caused a panic among women and children, and some of the warriors had started to flee, but Crazy Horse, throwing away his rifle, brained one of the incoming soldiers with his stone war-club and jumped upon his horse." Bourke's, *On the Border With Crook*, p. 415.

See also *Crazy Horse*, by Mari Sandoz, for his life history.

5. Lame White Man was killed in the Custer battle while leading a band of Cheyenne warriors up the ravine west of Custer Hill in the attack on the men of Troop E.

6. "Stirk (Richard C.) speaking of *Little Big Man*, says the Indians always speak of him as a squaw woman; they say he was not a brave man; he was a bad mischievous character, stirring up discord, trouble, but when he had fomented disturbance he stayed behind in camp and let the warriors face the difficulties he had created." *Ricker Interviews*, Tablet 8, p. 37.

"Little Big Man I did not like in those days; principally on account of his insolent behavior to the members of the Allison Commission at this same agency (Red Cloud), during the summer. In appearance he was crafty, but withal a man of considerable ability and force. He and I became better friends afterwards, and exchanged presents. I hold now his beautiful calumet and a finely beaded tobacco bag, as well as a shirt trimmed with human scalps, which was once the property of Crazy Horse." Bourke, *On the Border With Crook*, p. 415.

7. Letter of Ben Reifel to writer dated March 4, 1955.

8. Letter of Jake Herman to writer dated March 4, 1955.

9. Letter of Mari Sandoz to writer dated February 26, 1955.

10. *Ibid.*

11. *South Dakota Historical Collections*, Vol. 6, p. 228. This statement is borne out by that of Many Coups.

12. "*The Coup.* An Indian who shoots and kills an enemy gets no credit unless he touches him in some way. The reason for this is that he may kill him at a distance and this would be no sign of bravery; but, if he is near enough to touch his body it is evident that he was in proximity to exposure and danger, and so this is honorable and confers upon a warrior prestige, and he is rewarded accordingly. So the Indian who did not shoot at him at all; but was the first to touch him, says, 'I killed him first,' the one who did not shot at all but can truthfully say, 'I killed him second,' comes next in rank of honor, and this preference is carried to the third person or warrior. If this last be the man who actually shot him, he will be obliged to say, 'I killed him third,' and take the last degree.'" *Ricker Interviews*, Tablet 4, p. 123. Interview of Phillip F. Wells, half breed Indian scout and interpreter, at Kadoka, South Dakota.

13. Mari Sandoz, *Crazy Horse*, p. 315.

14. Stanley Vestal, *Warpath*, p. 187; Charles Eastman, "Story of the

Little Big Horn," *Chautauquan,* Vol. 31 (July, 1900), p. 356; Stanley Vestal, *Sitting Bull,* p. 155.

15. Burdick, *The Last Battle of the Sioux Nation,* p. 39.

16. Stanley Vestal, *Warpath and Council Fire,* p. 221.

17. *South Dakota Historical Collections,* Vol. 6, p. 228.

Chapter 6

1. Bourke, *Diary.*

It was difficult for me to believe that the double line of troops would be over five miles long so I wrote to Col. E. S. Luce, U. S. Army Retired, who replied in a letter dated March 27, 1954: "As to cavalry marching in the field, that always depends upon the terrain. When there are wagon trains accompanying the troops, they generally have a right wing and a left wing, with the wagons between the two wings. Cavalry in the field generally marches in columns of two's. The distance at 'Attention marching' order is 'Four feet from head to croup!' In 'Rout Order,' the distance varies, but is generally about ten feet from head to croup. There is a command in the cavalry known as 'Four feet from head to croup.' That means that you are to keep a closed-up alignment of your horse's head four feet from the hind end of the horse in front of you. In marching in the field, that entirely depends on the terrain, whether it is dusty or not. Your interval (right to left), is generally about three feet apart, but in some instances it can be as much as fifty feet apart. When I was stationed at Fort Wingate, N.M., many years ago, we hiked from that post to Albuquerque. Between Grants and Thoreau there is a black lava desert about 8 miles long, and our distance would be 100 feet and intervals about the same, so as to escape the rising black lava dust. Take a regimental front of 12 troops you would have normally in a platoon front, four squads of 16 men, three platoons to a troop. The distance of a platoon would be about 128 feet. If you brought up the whole regiment in one line, you would have a front of about 4,600 feet. If you had that regiment on the march in column of two's (four feet from head to croup) you would have a line of about 11,500 feet. With the 1310 mounted men, you would have a line of column of two's about 26,200 feet long."

The men were probably marching in "Route Order" because of the rough terrain, and the additional six feet of interval would add 7860 feet to the length of the column on the basis of a single line of two's. As eight companies were on the right side of the stream and twelve companies on the left side, the total length of the column on the left side, the longest, would be 20,436 feet or almost four miles. Probably the main reason for such a long line was that there would be considerable confusion and delay incident to the formation of the column. Some companies would not be ready to take their place and would have to hurry to make up the interval. The rear guard would follow at a considerable interval to the rear, so it was entirely possible that some of the men were still at the camp when the head of the column went into bivouac five miles down the stream.

2. The accounts differ as to the scouts who rode madly into camp with the news that the Sioux were approaching. All agree that the scouts

sent ahead that morning were Crows and that these met the scouts of
the Sioux unexpectedly at the high hill on the William Rowland place.
It is also true that some of the Shoshones were posted on the high crest
north of the field. It would seem probable that as soon as the returning
Crow scouts came in view of the Shoshones, the latter would immediately
carry the news down to the soldiers in the valley, arriving there before
the Crow scouts. This is borne out by the statement of Private W. E.
Helvie of the 4th Infantry, that it was Humpy, the little hunched back
Shoshone, who came tearing into camp with the news. See supra p. 170.
The Crow scouts, one of whom was severely wounded, probably followed
him into camp.

3. Finerty, *Warpath and Bivouac.*

4. Captain Thomas B. Dewees served all through the Civil War with
cavalry. "Dewees was an excellent story teller, and was gifted with an
open, generous nature, which made him a universal favorite in the
army. He was a man of large physique, and his laugh was of that hearty,
contagious quality which always sets a table in a roar." John F. Finerty,
Warpath and Bivouac, p. 323.

5. "Bainbridge Reynolds was born September 15, 1849, at West Point,
New York, where his distinguished father, General J. J. Reynolds, was
Principal Assistant Professor of Natural and Experimental Philosophy at
the time of his birth. He graduated number nineteen in the class of 1873
and was assigned to the Third Cavalry. As a cadet, he was noted for
his neatness of dress and military bearing as well as for his jovial, kindly
disposition and was extremely popular in his class. The writer was on
the most intimate terms with him, particularly during our first class year,
and has many pleasant recollections of his geniality. He died at his
mother's residence in Washington, July 10, 1901, after a protracted
illness due to cancer. He never married. Bainbridge Reynolds joined the
regiment the autumn of 1873 at Fort McPherson, Nebraska, a handsome,
robust specimen of early manhood, ambitious and teeming with energy.
The Third Cavalry then had stations along the Union Pacific Railway
from Fort McPherson to Fort Sanders, a line across the trails of the
numerous tribes of the great Sioux nation on the north and the southern
Indians in the Indian Territory and Texas. It was a particularly busy
time for the regiment and the hard work had to be done by small
commands under Lieutenants or Captains and the stations of the troops
amounted to but little more than bases of supplies. Young Reynolds,
always known by his associates as "B", took great pride in being an
officer and was as hardy as a knot. In the garrison, immaculate in his
dress, almost to vanity, and Chesterfieldian in his bearing, he threw
himself into the field work with interest, great energy, and zeal, and
was just as much at home in his rough scouting clothes, with coarse
campfare as the toughest one of us. At the Rosebud, the enemy was
fierce, daring, determined fighters and the brunt of the battle and most
of the losses fell upon four troops of the Third Cavalry, of which four
Reynold's troop was one. Seventeen years afterwards and several after
Reynolds had resigned from the service, he was tendered a brevet for
his gallantry in this battle. He was under fire at the numerous night
attacks in the winter campaign and in the fight at Crazy Horse village,
March 17, 1876; also at the fight on Tongue River, Montana, June 9th
and Slim Buttes, Dakota, September 9, 1876, in all of which he dis-

played the same marked zeal and bravery." *Annual Association of West Point Graduates* (1901).

6. Captain Peter D. Vroom was appointed to the army from New Jersey and served with New Jersey infantry and cavalry during the Civil War. He was brevetted for gallant and meritorious services during that conflict.

"Captain Vroom was then a magnificent speciman of the human race, tall, well built and good looking. He has since grown much stouter, the result, doubtless of the absence of Indian campaigns, which would now seem to be almost at an end." Finerty, *op. cit.* p. 70.

"On March 11, 1868, Apaches raided settlements near Tularosa, N. M. killing and mutilating 11 men and 2 women, capturing one child, running off about 2200 sheep and other stock. Pursued by Troop H 3rd Cav. under Lt. P. D. Vroom. Indians had 3 days start and escaped into Guaddoze Mts. Recovered some of the sheep." "Record of Indian Engagements," *U. S. Cavalry Journal,* (1903 and 1904).

7. Lt. Samuel M. Swigert came from Kentucky and graduated from West Point in the class of 1868.

8. Captain Elijah R. Wells served all through the Civil War and was brevetted for gallant and meritorious services in the battle of Beverly Ford, Va.; and Cedar Creek, Va. "The former (Captain Wells) was a veteran of the Civil War, covered with honorable scars, bluff, stern and heroic. "Finerty, *op. cit.,* p. 46.

9. Lt. Fred W. Kingsbury was born in Ohio and entered the service in June, 1870, having been appointed from the Military Academy of which he was a graduate.

10. Official Report of Captain Henry E. Noyes, 2nd Cavalry.

11. Official Report of Lt. Col. William B. Royall, 3rd Cavalry.

12. Captain Avery B. Cain was appointed 2nd Lieutenant 4th Infantry August 5, 1861, and was promoted 1st Lieutenant the same day. He was promoted Captain October 19, 1863. He was brevetted Captain for gallant and meritorious services at the battle of Chancellorsville, Va., May 3, 1863, and Major for gallant and meritorious services at the battle of North Anna River, Va., May 24, 1864. He served with the regiment during the operations before Yorktown, Va., and participated with it in the battle of Gaine's Mill, Malvern Hill and Bull Run (Second), Va., and Antietam, Md., in 1862; in the battle of Chancellorsville, Va., in 1863 and at Spottsylvania, Va., in 1864. He commanded the regiment in action at the battles of North Anna River and Popotomail Creek, Va.; and in the lines in front of the rebel defences of Petersburg, Va., in 1864. He was present in command of the regiment at Lee's surrender at Appomattox, Va., in 1865. *Army & Navy Journal,* Vol. 16 (April 12, 1879) p. 632.

Captain Cain served as commanding officer at Fort Fetterman, and was an officer of the old school in the strict enforcement of discipline: "In 1873, the 14th Inf. was relieved by the 4th Inf. This change brought my company to Fetterman. During the next five years there were numerous changes of military commanders. Major Alexander Chambers, Col. J. W. Mason, Maj. Powell, Capt. A. B. Cain, Maj. De Ruise and Capt. Edward M. Coates (to whose company I belonged) all following the usual routine of military duty except Capt. Coates . . ." Article of J. O.

Ward, late 1st Sergt., Co. "C" 4th U. S. A. printed in *Annals of Wyoming*, Vol. 4, No. 3, (January, 1927), p. 359.

In General Crook's "Starvation March" in the fall of 1876, Captain Cain betrayed symptoms of an unsound mind and was ordered to remain with the wagon train. He persisted in remaining with the column until the Yellowstone River was reached where his condition was so bad that he was ordered on board a transport boat with other men unfit for field service, and returned to the post. Bourke, *On the Border With Crook*, pp. 345, 361.

Captain Cain died suddenly at Fort Laramie on March 16, 1879, at his station, but he was buried elsewhere. Thus ended the career of a colorful figure who served his country well at the Rosebud.

13. "My usual good fortune attended me but poor Snow rode back to our lines badly shot through both arms near the elbows. (Interlined at top of page) Snow was helplessly crippled, discharged from service with pension to fullest extent allowed by law. He is now, May, 1878, a resident of Athol, Massachusetts." Bourke, *Diary*. Snow was later awarded the Congressional Medal of Honor.

14. Official Report of Captain Frederick Van Vliet of the battle.

15. Excerpt from letter of C. E. Faris.

16. There are several statements to the effect that the battle lasted until dark, but no detailed information has been found as to where such action occurred. In the October, 1924, issue of *Winners of the West* appears a letter from Sergeant Louis Zinzer of Company C, 3rd Cavalry: "The battle raged throughout the day until dark, when the Indians retreated to a nearby ravine. So we camped on the battlefield and took an inventory of our ammunition and found we averaged five rounds apiece. So you will understand that we were in no condition to make a fight. We had 150 rounds to the man to begin with. So you see we were not whipped by any means."

General Sherman in his annual report said, "The fight was on both banks of the Rosebud, and lasted into the night, when the Indians withdrew, leaving thirteen dead warriors." Report of the General of the Army Nov. 10, 1876, pp. 29,30; Report of the Secretary of War, 2d Sess., 44th Cong. Serial 1742. This action must have occurred during pursuit of the retreating Indians.

17. Robert Bebee David, *Finn Burnett, Frontiersman*, p. 340.

18. Oral narrative by Charles Young to writer in August, 1955.

19. "Crazy Horse's Story of Custer Battle," *South Dakota Historical Collections*, Vol. 6, p. 228.

20. *Army & Navy Journal* (July 29, 1876), p. 817.

21. *Ricker Interviews*, Iron Hawk Interview, Tablet 25, p. 131.

22. See note 3, Chapter 5.

23. *Ricker Interviews*, A. G. Shaw Interview, Tablet 11, p. 132.

Chapter 7

1. Mills, Op. Cit., pp. 404-409.

2. This is the only account I have found which belittles the actions of the Crows and Shoshones in the battle. All the others have only praise for them, some going so far as to claim the soldiers would have been

wiped out in the initial onslaught had it not been for the immediate action of the friendly allies.

3. Van Vliet's command did not join Royall's men on the left but went to the crest near Crook' Hill. See official reports of Captain Van Vliet and Major Evans of the battle.

4. Lt. Henry R. Lemly, Adjutant of the Third Cavalry at the time of the Rosebud Battle, was appointed to the Military Academy from North Carolina by his uncle, the Honorable I. G. Lash, Member of Congress, in 1868. He graduated in the class of 1872 and after several years service in the 3rd Cavalry was transferred to the Artillery and commanded a Light Battery in the Porto Rican Campaign in the Spanish-American War. In 1880 he accepted foreign service at Bogota, Columbia, where he became Instructor-General of the Army. In 1892 he was detailed as Military Attache' at Bogota and after retirement travelled all over the world. He was the author of a number of magazine articles and army manuels. He died in Washington, D. C. in 1925 with rank of Major. Lemly was the first of a long line of army and navy officers of that distinguished family which is proud of its tradition of service to our country.

5. Sergeant Van Moll was another soldier in the campaign who came to an unfortunate end.

"A despatch from Hat Creek, Wy. T., Dec. 15, says: At Silver Springs twenty-five miles south of here, a member of Co. A, 3d Cav., one of the three now en route to the hills, named Kennedy, while under the influence of liquor yesterday, threatened the life of a sergeant of his company, named Shaffer, but was prevented at the time from carrying his threat into execution. Shortly after arriving in camp in the evening, Kennedy procured a carbine, went to the tent where he supposed Shaffer would be found, and opening the flap, fired at the first man he saw, killing him instantly; but, instead of Shaffer, it proved to be John A. Van Moll, first sergeant of the Company. Kennedy was immediately disarmed and put under charge of a guard. Great excitement prevailed among the men of the company, by whom Van Moll was greatly respected, and some time during the night the guard was overpowered, and a blanket was thrown over Kennedy's head, and at daylight this morning his body was found suspended to a ridgepole of the guard tent by the neck, life extinct. Van Moll's body was brought here to day, and will be forwarded tomorrow to Fort Laramie for interment. An exchange gives the following sketch of Van Moll: He was born in Massachusetts in 1844. His father was a Belgian and his mother was Irish. He received a fair education, and when little more than fifteen years old, he joined one of the New England regiments as a drummer boy. In 1863 he dropped the drum and took up the rifle distinguishing himself particularly at Gettysburg, where he was promoted to a sergeancy. When Petersburg was taken he was recommended for a commission but the sudden collapse of the war spoiled his chances in that respect. After remaining a short time with his Massachusetts friends he enlisted in the 3d Cav., and was soon advanced to the position of first sergeant of Co. A, which he held at the time of his death. In Crook's Indian campaign of 1876 Van Moll was distinguished for his dashing bravery, and was recommended by some officers for a commission, and his name was on file for a lieutenancy at the War Department. He was a dashing rider, a splendid shot and a thoroughly sober and conscientious non-commissioned officer. In his death the 3d Cav., has sustained a severe loss, for he set an example of heroism and honor to the entire command. On the march, in unison with his staunch friend, Corporal Bessie, he always kept the company enlivened by his sweet singing. This faculty made him a most agreeable bivouac fire comrade." *Army & Navy Journal,* Vol. 15 (Dec. 29, 1877), p. 324.

6. This was the charge made by the Sioux at approximately 10:30. Considering all of the accounts, it seems that during this charge a party of Cheyennes rode down the Rosebud to capture the extra horses of the Shoshones herded by the small boy but were driven off by the fire of Van Vliet's men on the bluff to the south. This incident is not to be confused with the attack by a large band of Indians down the Rosebud and over the campground of that morning whereby Crook's command was entirely encircled after Mills' had gone down the canyon. The two attacks are separate and the first occurred about 10:30 in the morning while the latter must have been near the end of the fight, about 1:00 in the afternoon.

7. The third ridge was the large conical hill to the northwest about 1200 yards distant from Crook's Hill which was occupied by the three infantry companies.

8. Lt. Adolphus H. Von Luettwitz was a Prussian who had served with New York Volunteers during the Civil War.

Finerty first met Von Luettwitz on the railroad station at Sidney, Nebraska, on his way to join the troops: "The platform was crowded with citizens and soldiers, the barracks of the latter being quite close to the town. Nearly all the military wore the yellow facings of the cavalry. I was particularly struck by the appearance of one officer—a first lieutenant and evidently a foreigner. He wore his kepi low on on his forehead, and beneath it, his hooked nose overhung a blonde mustache of generous proportions. His eyes were light blue; his cheeks yellow and rather sunken. He was about middle stature and wore huge dragoon boots. Thick smoke from an enormous pipe rose upon the morning air, and he paced up and down like a caged tiger. I breakfasted at the railroad restaurant, and, as the train was in no hurry to get away, I had a chance to say a few words to the warrior already described.

'Has your regiment got the route for the front yet, Lieutenant,' I inquired.

'Some of it,' he replied in a thick German accent, without removing his pipe. 'Our battalion should have it already, but 'tis always the vay, Got tamn the luck! 'Tis alvays the vay!'

'I guess 'twill be all right in a day or two, lieutenant.' I remarked.

'Vell, may be so, but they're alvays slighting the 3rd Cavalry, at headquarters. Ve ought to have moved a veek ago.'

'I saw General Crook at Omaha, and he said he would be at Fetterman by the 15th.'

'You don't zay so? Then ve got off. Vell, dat is good. Are you in thet army?'

'No; I am going out as correspondent for the Chicago *Times.*'

'Vell, I am so glad to meet you. My name is Von Luettwitz. The train is going. Good-bye. We shall meet again.'" Finerty, Op Cit., p. 30.

With the same ill fortune that seemed to dog the footsteps of so many of the officers at the Rosebud, Von Luettwitz was shot in the right knee joint on the following September 9th at the battle of Slim Buttes, and his leg was amputated at Deadwood City a few days later. He was retired on a pension in 1879. "Almost at the first shot Lieut. A. H. Von Luettwitz, of Troop E, 3d Cavalry, fell with a bullet through his right knee joint. This gentleman had served in the Austrian and Prussian armies, had fought at Montebello, Magenta, Solferino, all through the Italian campaign of '59, had distinguished himself at Gettysburg and other great battles of our war, and had escaped comparatively unscathed. Yet his hour had come, and he fell wounded in a miserable Indian skirmish the very first man." Finerty, Op. Cit., p. 251.

9. It is not known how many statements Crazy Horse made at the Agency but in the light of statements of other Sioux who were in the battle, it is very doubtful if Crazy Horse ever said that he had 6500 in the fight of whom 5000 were concealed behind the bluffs and hills. What he probably said was that he had 6500 Indians in his encampment all together and that 1500 of these were in the battle. The interpreters in those days, and in many cases the Indians themselves, would twist the meaning of words so as to give the desired answers. Stanley Vestal, *Warpath and Council Fire*, pp. 221, 229.

10. This high point is believed to be the high rocky hill just west of the head of Kollmar Creek which Captain Andrews had occupied earlier in the battle. We will probably never know absolutely about this because even if shells were found on this hill, they could have been those used by Captain Andrews' men. There is another high point about a half mile east of Andrews Point, on the crest, which might be the one mentioned by Bourke, but its slope on the west side is not a steep bluff. Horsemen could ride down the slope. Lt. Morton's map shows a ridge southwest of the "high point" standing off by itself and to which the Sioux retreated, and there is such a ridge southwest of Andrews' Point.

11. Grinnell, *The Fighting Cheyennes*, p. 321; Stanley Vestal, *Warpath and Council Fire*, pp. 221, 229. Every person I have talked to who has seen this little valley scouts the idea of it having been a trap. The general impression is that the talk of an ambush was just a "whitewash" for General Crook, to make it appear that he won a victory by not going further.

12. The exact wording of the interview as reported by Charles Diehl, special correspondent of the Chicago *Times* and published in that newspaper on May 27, 1877, on this point, is as follows: "The first attack of the troops was made by Cheyennes, Oglalas, Minneconjous and Sans Arcs, whose combined force was about 1500. Above the point where the attack was made about 8 miles Crazy Horse and Sitting Bull with about 5000 Indians were camped. The attack was made with the idea that when the Indians retreated the troops would then fall into their stronghold. It shows as much generalship to avoid defeat and massacre as to win a battle and in this case just such generalship was shown by General Crook."

13. All technical data relating to firearms and ammunition in the battle have been furnished by Philip Jay Medicus, 18 Fletcher Street, New York 7, New York, a recognized authority on the subject. All shells and bullets found on the field and referred to herein have been examined by Mr. Medicus who has furnished written opinions on them.

Chapter 8

1. Not much is known about Lt. William L. Carpenter except that he served in the Civil War and was appointed a commissioned officer from the ranks.

2. Lt. Edgar Brooks Robertson was from Massachusetts and graduated from the Military Academy in the class of 1874. For twelve years after his graduation he served on frontier duty at various stations in the Northwest. He died August 1, 1924, at San Francisco, California, at the age of 71 years, after a long and successful career in the Army.

3. Grinnell, *The Fighting Cheyennes*, p. 321.

4. Not much is known about Lt. Henry Seton except that he was appointed to the army from New York.

5. Lt. Thaddeus H. Capron served with the 55th Illinois Volunteers during the Civil War and was appointed an officer from Illinois. During the Rosebud campaign Lt. Capron kept a Diary and wrote back letters to his wife, Cynthia J. Capron. Extracts from the Diary and letters were published in the January, 1921, issue of the *Journal of the Illinois State Historical Society*, at page 476. The article is interesting reading but does not contribute anything towards our knowledge of the campaign.

6. Lt. Charles Morton was from Missouri and served with infantry during the Civil War, starting in as a private. He graduated from the Military Academy in the class of 1869. He enjoyed a long and successful career in the army and finally attained the rank of a general. He died December 20, 1914, at Washington, D. C., at the age of 69.

7. Schmitt, *General George Crook: His Autobiography*, p. 194.

8. Joe DeBarthe, *Life and Adventures of Frank Gruard*, p. 125 (Reprint Edition).

9. This is undoubtedly another description of the wounding of Trumpeter Elmer A. Snow as seen by Frank Gruard at or near Crook's Hill. The only other soldier suffering similar injuries was Sergeant Andrew Grosch of Company I, Third Cavalry, who received "very severe gunshot left arm and chest. Both arms fractured." This could not have been the man referred to by Gruard as he was in Captain Andrews' company away off on the left flank.

10. Probably Captain Andrew S. Burt, Company H, 9th Infantry.

11. Crook had become acquainted with Nickerson right after the Civil War when both were on shipboard on the way to west coast assignments. Becoming attached to the younger man, the General arranged his transfer to his command. They served together through the Indian wars in Oregon and Arizona.

12. Henry W. Daly, *American Legion Magazine*, (April, 1927).

Chapter 9

1. Lt. William W. Robinson, Jr., was from Wisconsin and graduated from the Military Academy in the class of 1869. He was transferred to the Seventh Cavalry June 26, 1876, shortly after the battle. He was in Captain Henry's company but did not serve with the company during the battle.

2. Lt. Albert D. King served as a private in the Second California Cavalry during the Civil War and was appointed from California.

3. "Captain Nickerson of General Crook's staff brought, attended with great personal danger (as the Indians seemed to divine his mission) orders for Col. Royall to retire or connect his line with General Crook's. This was affected instead of by a forward movement, by a sort of left about wheel, or retreat . . .

"Royall by maintaining successive lines of retreat, aided by the great gallantry of his men and officers, succeeded, with loss, in joining Crook's command. This loss was diminished by the charge made by our allies and two infantry companies from Crook's left upon the advancing Sioux. This charge should have been made when we first commenced our retreat movement." Unknown correspondent for the *Army and Navy Journal* (July 22, 1876), p. 801.

4. There are many conflicting accounts of how Vroom's company became surrounded. Several of these claim that the Indians, in order to deceive the soldiers, wore strips of cloth in imitation of the Crows and Shoshones, who wore a similar adornment so as to be distinguishable from the enemy, and that Vroom's men followed some of the Indians too far in the belief that they were allies. The quoted portion of the report of Colonel Royall is believed to contain the true reason why Vroom's men were separated from the rest of the command. They were sent to line the crest for the protection of the rest of the command in their passage over the defile.

5. Lewis F. Crawford, *Rekindling Campfires,* p. 256.

6. A Foragers charge is made in pairs of men, and it is usually *en melee,* and the pistol is used. The interval between men in charging platoon or company front in a cavalry charge was 9 feet from the horse's nose to horse's nose. The distance between platoons or companies in charging was about 60 feet, but a lot depended upon the kind of ground being charged over.

7. Lt. Emmet Crawford was appointed to the army from Pennsylvania. He served with Pennsylvania troops during the Civil War and was brevetted for "meritorious conduct" during that conflict. "He was over six feet high, with a genuine military face, and a spare but athletic form." Finerty, *Op. Cit.* p. 75.

He had had some experience fighting Indians before. "Nov. 20, 1875, a detachment of Troop G. 3rd Cav. under Lt. E. Crawford had a fight with Indians near Antelope Station, Nebraska." "Record of Indian Engagements," *U. S. Cavalry Journal* (1903-1904).

" 'Crawford was born 1000 years too late,' says Lt. Davis, 'Sans peur et sans reproche' would have been sung of him in ballads of the Middle Ages. Mentally, morally, and physically, he would have been an ideal knight of King Arthur's Court. Six feet one, gray eyed, untiring, he was an ideal cavalryman and devoted to his troop, as were the men of it to him.' " *Winners of the West* (May, 1940). Crawford was highly idealistic and never married.

In the latter part of 1885 Crawford was given command of a band of troops and Indian scouts for the purpose of pursuing Geronimo into Old Mexico and catching him. On January 11, 1886, his command was attacked by some Mexican Irregular troops who were also after Geronimo. In an attempt to explain that his men were American and were in pursuit of Geronimo also, he stood up on a high rock in sight of both forces, waving a white flag. But there came a shot which hit Crawford in the head and he died January 17th without regaining consciousness. He at least lived longer than many of the other officers who served their country in the Rosebud campaign.

8. C. T. Brady, *Indian Fights and Fighters*, p. 204.

9. T. B. MacMillan, *Chicago Inter-Ocean* (June 24, 1876).

Chapter 10

1. This action might have been the charge of the Snakes.

2. Chief Red Cloud was the head of the Red Cloud Agency and was at peace with the white man during this period. The government had previously given him a Winchester rifle with his name engraved on it, in token of its friendship. His son, young Jack Red Cloud, carried the rifle in the Rosebud battle where it was captured by the Crow scouts.

3. The fight with Royall's men could have been that referred to here.

4. This monument commemorating the Battle of the Rosebud was erected and dedicated largely through the efforts of Mrs. R. C. Dillavou of Billings, Montana, who was State Regent, National Society Daughters of American Revolution at that time. Her son George and her daughter, Harriet Louise, unveiled the marker on the anniversary of the battle, June 17, 1934.

5. For many years it was believed that Crook came from the south over the Decker-Busby road which runs by the east bend, and then marched westward along the Creek. This was incorrect and may have been caused by the fact that after the action commenced many of the soldiers were marching westward to take their place in the line.

6. The writer undoubtedly meant that the soldiers were scattered from the big bend to the site of their camp the night before to the southwest near the divide. By "Sioux Pass" he evidently refers to the divide near the camp of the night before. Sioux Pass, as known at the present day, is about three miles north and six miles west of the field.

Chapter 11

1. John F. Finerty, *op. cit.* p. 137.

2. *Ibid.*, p. 200.

3. Bourke, *On the Border With Crook*, p. 345.

4. W. F. Beyer and O. F. Keydal, *Deeds of Valor*, Vol. 2, p. 210.

5. *Ibid.*

Chapter 12

1. Report of the General of the Army, Nov. 10, 1876, pp. 29-30. *Report of Secretary of War*, 2d Sess., 44th Cong. Serial 1742.

2. Report Nov. 10, 1876, p. 442. *Report of Secretary of War*, 2d Sess., 44th Cong. Serial 1742.

3. *Army & Navy Journal*, (Sept. 16, 1876), p. 86.

4. *Army & Navy Journal*, (December 23, 1876), p. 315.

5. Hebard, *op. cit.*, p. 203.

6. Mills, *op. cit.*, p. 410.

7. *Army & Navy Journal*, (Sept. 8, 1883), p. 106.

Appendix A

NAMES OF TROOPS IN THE CAMPAIGN

The names of troops who were in the Rosebud battle are taken from the Muster Rolls which were filed on June 30, 1876, by the various Companies. The officers and men who belonged to these organizations but who for various reasons were not in the campaign are omitted. Many of these were on detached service, in the hospital, or in confinement; some had deserted. The five infantry companies were stationed at Camp North Side, Fort Fetterman, at the date of the muster rolls.

COMPANY C NINTH INFANTRY

Samuel Munson, Captain
Thaddeus H. Capron, 1st Lieutenant
James Whelan, 1st Sergeant
Stephen Malloy, Sergeant
William W. Butler, Sergeant
Jesse N. Farmer, Sergeant
Andrew J. O'Leary, Sergeant
Marshall Crocker, Corporal
Andrew Murphy, Corporal
George Kressig, Corporal
William S. Parsons, Corporal
Frank Clarke, Bugler
William H. Smith, Artificer
Sylvester Blanwell, Private
Howard Boyer, Private
Edward Burns, Private
James W. Butler, Private
William B. Colcroft, Private
Harley Crittenden, Private
Michael Deegan, Private
Christopher Dillon, Private
Edward Donnelly, Private
Michael Dougherty, Private
John C. Eisenberg, Private

Charles Edwards, Private
Barney Flanagan, Private
Samuel Gibson, Private
Thomas W. Granberry, Private
Frank I' ill, Private
Frederick Hanshammer, Private
Julius Hoppi, Private
Solomon Herschberg, Private
Thomas Hughes, Private
Samuel Hunt, Private
Samuel Jacob, Private
Andrew Johnson, Private
Daniel Mahoney, Private
George W. McAnnulty, Private
Hugh McLean, Private
Ernest Melin, Private
Henry Mell, Private
Oliver Navarre, Private
Charles A. Nichols, Private
Calvin Rainsome, Private
Walter C. Smith, Private
Ole Tothamer, Private
Luther B. Wolfe, Private
Albert Zimmerman, Private

Total officers and men in campaign was 48. This report stated that there were no casualties in this Company. Seven privates had been left at Fort Laramie, where they had been on detached service since May 22, 1876. Second Lieutenant Hayden DeLaney was on detached service at Camp Sheridan.

COMPANY G NINTH INFANTRY

Thomas B. Burrowes, Captain
William L. Carpenter, 1st Lieutenant
John C. Rafferty, 1st Sergeant

Frances Doyle, Sergeant
Frederick Klein, Sergeant
Frank McCarthy, Sergeant

199

James Delaney, Corporal
Timothy O'Sullivan, Corporal
Rudolph Ormann, Corporal
Joseph S. Wrisley, Corporal
William Doody, Trumpeter
Hugh Thomson, Trumpeter
Joseph Holtz, Artificer
John Anderson, Private
Richard L. Case, Private
Edward Conlin, Private
Patrick Dwyer, Private
William Ecrestain, Private
William Faulman, Private
James Gaskill, Private
William E. Glick, Private

William R. Hardin, Private
Michael Healey, Private
August Hocksmith, Private
Frederick Lafine, Private
Gineral A. Lee, Private
Alexander M. Lowrie, Private
Michael Murphy, Private
John G. Newman, Private
John Norton, Private
Samuel Smith, Private
John Thomas, Private
Charles W. Wilson, Private
Samuel H. Woollen, Private
Samuel C. Wynkoop, Private
Rudolph Zysset, Private

Total officers and men in the campaign was 36. Second Lieutenant Walter S. Wyatt was on detached duty at U. S. Military Academy. The report stated that there were no casualties in the Company. Two Privates were on detached service.

COMPANY H NINTH INFANTRY

Andrew S. Burt, Captain
Edgar B. Robertson, 2nd Lieutenant
August Lange, 1st Sergeant
Henry Stoll, Sergeant
Charles F. Hiller, Sergeant
Danford R. Langley, Sergeant
John Smith, Sergeant
John McFarlane, Corporal
Sylvester Poole, Corporal
Bernhard Blomer, Trumpeter
Julius Permell, Trumpeter
Louis Allison, Private
John H. Atwood, Private
Joseph S. Bennett, Private
Charles Beyschlag, Private
Samuel B. Brown, Private
George Coy, Private
David N. Eshelman, Private

Henry Robert Fritz, Private
Thaddeus N. Hendricksen, Private
George E. Leggatt, Private
John McCann, Private
John McCormick, Private
James Morgan, Private
William Nobles, Private
Richard O'Hearn, Private
Daniel P. Reddy, Private
Charles Riesch, Private
John Seery, Private
Aaron Smith, Private
John Stephenson, Private
Warren Taylor, Private
John Walsh, Private
Richard Walsh, Private
James Waters, Private
Peter Winegardner, Private

Total officers and men in campaign was 36. This report stated that there were no casualties in the Company. Five privates had been left at Fort Laramie, where they were on detached service. 1st Lieutenant William E. Hofman was on detached service. In his report Captain Burt stated that Company H was "ordered with Company G to occupy a hill and 'stop those Indians'." It seems clear from this that the two companies occupied only one hill and did not occupy the one several hundred yards south of it.

COMPANY F FOURTH INFANTRY

Gerhard L. Luhn, Captain
John D. O'Brien, 1st Sergeant
George Russell, Sergeant

William Miller, Sergeant
John H. Neiss, Sergeant
Ludwig Roper, Corporal

George Wood, Corporal
John C. Cain, Corporal
Lucius E. Stearns, Corporal
Peter Cassidy, Musician
Jay E. Brandow, Artificer
Oscar Baker, Private
John Baptiste, Private
Oliver F. Bowden, Private
Edward Buird, Private
Michael Cunningham, Private
Robert Dickson, Private
James Ferguson, Private
William Frisby, Private
John Galliger, Private
William Green, Private
August Gunker, Private
John Healey, Private

William E. Helvie, Private
William Johnston, Private
William Kent, Private
Christopher Larsen, Private
Patrick Lonangan, Private
David Mesirola, Private
John McCarty, Private
Patrick McEnery, Private
Richard C. Sullivan, Private
George Richberg, Private
Oscar Sloan, Private
William Stillwell, Private
William Swain, Private
Jacob Schumaker, Private
Frederick Tostika, Private
Joseph Turner, Private
William E. Wolfe, Private

Total officers and men in campaign was 40. The report stated that George W. Gibbs, Thomas Malford, and James Malford, Privates, deserted on June 28th, but were apparently in the campaign. There were no casualties in the Company. 1st Lieutenant David P. Ezekiel was on leave and not in the campaign. Sergeant Thomas Doolan had been on detached service at Fort Fetterman since May 27th, and Private George Bloomingdale was left behind at Fort Fetterman because of sickness.

COMPANY D FOURTH INFANTRY

Avery B. Cain, Captain
Henry Seton, 1st Lieutenant
Reichert Z. Dexter, 1st Sergeant
Bernard Degnan, Sergeant
Joseph Lister, Sergeant
Smith Chittenden, Sergeant
Alfred F. Funk, Corporal
John F. Cochrane, Sergeant
Thomas Conley, Corporal
Alfred Smith, Trumpeter
James Connelly, Trumpeter
Charles McMahon, Artificer
John Benazet, Private
Charles R. Bill, Private
John H. Bishop, Private
George W. Bowley, Private
Carl Dahlman, Private
Peter Decker, Private
James Devine, Private
James Devlin, Private
David F. Dowling, Private

John Edwards, Private
Louis Eiskamp, Private
Richard Flynn, Private
Phillip George, Private
Richard Haney, Private
Irving Heaslip, Private
Patrick Higerty, Private
John Hall, Private
Leon Lawrence, Private
Gilbert Long, Private
Thomas Maher, Private
Daniel McCormick, Private
Ezekial Morgan, Private
William Perry, Private
Lawrence Schneiderhan, Private
Joshua Scott, Private
Charles Stollnow, Private
John H. Terry, Private
Albert Wagner, Private
Edward Williams, Private

Total officers and men in campaign was 41. This report, which stated that Privates James Devine, Richard Flynn, and John H. Terry were wounded in the battle, checks with General Crook's Report. Sergeant Frank Smyth and two Privates had been on detached service at Fort Steele since May 13, 1876.

COMPANY A THIRD CAVALRY

Joseph Lawson, 1st Lieutenant
Charles Morton, 2nd Lieutenant
John W. Van Moll, 1st Sergeant
Henry Shafer, Sergeant
Gottlieb Bigalsky, Sergeant
Frederick Stanley, Sergeant
William J. Armstrong, Sergeant
Charles Anderson, Sergeant
John Patton, Corporal
Charles A. Bessey, Corporal
William H. Finch, Corporal
Walter Wells, Trumpeter
George Hammer, Trumpeter
Karl Dreher, Saddler
Michael Conway, Blacksmith
James Allen, Private
John Anderson, Private
Maurice Breshnahan, Private
Frederick Bartlett, Private
William Babcock, Private
Conrad Baker, Private
Robert Blackwood, Private
Joseph Boyle, Private
John Bigley, Private
John Cook, Private
John Downey, Private
William Davis, Private
Michael Fitzgerald, Private
William Featherall, Private

Edwin M. Griffin, Private
Thomas Gynau, Private
James Golden, Private
Charles Gordon, Private
Lawrence L. Grazierni, Private
Maurice Hastings, Private
Robert Harry Heinz, Private
Lawrence Kennedy, Private
Herman J. Kaider, Private
Charles Kolaugh, Private
John A. Lowder, Private
Henry Leonard, Private
John Lynch, Private
John McCann, Private
Florence Neiderst, Private
Samuel Peterson, Private
John Reilly, Private
James L. Roberts, Private
Henry Rompton, Private
Albert Simons, Private
Alfred S. Southon, Private
James E. Snepp, Private
James Taggart, Private
Ernest Therion, Private
William H. Vince, Private
John Wenzel, Private
George White, Private
James Wood, Private

Total officers and men in campaign was 57. Captain William Hawley had been sick at Fort D. A. Russell since May 18. Five privates were not in the campaign for various reasons. The Company left Fort D. A. Russell with 2 officers and 53 enlisted men, and seems to have acquired two men along the way, because the total in the muster roll was 2 officers and 55 men. No casualties are reported. The cavalry companies were all stationed at Camp Cloud Peak on June 30th, the date of the muster roll.

COMPANY B THIRD CAVALRY

Charles Meinhold, Captain
James F. Simpson, 2nd Lieutenant
Charles Witzemann, 1st Sergeant
Robert Stewart, Sergeant
John Moriarity, Sergeant
Maurice Connell, Sergeant
James A. Boggs, Sergeant
Charles S. Abbott, Sergeant
John Tighe, Corporal
Thomas M. Clarke, Corporal
Joseph Kirby, Corporal
George G. Criswell, Corporal

Hugh Carton, Trumpeter
Robert Roulston, Farrier
Henry N. Tucker, Saddler
James A. Chaffee, Blacksmith
William E. Anthon, Private
James E. Anderson, Private
Charles R. Appleton, Private
Conrad Allbright, Private
George Allen, Private
William Brindley, Private
Edward Bushlepp, Private
John W. Barrow, Private

William E. Baldwin, Private
Joseph Bennett, Private
Hugh Curry, Private
James Cleveland, Private
John Davis, Private
Michael J. Fitzpatrick, Private
Thomas Flood, Private
Charles Foster, Private
James Calvin, Private
Joseph Gallagher, Private
John W. Hobbs, Private
Francois Jourdain, Private
John Kramer, Private
William B. Lewis, Private
Reginald A. Loomis, Private
John Longrigg, Private
William Lee, Private
Andrew Lee, Private
Julius Murray, Private
Hugh McConnell, Private
Franklin A. Maricle, Private

Martin M. Moore, Private
Francis Mayer, Private
William Pattison, Private
Henry L. Quinn, Private
John Ritchie, Private
Robert Rice, Private
Frank Smith, Private
John H. Smith, Private
George Stickney, Private
Thomas Slater, Private
James Sweeney, Private
Thomas D. Sanford, Private
Henry Steiner, Private
David A. Tilson, Private
John H. Thorison, Private
William Walton, Private
Edwin D. Wood, Private
Francis A. Wilbur, Private
William Wilson, Private
Frederick Winters, Private

Total officers and men in campaign was 65. Lieutenant John P. Walker was absent under suspension for two years. This report stated that 64 enlisted men left Fort McPherson, Nebraska, for the campaign. Casualties in this Company were Private Henry Steiner wounded and one horse killed. Two privates were on detached service and not in the campaign.

COMPANY C THIRD CAVALRY

Frederick Van Vliet, Captain
William Riley, 1st Sergeant
John J. Mitchell, Sergeant
Joseph Manly, Sergeant
John Welsh, Sergeant
Otto Ahrens, Sergeant
Hermann Guenther, Sergeant
Michael F. Lanigan, Corporal
William Stewart, Corporal
Joseph N. Hobsen, Corporal
Eugene Bessiers, Corporal
Alfred Helmbold, Trumpeter
George Steele, Trumpeter
William Johnson, Farrier
John Mathews, Saddler
Heinrich Glucing, Blacksmith
Henry Wellwood, Waggoner
James Allen, Private
Henry Bartley, Private
George W. Bickford, Private
Henry Burmeister, Private
William B. Dubois, Private
Wentelin Ehrig, Private

Perry A. Elden, Private
Walter Gau, Private
John N. Green, Private
William Hart, Private
William Herd, Private
Henry Johnson, Private
John D. Leak, Private
Fred Lehman, Private
Arthur Leroy, Private
William Larkingland, Private
George P. Lowry, Private
William P. McCandless, Private
William J. McClinton, Private
William McDonald, Private
John Miller, Private
James Mulney, Private
James Nolan, Private
Fred Paul, Private
James Perkins, Private
Frank Quado, Private
John Reed, Private
John W. Reppert, Private
Francis Rodgers, Private

Louis Sachs, Private
George E. Sanderson, Private
John H. Sherman, Private
David O. Sloan, Private
John A. Smith, Private
Harry Snowdon, Private

Andrew Tierney, Private
William M. Walcott, Private
Arnold Weber, Private
Henry Weyworth, Private
George Williams, Private
Louis Zinzer, Private

Total officers and men in campaign was 59. Lieutenant James Allen was on detached service. The report showed no casualties in the Company and four privates not with the command for different causes.

COMPANY D THIRD CAVALRY

Guy, V. Henry, Captain
John G. Bourke, 2nd Lieutenant
Joseph Robinson, 1st Sergeant
Patrick Flood, Sergeant
John Knox, Sergeant
John D. Lindsay, Sergeant
Richard J. McKee, Sergeant
Charles Taylor, Sergeant
William Blair, Corporal
John McDonald, Corporal
William Ferguson, Corporal
John F. Sanders, Corporal
Frank Ropetsky, Trumpeter
John Robinson, Farrier
George W. Hutchinson, Blacksmith
Sidney F. Bates, Private
Michael Bolton, Private
James Caraley, Private
Frank Cunningham, Private
Frank DeHaven, Private
John Delmont, Private
John F. Doherty, Private
August Dorn, Private

Charles Dougherty, Private
John W. Elder, Private
Robert Flint, Private
Eugene Jones, Private
John Kearney, Private
James Kelly, Private
Jacob Knittell, Private
James Loun, Private
John Miller, Private
John McDonald, Private
John Phillips, Private
Charles H. Pulli, Private
Alfred Rowcliffe, Private
Thomas Riley, Private
Francis Stahl, Private
George Steine, Private
John Stevens, Private
Dennis Sullivan, Private
Charles Ward, Private
Jacob R. Webb, Private
Frederick Weber, Private
J. Franklin Webster, Private
Henry Wielenburg, Private

Total officers and men in campaign was 46. Lt. William W. Robinson, Jr., was reported as "Dropped. Relieved from duty with company on May 13th." It would seem that he served through the campaign with this company as General Crook in his General Order No. 1 assigned him to it.

Six privates are listed as on detached duty or sick at Fort D. A. Russell. The only casualty listed in the battle was Captain Guy V. Henry; but seven men are listed as deserting, and two more discharged for disability, before the campaign started. The seven deserters listed for the two months period seems rather high. Since this company was heavily engaged under Colonel Royall, one wonders if the seven men listed as deserters and the two discharged for disability could have been additional casualties in the fight. Perhaps four of them were the "mortally wounded."

COMPANY E THIRD CAVALRY

Alexander Sutorius, Captain
Henry R. Lemly, 2nd Lieutenant
  Attached

A. H. Von Luettwitz, 1st Lieutenant
Jeremiah Foley, 1st Sergeant
Edward Glass, Sergeant

Frank P. Secrist, Sergeant
Morgan B. Hawks, Sergeant
Joseph Nemour, Sergeant
William Miller, Corporal
Edwin F. Ambrose, Corporal
Charles N. E. Williams, Corporal
Evan S. Worthy, Trumpeter
George Hoffstetter, Trumpeter
Samuel Stanley, Farrier
George Hanernas, Blacksmith
Peter Jansen, Saddler
Christopher Ayers, Private
Daniel Akley, Private
John Beatts, Private
Henry Burton, Private
Michael Brannon, Private
Joseph Budka, Private
James Conway, Private
William H. Clark, Private
Andrew Dolfer, Private
Patrick J. Dowling, Private
Richard Dillon, Private
Malachi Dillon, Private
Orlando H. Duren, Private
Charles F. Eichweitzel, Private
John Foley, Private
Thomas Ferguson, Private
Lewis S. Grigsby, Private
Michael Glannon, Private
Patrick Hennessey, Private

Henry Herald, Private
Marcus Hansen, Private
William G. Hill, Private
Peter Hollen, Private
Patrick Kelly, Private
Bernard Kelly, Private
Thomas Lloyd, Private
Edward Lavelle, Private
Allen Lupton, Private
William C. C. Lewis, Private
John Langan, Private
Thomas McNamara, Private
James Montgomery, Private
Edward McKiernan, Private
Marcus Magerlein, Private
Thomas Nolan, Private
Joseph Peterson, Private
Henry Perkins, Private
William Pease, Private
James Quinn, Private
Alexander Reardon, Private (in hospital at Camp Cloud Peak since June 7th.)
William Rice, Private
Daniel C. Ross, Private
William Schubert, Private
Patrick Scully, Private
Alexander Shire, Private
Daniel Timmey, Private

Total officers and men in campaign was 62. Lieutenant George E. Ford was absent on sick leave. There were three deserters reported, and four privates were absent on account of sickness or detached duty. The sole casualty reported was Private Herald wounded. In the skirmish at Prairie Dog Creek one horse of this company was reported wounded in the back near the rump, while at the Rosebud one horse was wounded in the right fore leg and another in the left hind leg. In the cavalry there was a strong bond of friendship between the troopers and their horses, and whenever a horse was wounded it was as if the rider had lost a close friend.

COMPANY F THIRD CAVALRY

Bainbridge Reynolds, 2nd Lieutenant
Michael A. McGann, 1st Sergeant
Thomas Hackett, Sergeant
John C. A. Warfield, Sergeant
Robert Emmet, Sergeant
Frank Rugg, Sergeant
John Gross, Sergeant
Dennis Giles, Corporal
John Kohn, Corporal
John Fry, Corporal
Arthur N. Chamberlin, Trumpeter

Richard O'Grady, Farrier
Averius S. Varney, Blacksmith
Jeremiah Murphy, Saddler
Spencer Bates, Private
Otto Brodersen, Private
Henry Carson, Private
William Chambers, Private
Thomas Cramer, Private
Charles Dennis, Private
Michael T. Donahue, Private
Peter Dyke, Private

Frank W. Estabrook, Private
William Featherly, Private
Edward Glasheen, Private
John Hecker, Private
Frederick Hershler, Private
Julius Jansen, Private
John W. Jordan, Private
Henry Kett, Private
John Lannen, Private
David Lindsay, Private
Robert Livingston, Private
Richard Lynch, Private
Oliver Meserby, Private
John Meyer, Private
James Moran, Private

William Mulroy, Private
John Murphy, Private
Michael McGraine, Private
Alexander Noterman, Private
Gerold J. O'Grady, Private
Michael O'Hearne, Private
Ferdinand Rutten, Private
Albert Salice, Private
John Semple, Private
John Staley, Private
John Tischer, Private
Phineas Towne, Private
Charles R. West, Private
Francis Woltering, Private

Total officers and men in campaign was 51. Captain Alexander Moore was under arrest at Fort D. A. Russell, as he was believed to have been partly responsible for the fiasco at Crazy Horse Village on March 17, 1876. Lieutenant A. D. Bache Smead was on extended leave, and Lieutenant Bainbridge Reynolds was in command of the company. Four privates were reported sick or detached. During this two month period ten men had deserted from the company of whom five had been apprehended and fined. These five are included above as they were in the campaign. Sergeant David Marshall and Private Gilbert Roe were reported killed; and Privates Brodersen, Featherly and Towne were reported wounded in the Rosebud battle. This is in accord with General Crook's report on casualties.

COMPANY G THIRD CAVALRY

Emmet Crawford, 1st Lieutenant
William Cambell, 1st Sergeant
Fritz W. Henry, Sergeant
Hugo Deprizin, Sergeant
William Conklin, Sergeant
William Mason, Sergeant
Jacob Bender, Corporal
Allen J. Rosenberry, Corporal
Fred Gahlsdorf, Corporal
Joseph Billow, Trumpeter
Robert McMurray, Trumpeter
Patrick Tooel, Farrier
Charles P. Hansen, Blacksmith
Charles F. Smith, Saddler
Frank McConnell, Wagoner
Hubert Beohnke, Private
James H. Bell, Private
Edward M. Courtney, Private
John B. Comber, Private
Patrick Delmage, Private
George M. Edgar, Private
Frederick P. English, Private
Byron D. Ferguson, Private

Frederick W. S. Fonss, Private
Patrick Freeman, Private
Henry Feister, Private
Thomas Glanon, Private
James Gandley, Private
John Hale, Private
Alonzo Hogland, Private
Edwin Hamilton, Private
Jacob Hekel, Private
Thomas Kirby, Private
Adolph Kalber, Private
Edward C. Leitelt, Private
William Moore, Private
John Martin, Private
James McChesney, Private
Edward McCloskey, Private
John McClain, Private
John Miner, Private
Gotthilf Osterday, Private
Henry Olsson, Private
Thomas Phelan, Private
Thomas Quinn, Private
Fred Ray, Private

Charles W. Ruffle, Private
James E. Rose, Private
Henry Schmidt, Private
John Smith, Private
William Smith, Private

George Spreight, Private
Peter Schweikart, Privtae
William Taylor, Private
John A. Taylor, Private
James Welsh, Private

Total number of officers and men in campaign was 56. Captain Dean Monahan was absent on detached service as was Lieutenant Edgar Z. Steever. Eight men were on detached service and one desertion was reported. There is nothing to indicate casualties in the battle.

COMPANY I THIRD CAVALRY

William H. Andrews, Captain
Albert D. King, 1st Lieutenant
J. E. H. Foster, 2nd Lieutenant
John Henry, 1st Sergeant
John Sullivan, Sergeant
Peter Foster, Sergeant
George W. Lowry, Sergeant
Andrew Grosh, Sergeant
John I. Byrons, Corporal
William H. West, Corporal
Frederick Ashwall, Corporal
Tobias Carty, Corporal
Michael O'Reilley, Farrier
Dick C. Kingston, Blacksmith
Frank S. Connells, Saddler
Henry Blake, Private
George H. Bowers, Private
Peter Butler, Private
John Carroll, Private
John Conley, Private
Edward Flood, Jr., Private
Frank W. Hitchcock, Private
Benjamin Heald, Private
Charles H. Hines, Private
George Holledered, Private

John Hubert, Private
James M. Hurt, Private
Anselm Langman, Private
William Leary, Private
John Losciborski, Private
Frank Maginn, Private
James Martin, Private
Michael McMahon, Private
Robert Neal, Private
James O'Brien, Private
Robert F. Pratt, Private
William Ray, Private
James Reilley, Private
Robert Roberts, Private
Patrick Ryan, Private
Lewis C. Singleton, Private
William Schubert, Private
Daniel Shields, Private
Francis Smith, Private
John Smith 2nd, Private
Fritz Strickert, Private
Charles W. Stuart, Private
Herbert W. Weaver, Private
Thomas Welch, Private
Louis Wilmer, Private

Total officers and men in campaign was 50. Five privates were absent on account of sickness or detached service. Privates William W. Allen and Eugene Flynn were reported killed, and eight men were reported wounded, two only slightly. The six mentioned as wounded were Sergeant Andrew Grosh, and privates John Losciborski, James O'Brien, James Reilley, Francis Smith, and Charles W. Stuart. Eight horses were reported wounded.

COMPANY L THIRD CAVALRY

Peter D. Vroom, Captain
George F. Chase, 2nd Lieutenant
Joseph Howe, 1st Sergeant
Roswell E. Patterson, Sergeant
Samuel Cook, Sergeant
Fuller H. Chepperson, Sergeant
Eugene M. Prince, Corporal
Edward Walker, Corporal

David H. Connell, Corporal
Otto Tigerstraim, Corporal
William H. Edwards, Trumpeter
Marcellus Goddard, Trumpeter
Charles Webster, Blacksmith
George B. Oaks, Farrier
Charles L. Fisk, Saddler
Henry J. Bowler, Private

John Creme, Private
John Clements, Private
Richard Callahan, Private
Michael Cassidy, Private
Christopher Camp, Private
William Griffith, Private
Harrison Hiricer, Private
Thomas Hill, Private
Daniel Harrigan, Private
John Hanrahan, Private
John Kremer, Private
Theodore Lowe, Private
George H. McDonald, Private
Fred Mayer, Private
William Miller, Private
Charles Miller, Private
Thomas F. Maxwell, Private

James O'Donnell, Private
Louis Phister, Private
James L. Parks, Private
George Ray, Private
Claud Schmidt, Private
Michel Sullivan, Private
Antony Schenkberg, Private
John T. Smith, Private
George A. Serila, Private
George Sproul, Private
James F. Todd, Private
Thomas Walker, Private
William M. Ward, Private
Richard H. White, Private
Rudolph Winn, Private
Azabel R. Van Seer, Private
Alexander Yates, Private

Total officers and men in the campaign was 50. One sergeant and four privates were absent on account of sickness or detached service. Sergeant Anton Newkirken and privates Richard Bennett, George Potts, Brooks Connors, and Allen J. Mitchell were reported killed in the battle. Sergeant Samuel Cook, Trumpeter William H. Edwards, and Private John Kremer were reported wounded. This accords with the official report of casualties of the battle.

COMPANY M THIRD CAVALRY

Anson Mills, Captain
Augustus C. Paul, 1st Lieutenant
Fred Schwatka, 2nd Lieutenant
Frank Rittel, 1st Sergeant
Charles Kaminski, Sergeant
Frank V. Erhard, Sergeant
Franklin B. Robinson, Sergeant
Alexander B. Ballard, Sergeant
John A. Kirkwood, Corporal
Gilbert Exford, Corporal
Mathew Grappenstetter, Corporal
Peter L. Hogebroom, Corporal
Elmer A. Snow, Trumpeter
Frank Serfas, Trumpeter
Albert Glaurniski, Blacksmith
Charles H. Lindenberg, Saddler
Myron P. Boyer, Private
John H. Bryce, Private
Henry Badgery, Private
Bernard F. Cullen, Private
Carlos L. Chamberlin, Private
Henry E. Curley, Private
Dave S. Drake, Private
Dennis B. Duggan, Private
Bernard Deringer, Private
John E. Douglass, Private
George Foster, Private

John A. Foster, Private
Isaac J. Kelton, Private
Dennis W. Larkin, Private
Hugh H. Massey, Private
Patrick I. Maguire, Private
Timothy McCarthy, Private
Jeremiah Murphy, Private
Albert Morganthaler, Private
William McGinness, Private
Joseph W. Morgan, Private
James B. Miller, Private
Thomas I. O'Keefe, Private
Adam Pringle, Private
William H. Reynolds, Private
George Raab, Private
Dave C. Renear, Private
Fred Schuttle, Private
Blaseus Schmalz, Private
Joseph Schmitz, Private
James Shanley, Private
Robert Smith, Private
John W. Singer, Private
John I. Stevenson, Private
John Sweeney, Private
Charles E. Trevick, Private
Soren O. Very, Private
Joseph Walzer, Private

Total officers and men in campaign was 54. Trumpeter Elmer A. Snow was reported wounded but no other casualties were mentioned. There had been ten deserters during the two months period covered by the report.

COMPANY A SECOND CAVALRY

Thomas B. Dewees, Captain
D. C. Pearson, 2nd Lieutenant
Gregory P. Harrington, 1st Sergeant
William H. Butterworth, Sergeant
Charles A. Maude, Sergeant
Alexander Albrecht, Sergeant
John A. Carr, Sergeant
James Ellis, Sergeant
Charles Wintermute, Corporal
Antonio Brogerri, Corporal
Charles Angus, Corporal
John Naaf, Corporal
John W. Vincent, Trumpeter
William F. Somers, Trumpeter
John A. Bott, Farrier
Bernard Schnable, Blacksmith
Frederick France, Saddler
Charles Austin, Private
James Branagan, Private
Henry C. Campbell, Private
Marvin Collins, Private
John A. Courtney, Private
Thomas J. Dickinsen, Private
Uriah Donaldson, Private
John Durkin, Private
Henry Glock, Private
Hugh Green, Private
George Greenbauer, Private
James Hayes, Private

James P. Henry, Private
John Kelly, Private
Charles King, Private
Ferdinand Knupper, Private
Edward Lewis, Private
Rudolph Laffelbein, Private
Henry A. McCook, Private
James McDuff, Private
William H. Merritt, Private
Christopher McIntyre, Private
Daniel Morgan, Private
Daniel Munger, Private
John Murphy, Private
Robert Noonan, Private
David W. Neil, Private
William F. Norwood, Private
William J. Porter, Private
William L. Regan, Private
George B. Robinson, Private
Michael Reynolds, Private
Thomas A. Secord, Private
Charles M. Sheldon, Private
Charles Spencer, Private
George W. Sweeney, Private
John F. Vincent, Private
Alonzo A. Vincent, Private
James Walsh, Private
John Wray, Private
Michael Duffy, Private

Total officers and men in campaign was 58. Michael Duffy was discharged at Fort Fetterman on June 27th. No casualties were reported. Three men had deserted at Fort Fetterman just before the campaign started. Lieutenant M. E. O'Brien was on detached duty at Fort Fetterman.

COMPANY B SECOND CAVALRY

William B. Rawolle, 1st Lieutenant
Charles S. Alter, 1st Sergeant
Bartholomew Shannon, Sergeant
William J. Cunningham, Sergeant
Charles W. Day, Sergeant
Thomas Murray, Sergeant
John Howard, Sergeant
Alexander Huntington, Corporal
Thomas Aughey, Corporal
James Mitchell, Corporal
Eugene H. Glasure, Corporal

Robert Dyer, Trumpeter
John Friegel, Trumpeter
Charles F. Jones, Farrier
Edmund Grady, Blacksmith
John Graninckstrotkin, Saddler
John Atkin, Private
Daniel Austin, Private
Henry Baldwin, Private
Henry Chambers, Private
Henry G. Coffman, Private
James Corniff, Private

Charles P. Corliss, Private
James Cosgriff, Private
William Coulton, Private
William Cogan, Private
Robert Coster, Private
Louis Craft, Private
Richard N. Criswell, Private
Benjamin Domeck, Private
Patrick Doherty, Private
William J. Daughty, Private
John Davis, Private
Charles F. Edwards, Private
Adam Fox, Private
Wesley Gable, Private
Thomas B. Glover, Private
Alexander Graham, Private
Paul Gutike, Private
Michael Graemer, Private
Francis Hart, Private
Patrick Hanson, Private

Herman Harold, Private
William A. Hills, Private
Thomas Kelly, Private
Eggert Kohler, Private
Theodore P. Leighton, Private
William W. Lyman, Private
Daniel McClurg, Private
Henry Morris, Private
Francis O'Connor, Private
Charles S. Podge, Private
James Ramer, Private
Peter J. Redmond, Private
George W. Rowlau, Private
Mark B. Rue, Private
William H. Tailor, Private
Augustus Thompson, Private
George D. Vickers, Private
Patrick Wall, Private
Herbert Witmer, Private

Total officers and men in campaign was 61. Captain James I. Peale was under suspension at Fort D. A. Russell since March 17th. Lieutenant Frank W. Robinson was sick at Fort D. A. Russell since May 18th. No casualties were reported. Four privates deserted at Fort D. A. Russell just before the campaign commenced. Three privates were sick or on detached duty.

COMPANY D SECOND CAVALRY

Samuel M. Swigert, 1st Lieutenant
Henry D. Huntington,
   2nd Lieutenant
James W. Marcy, 1st Sergeant
Frederick W. Evans, Sergeant
John L. Joisteen, Sergeant
Patrick O'Donnell, Sergeant
Oscar R. Cornwell, Sergeant
George C. Williams, Sergeant
Russell W. Payne, Corporal
Henry C. Harrington, Corporal
William Madigar, Corporal
William I. Webb, Corporal
Gustavus Nicolai, Trumpeter
Joseph A. Wadsworth, Trumpeter
Henri Heynimann, Artificer
William L. Webb, Blacksmith
William H. Haynes, Saddler
William Allen, Private
James Anthony, Private
Otis Clark, Private
Davis Connors, Private
Michael Connors, Private

Jeremiah Cory, Private
Samuel J. Curtis, Private
James Darcy, Private
George Daum, Private
Henry DeMott, Private
Edward Devinney, Private
William Dudley, Private
John Flemming, Private
James Forrestel, Private
William Fryling, Private
James Galvin, Private
John T. Harris, Private
Carl Hecht, Private
Samuel W. Hine, Private
Eugene Isaac, Private
John Jackson, Private
Abraham Jacobs, Private
Washington Jones, Private
Harry Kiel, Private
James Koelman, Private
William Lang, Private
Joseph Laverty, Private
John Lewis, Private

John McCormack, Private
George McKnight, Private
William McManus, Private
Jacob Mack, Private
Frank Mackenzie, Private
William Madden, Private
William H. Moffitt, Private
John Moore, Private
Charles E. Parker, Private
John C. Putnam, Private
Emile Renner, Private

John Shields, Private
George A. Stone, Private
Carlton Torman, Private
Joseph Ward, Private
Edward A. Watson, Private
Thomas H. White, Private
William H. Williams, Private
James Wilson, Private
Joseph Wilson, Private
John F. A. Witt, Private

Total officers and men in campaign was 66. Captain David S. Gordon did not go on the expedition. Sergeant Patrick O'Donnell was reported wounded "the ball passing through right arm."

COMPANY E SECOND CAVALRY

Elizah R. Wells, Captain
Frederick W. Sibley,
  2nd Lieutenant
William Land, 1st Sergeant
Louis Gilbert, Sergeant
William P. Cooper, Sergeant
George L. Howard, Sergeant
Weaver Dollmair, Sergeant
Orson M. Smith, Sergeant
John Hollenbacker, Corporal
William C. Kingsley, Corporal
Otto C. Mendhoff, Corporal
Peter Waag, Bugler
Joseph F. Long, Saddler
John Bach, Private
Nicholas Burbach, Private
Leo Baader, Private
William I. Croley, Private
Patrick Clark, Private
George Coyle, Private
William J. Dougherty, Private
George Douglas, Private
Milton F. Douglass, Private
Lawrence Delaney, Private
William T. Englehorn, Private
Frank Foster, Private
Daniel Gabriel, Private
John Glancey, Private

Jacob Heird, Private
David Hogg, Private
John Hoffman, Private
Howard Krapp, Private
Alfred Logan, Private
Austin E. Lemon, Private
Montgomery McCormick, Private
William C. Murray, Private
Gustav Martini, Private
Thomas McCue, Private
Edward Nagle, Private
Linden B. Perry, Private
Richard Parkington, Private
William F. Paul, Private
Valentine Rufus, Private
Oliver Remley, Private
George Rosendale, Private
Oscar Rollan, Private
Cody Robertson, Private
James A. Scott, Private
Charles H. Sargent, Private
Patrick Sullivan, Private
James Smith, Private
Charles Tausher, Private
Jeremiah Twiggs, Private
William Volmer, Private
James Vance, Private
Hugo Wagner, Private

Total officers and men in campaign was 55. Lieutenant Randolph Norwood was absent on detached service. No casualties were reported. Six privates were either sick or on detached service while the company had 15 deserters during the two months period.

COMPANY I SECOND CAVALRY

Henry E. Noyes, Captain
Fred W. Kingsbury, 2nd Lieutenant
William Kirkwood, 1st Sergeant
William Taylor, Sergeant
William Skinner, Sergeant
Thomas Meagher, Corporal
Amos Black, Corporal
Thomas C. Marion, Corporal
John P. Slough, Corporal
George Fisher, Farrier
Henry Knapper, Saddler
Hermann Ashkey, Private
George M. Bickford, Private
Phillipp Burnett, Private
John E. Collins, Private
Charles Emmons, Private
Frank W. Foss, Private
John Gallagher, Private
Charles G. Graham, Private
John G. Hall, Private
Robert Johnson, Private
Walter B. Keenright, Private

Peter King, Private
George H. Liddle, Private
Martin Maher, Private
Charles Minarcik, Private
John Moran, Private
Charles Morrison, Private
Gustav Ohm, Private
James H. Ray, Private
John Reynolds, Private
George Rhode, Private
Gottlieb Ruf, Private
John Russell, Private
Konrad Schmid, Private
John M. Stevenson, Private
Irvine H. Stout, Private
William Strong, Private
Patrick H. Wall, Private
Daniel Walsh, Private
George J. Walters, Private
George Watts, Private
Thomas Wingfield, Private

Total officers and men in campaign was 43. Lieutenant Christopher F. Hall was not in the campaign and two sergeants and seven men were also absent. Eighteen men had deserted. Corporal Thomas Meagher was listed as wounded in action but no other casualties were reported.

Appendix B

OFFICIAL REPORTS OF THE BATTLE

"General Crook and all of us wrote out brief reports of the battle, having little pride in our achievement"—Anson Mills.

This Appendix contains copies of all of the official reports of the Rosebud battle which are now in the files of the National Archives. The telegraphic report of General Crook dated June 19th and his official report of June 20th are set forth first and are followed by that of Major Andrew W. Evans, who was next in command to Col. Royall. The reports of the infantry officers are all intact and are grouped together. Captain Noyes was the only officer to make a report on behalf of the Second Cavalry, and it follows those of the infantry. At the last are grouped the reports of the Third Cavalry officers with Colonel W. B. Royall's first, followed by those of his company commanders. No official reports have been found in the National Archives by Lt. Emmitt Crawford, Lt. Bainbridge Reynolds, Captain Peter D. Vroom, and Captain Sutorius, who were all company commanders in the Third Cavalry. These reports are all unaltered and are set forth just as they appear in the faded handwriting of the officers or their clerks.

TELEGRAPHIC REPORT OF GENERAL CROOK

Camp on South of Tongue River, Wy June 19 via Ft Fetterman.
Lt Gen Sheridan, Chicago Ill.
Returned to camp today having marched as indicated in my last telegram. When about forty miles from here on Rosebud Creek Mont morning Seventeenth inst Scouts reports Indians in vicinity and within a few minutes we were attacked in force the fight lasting several hours we were near the mouth of a deep canyon through which the creek ran. The sides were very steep covered with pine and apparently impregnable the village supposed to be at the other end about eight miles off.

213

They displayed strong force at all points occupying many and such covered places that it is impossible to correctly estimate their numbers The attack however showed that they anticipated that they were strong enough to thoroughly defeat the command during the engagement I tried to throw a strong force through the canyon but I was obliged to use it elsewhere before it had gotten to the supposed location of the village the command finally drove the Indians back in great confusion following them several miles the Scouts killing a good many during the retreat our casualties were nine men killed and fifteen wounded of third cavalry two 2 wounded Second Cavalry three men wounded fourth infantry and Capt Henry Third Cavalry several wounded in the face it is impossible to correctly estimate the loss of the indians many being killed in the attacks others being gotten off before we got possession of that part of the field 13 thirteen dead bodies being left we remained on the field that night and having but what each man carried himself we were obliged to return to the train to properly care for our wounded who were transported here on mule litters and lie now comfortable all doing well I expect to find those indians in rough places all the time and so have ordered five (5) companies of infantry and shall not probably make any extended movement until they arrive officers and men behaved with marked gallantry during the engagement.

Crook Brig Genl

OFFICIAL REPORT OF GENERAL CROOK

Headquarters Big Horn and Yellowstone Expedition
Camp Cloud Peak
Base Big Horn Mountains W. T.
June 20th 1876.

To the
    Assistant Adjutant General
        Headqrs Mil Dis of the Mo
          Chicago, Ills.

Sir

I have the honor to report that the detachments of Crow and Shoshone Indians Scouts I had been negotiating for, reached me on the night of the 14th instant. I immediately packed my trains, pack animals etc in a secure place so arranged that the civilian employes left with them, could if necessary, defend them till our return, and marched on the morning of the 16th with every available fighting man and four days rations carried by each officer and man on his person or saddle. I allowed no lead horses, each officer and man being equipped alike, with one blanket only, and every man who went whether Citizen, servant or soldier, armed and with some organization for fighting purposes only.

The Crow Indians were under the impression that the hostile village was located on Tongue River or some of its small tributaries and were quite positive we should be able to surprise it. While I hardly believed this to be possible as the Indians had hunting parties out who must necessarily become aware of the presence of the command, I considered it worth while to make the attempt. The Indians (ours) of course being expert in this matter I regulated movements entirely by their efforts to secure this end.

Marching from our camp on the South Fork of Tongue River, or Goose Creek as sometimes called, towards the Yellowstone, on the end of the first days march we came to a small stream near the divide that separates the waters of the Tongue and Rosebud we discovered that a small party of hunters had seen us. We crossed the divide that evening and camped on the headwaters of a small stream laid down on the map as Rosebud Creek and about thirty five or forty miles from our camp on Tongue River.

Pushing on the next morning down the Rosebud with my Indian scouts in front, when about five miles down the stream, near the mouth of a deep cañon, the scouts came into camp reported that they had seen something, and wished me to go into camp where we were lying close till they could investigate, and very soon after others came in reporting the Sioux in the vicinity and within a few minutes we were attacked by them in force.

The country was very rough and broken the attack made in greater or less force on all sides, and in advancing to meet it the command necessarily became separated. Under the circumstances I did not believe that any fight we could have would be decisive in its result, unless we secured their village supposed to be in close proximity. I therefore made every effort to close the command and march on their village.

I had great difficulty in getting the battalions together, each command being pressed by the Indians as the effort to concentrate them was made, the roughness of the ground facilitating this. The Indians apparently being aware of the reason of the movement and assembling on the bluffs overlooking the canon through which the command would have to pass.

While the engagement was in progress I succeeded however in throwing a portion of the command into and down the cañon for several miles but was obliged to use it elsewhere and before the entire command was concentrated it was believed that the cañon was well covered. Our Indians refusing to go into it saying it would be certain death. The bluffs on the side of the cañon being covered with timber they could fire upon the command at short range while a return fire would be of no effect.

The troops having repulsed the attack and in connection with the Indian Scouts drove the Sioux several miles and our Indians refusing to go down the cañon to the supposed location of the village, it remained to follow the retreating Sioux without rations, dragging our wounded after us on rough mule litters, or return to our train where they could be cared for, the latter being the course adopted we camped that night on the field, and marched next morning, and reaching camp yesterday evening, having been absent as intended when we first started four days.

Our casualties during the action, were 10 killed including one Indian Scout, and 21 wounded, including Captain Guy V. Henry, 3rd Cavalry, severely wounded in the face. It is impossible to correctly estimate the loss of the enemy as the field extended over several miles of rough country including rocks and ravines, not examined by us after the fight. Thirteen of their dead bodies being left in close proximity to our lines.

I respectfully call attention to the enclosed reports of Lieut. Colonel Royall 3rd Cavalry and Major Chambers 4th Infantry, commanding the Cavalry and Infantry battalions respectively and commend the gallantry and efficiency of the officers and men of the expedition as worthy of every praise.

Lieut Col Royal and Major Chambers have given me great strength by the able manner in which they commanded their respective columns.

I am particularly grateful to them for their efficiency during the trip and the engagement.

I am Sir

Very respectfully

Your Obedt Servt

(signed)   George Crook

Brigadier General Commanding

True Copy from original M.S

(Sig'd) A. H. Nickerson

Captain 23rd Infantry

A. D. C. & A. A. A. G.

Official Copy for file

OFFICIAL REPORT OF MAJOR ANDREW W. EVANS

Camp on South Goose Creek

June 20, 1876

Act. Asst. Adjt. Genl

Hd Qrs Cavalry, G, H, & Y Exp:

Sir,

In compliance with your instructions to report the part taken by the battalion, 3rd Cavalry, in the engagement with Indians on the 17th inst. I have the honour to do so, as follows: so far as the same came under my observation: The command marching down Rosebud Cr. on the morning of that day, had halted & unsaddled about three miles below the camping ground of the night before, when an alarm of the approach of hostile Indians was given, who soon made their appearance over a high hill to the N. W. Immediately after saddling I sent Capt Van Vliet's squadron (C & G Cos) to occupy the commanding ridge on the S, and Capt Henry was directed to place two Cos a short distance up the creek, on a lower ridge commanding the approach down the valley in that direction. He obeyed by going with his own Co. for one of these. The positions thus taken up were all on the right bank of the creek, on which side the 3rd had been marching. The battalion was then directed to cross the creek to the left bank (crossing bad and boggy); and receiving no further orders it was massed behind a low hill: in numbers six Cos; being Capt Mills' battalion and two cos of Henrys. I rode up to another ridge on the left front, to observe the engagement then going on, and had scarcely reached its crest when I was followed by Col Royall, leading the six cos in column, who directed me to deploy them as skirmishers in line forward and then proceeded to the front with his staff. I was endeavoring to deploy Mills' cos, when the command was again thrown forward in column, I believe by Col Royall's direct order, going up the hills at a rapid gallop & leaving me necessarily in their rear. I followed as speedily as my horse would carry me to the high ridge where the enemy had first appeared & where I supposed Col Royall had gone. He had however inclined to the left, followed by Cos B & L of Henry's battalion & I of Mills', and I found on the ridge only the latter with three Cos (A, E & M) deployed as skirmishers dismounted, and exchanging distant shots with the enemy. I was directed by Genl Crook to withdraw this line, a little while after, to mount & to prepare for a movement upon the Indian village (supposed to be in the neighbourhood), but I was obliged upon pressure from the enemy to reestablish it. By Genl Crook's order I also withdrew Van Vliet & was joined by him upon the hill in due time. Subsequently, the engagement slackening on this side, Capt Mills, with his three cos, was detached by Genl Crook under special orders, and moved down the hills, and I was ordered to hold another portion of the ridge with Capt Van Vliet's squadron, where, however, no firing worth mentioning was encountered. Meanwhile Col Royall, hotly engaged on the far left & front, had ordered to join him Henry's two Cos (F & D), withdrawing them from the position where I had placed them; and of the operations of these five cos (B, D, F, I & L) I had only a distant & imperfect view. The Cavalry Commander, Col Royall, under whose personal orders they were, knows best how well they behaved. I regret exceedingly that Capt Henry's severe wound renders it quite out of the question that he should make a written report of the operations of his battalion. The reports of Capts Mills & Van Vliet are enclosed herewith. The subsequent movements of the day, after the withdrawal of the

Indians, are not, I presume, included in your instructions. The casualties in the 3rd Cav were one officer, (Col Henry) severely wounded; 9 enlisted men killed & 17 wounded. Upon reviewing the above my attention is called that the withdrawal, by Col. Royall, of the two Cos of Henry from the position in which I had placed them in the valley, took place before the charge up the hill. I need scarcely add that throughout the affair the officers & men of the Reg't conducted themselves with great coolness & gallantry. Of the 5 Cos with Col Royall, it is proper to mention that one (B—Capt Meinhold) was sent off by him under orders, and joined me on the high ridge before the close of the fight. Capt Meinhold has taken down from Col Henry's lips his report of the operations of his battalion previous to his wound, and supplemented this by a report of its subsequent movements: both of which are enclosed.

Very Respectfully
Your Obt Serv't
A. W. Evans, Major 3rd Cavalry

OFFICIAL REPORT OF CAPTAIN HENRY E. NOYES

Camp on Goose Creek, Wyo. Ty
June 20th, 1876

Lieut. H. R. Lemley. 3rd Cavalry
    Adjutant Cavalry Battalions
Sir

In obedience to Par II of Circular of this date from HdQrs Battalion 2nd and 3rd Cavalry, I have the honor to respectfully report that my command was resting at the first halting place after leaving Camp on 17th inst. the horses being unsaddled and grazing, in obedience to orders received. We had been unsaddled but a short time, when I received orders to saddle up and await further orders. The Battalion was but just saddled, when some of the friendly Indians came running over the bluffs, at the foot of which we were, and by their words and actions informed us that the Sioux were coming in large numbers. As there was considerable discharging of firearms in the direction indicated, and every sign of the close proximity of the Sioux, *Without awaiting further orders*, I ordered four of the five companies of my Battalion forward on foot, leaving Co. A (Capt Dewees) in charge of the led horses of the other companies. We reached the top of the bluff as soon as possible, and drove the Sioux from that part of the ridge to the left of the ravine that cut through it (and at the mouth of which we had been resting).

Company B (Lieut. Swigert) was posted on the knob to the right of this ravine which was very rough and rocky and afforded cover for quite a number of Sioux.

Company E (Capt Wells) was posted on the knob and Crest to the left of this ravine, and the other two companies (Co B. Lieut Rawolle, and I, Lieut. Kingsbury) were on the ridge to the left of Co. E. Co D reached the crest just before the arrival of the Sioux, who were found in force just beyond. The companies to the left of this ravine found the Sioux on the crest, but drove them from it and they retreated toward our left along the crest, whence they were subsequently driven by troops further to the left.

The command was halted on the crest to await orders: the only casualties attending the occupation of this ridge was the wounding of First Sergeant Thomas Meagher, Co I. 2nd Cavalry, and Sergeant Patrick O'Donnell, Co. D. 2nd Cavalry, each of whom was wounded in the arm.

In about an hour, Capt Dewees reported with the led horses, having been ordered forward by the Brigadier General commanding. Not long after the arrival of the led horses, I received an order (through Lieut Bourke A.D.C.) to withdraw my command from the crest, mount and follow Capt Mills' battalion down the creek. This was done without delay, and the Battalion had been travelling very rapidly for about half an hour, in the direction ordered, when Capt Nickerson A.D.C. overtook us and recalled us to rejoin the command. Which we did, cutting across the country and passing over the ground on which the Sioux had been but a short time previous. On the way back I saw a large party of Sioux, leaving the field, a mile or more to our right and rear. After rejoining the command, we marched a short distance toward the front, halted a short time, and countermarched to a camp near where we had been resting when the affair commenced. I saw nothing in the conduct of either officers, or men, of my command, but that was deserving of commendation.

The amount of ammunition expended averaged about twelve rounds per man. There were present nine officers and two hundred and sixty enlisted men of the Second Cavalry.

I am, Sir,

Very respectfully

Your Obedient Servant.

Henry E. Noyes.

Captain 2nd Cavalry

Comdg Battalion 2nd Cavy

OFFICIAL REPORT OF MAJOR ALEX CHAMBERS

Hdgqrs Infantry Battalions B.H. & Y Expedition
Camp. Goose Creek June 20, 1876

Acting Asst. Adjutant General

Big Horn and Yellowstone Expedition

Sir:

I have the honor to make the following report of the part taken by the Infantry battalion composed of Companies D and F 4th Infantry, and C G and H 9th Infantry in the four (4) days scout of the troops composing the B. H. and Y. Expedition.

The command left camp on Goose Creek, mounted on mules, at 6 o'clock A.M., and marched about thirty five (35) miles to headwaters of Rosebud. Marched the morning of the 17th about five (5) miles and camped. A short time after camping, shots were heard behind the bluffs in rear of camp, and cries that hostile Indians were coming. I sent, as ordered, two companies, dismounted, to the edge of the bluffs to protect that point: posted as skirmishers. Shortly after the three (3) remaining companies formed a skirmish line on top of the ridge. After occupying this position for some time. I was ordered to have the Battalion mounted, and marched to the crest of the ridge, which was done, as soon as the companies on the skirmish line could be recalled for that purpose, one returning for their animals, and the mules of the other companies, the men and animals being kept concealed as much as possible. The left of the cavalry line retiring closely pursued by the Indians. Two (2) companies of the 9th Infantry. G and H were sent to protect the withdrawal of Cavalry. the three companies remaining were sent as a skirmish line across the plateau to drive off a body of Indians, behind a conical hill, who kept up a constant fire. This was successfully accomplished, and the Indians disappeared. I then took up a position on the hill and remained until 7 P.M., when the command returned to camp on the banks of the river. The command marched next day in rear, to head of creek or branch of Tongue River twenty (20) miles. Next day twenty (20) miles, to near the camp left on the 16th. Each of the command performed this duty cheerfully and with credit. Casualties were, three enlisted men wounded of Company D 4th Infantry viz: Corporal James A. Devine wounded in head. Private John H. Terry severely wounded in left leg. Private Richard Flynn slightly wounded in left shoulder. For detailed reports I respectfully refer to reports of company commanders, enclosed.

I am sir very respectfully
Your Obedient Servant.
(sgd) Alex Chambers
Major 4th Infantry
Commanding.

Official Copy for file
A. A. General.

OFFICIAL REPORT OF CAPTAIN SAMUEL MUNSON,
Co C 9th Infantry.

The Adjutant.   Goose Creek (Upper Part)
Infantry Battn.   B. H. and Y. Expedition
Sir.   June 20th, 1876

I have the honor to submit the following report for the information of the commanding officer, Infantry Battn, Big Horn and Yellowstone Expedition.

On the morning of the 17th June 1876, Co C 9th Infantry, was unsaddled when the firing on the bluffs commenced. I immediately formed my company as previously directed and waited for orders. The first order I received was to take my men dismounted up the bluffs and report to General Crook. I took my Co to point indicated, but, did not find the General. The men were directed to lie down on the edge of the bluffs and reserve their fire until the Indians had approached near them. At this time I formed part of the line of Infy. and Cavalry holding the second line of bluffs. Before we had time to accomplish anything I was ordered to go back into the valley, saddle up, and then take the Co to the shelter of the nearest hill, and wait for orders. This I did and when joined by two other companies we were directed to proceed up the hill, which we did advancing about 1½ miles; at this point we remained for some time. During this halt, the call was given for help, and I was directed to take six of my men, sharpshooters, to some rocks and broken ground on the crest of the hill, and drive back the Sioux who were then charging. this I did, and held the position with the aid of about a dozen men of other companies and about twenty friendly Indians. We were then ordered to fall back and rejoin our companies, who were then preparing to form a skirmish line. When this line was formed, my company occupied the right, my skirmishers taking up the ground between the top of the hill and valley below. We met no resistance on that side of the hill—the Sioux retiring—a few only showing themselves at long distance. The action being over, we were ordered to the top of the hill which we occupied until dark. No officer or man of Co C, 9th Infantry was injured.

I have the honor to be Sir Your obedient Servant
S. Munson Captain Commanding Co C 9th Infantry

OFFICIAL REPORT OF CAPTAIN T. B. BURROWES, Co. G 9th Infantry.

Adjutant Batt Inf
In the field
Sir

Camp on Goose Creek W. T.
June 20th, 1876.

In compliance with verbal instructions, this day received from your Head Qrs. I have the honor to submit the following report. Company G 9th Inf. consisting of Captain *T. B. Burrowes* 9th Inf. commanding, 1st Lieut. *W. L. Carpenter* 9th

Inf. with thirty one enlisted men formed part of the Big Horn and Yellowstone Expedition against the Sioux. The Company left the camp of the expedition, on Goose Creek, as a portion of the Infantry Battalion, as mounted Infantry, on the morning of the 16th Inst. at 1 o'clock A. M. Company marched to the head of the Rose Bud Creek that day camped at 9 P.M. distance marched 37 miles. On the morning of the 17th Inst. Company marched 4 miles down the Rose Bud Creek, and at 8:30 A.M. was ordered into action against the Sioux. Company remained in action and under desultory fire for about 4 hours. At about 10:30 A.M. Company was ordered forward to check advance of Indians on a retiring line.—Advance was made and Indians checked. After engagement Company remained on picket duty until nightfall, when it was ordered to camp with the remainder of the column. Company marched with expedition on the 18th inst. forming a part of the rear guard of the column; camped on a tributary of the Tongue River, distance marched 20 miles. On the 19th inst. Company returned with expedition to supply camp on Goose Creek W. T. distance marched 22 miles.

Casualties in company during engagement on the 17th inst. none.

I am Sir very respectfully

Your Obt. Servant

T. B. Burrowes

Captain 9th Infantry Company G

OFFICIAL REPORT OF CAPTAIN A. S. BURT,
Co. H 9th Infantry

Camp on Goose Creek Wyo.
June 20, 1876

Lieut. Seaton
Batt. Adjutant

Sir:

In obedience to orders I forward following report of the four days scout of my company to the Rosebud and return. On the 15th I was ordered to receive from Capt Fleury Q.M. necessary number of mules and saddles to mount my company which after much vexations delay was accomplished. On the 16th my company as part of Col Chambers Batt marched thirty six miles to Rosebud Creek. On the 17th about 8 o'clock A.M. while in camp our Crow Scouts discovered the Sioux Indians in force near by. My company with rest of Infty Batt. fell in dismounted and occupied adjacent hills, expecting the Crow and Snake Indians to draw the Sioux by feigned retreat to this position. We were discovered and this plan frustrated. Shortly after this, orders were received to return to camp and mount my company and join Col. Chambers on the hill; which was done in about an hour. This length of time was taken up because of report made to me by Lieut of Seaton of wounded men being in camp and that my company was the last there. I directed him to report to me when the surgeon was ready to move with every wounded man. This was done and then my company, the wounded and the mules of D Co. 4th Infty moved out and to the hill.

Subsequently while waiting on this hill in line I received orders with Maj. Burrowes "to stop those Indians and occupy that ridge." The ridge referred to was across a ravine and toward the left of the general line some several hundred yards away. The Indians were the Sioux pursuing a battalion of cavalry. We dismounted and moved forward at double time and on reaching the ridge stopped the Indians quickly and decisively without loss on our part, my company disabled two Indians and three ponies. I make this statement carefully believing greater damage was done the enemy. On the evening of the 17th my company went into the old camp on Rosebud Creek. On the 18th my company as part of Col. Chambers Battalion marched 22 miles across Wolf Mountains and camped on a small stream emptying into Tongue River.

On the 19th we returned to camp on Goose Creek. Distance marched 25 miles. Total enlisted men of the company who took part in the scout was 32; 5 sergeants, 2 corporals, 2 buglers and 23 privates. Lieut. Robertson, the non commissioned officers; Buglers and Privates of my company did their duty on the Rosebud Scout.

I am respt-

Yrobt Svt-

A. S. BURT

Captain commanding Co. H, 9th Inf.

OFFICIAL REPORT OF CAPTAIN A. B. CAIN,
Co. D, 4th Infantry

Big Horn Expedition
Camp on Goose Creek W. T.
   June 20, 1876
Lieut. Henry Seton, 4th Infantry
Adjutant Infantry Battalion
Sir:

   I have the honor to submit the following report:

   My Company D, 4th Infantry moved from camp on Rosebud Creek, W. T. at about 8 A.M. on the 17th instant, and as skirmishers engaged the enemy Sioux Indians and assisted the Crow and Snake Indians in driving them from their position. My loss was two Privates wounded.

   At about 11 A.M. my Company D with Company F 4th Infantry, Captain Luhn and Lieut. Seton, Company C 9th Infantry, Captain Munson and Lieut. Capron, all under my immediate command, moved upon the enemy, and drove him from his position. My loss was one (1) private wounded.

   This command was then relieved from the line by a cavalry force.

   The officers and enlisted men are entitled to great credit for their good conduct. I respectfully call attention to the following named officers and enlisted men for their gallantry and bravery. Captain Munson and Lieut. Capron 9th Infantry. Captain Luhn and Lieut. Seton 4th Infantry. 1st Sergeant Dexter, Sergeant Lister, Corporals Funk and Conboy, and Private Terry Co D 4th Infantry.

   I am Sir Very Respectfully Your Obediant Servant

A. B. CAIN
Captain 4th Infantry Comdg Company D
Camp Goose Creek
June 20, 1876

To the Adjutant Infantry Battalion
B H & Y Expedition
Sir:

I have the honor to report that Company F 4th Infantry consisting of one (1) commissioned, six (6) non commissioned, officers, and thirty three (33) privates, mounted on mules with four (4) days rations and one hundred rounds of ammunition per man, took the following part in a four (4) days campaign against the Sioux from Goose Creek.

Left camp on Goose Creek on the morning of the 16th inst. marched to Rosebud and camped: left camp about 6 A.M. on the 17th marched about five (5) miles, when the Battle of the Rosebud commenced. The company was deployed as skirmishers and remained on the field of battle until sundown, then marched to the Creek and camped: left camp on the 18th about 6:30 A.M. and marched to Rosebud Mountain and camped: left camp about 6 A.M. on the 19th and marched to Goose Creek.

Very Respectfully
Your Obdt Servant
G. L. LUHN
Captain F Company 4th Infantry
comdg Company

OFFICIAL REPORT OF LT. COLONEL W. B. ROYALL, 3rd Cavalry

Headquarters Cavalry Battalions, Big Horn &
Yellowstone Expedition
Camp South Fork Tongue River W. T.
June 20, 1876

Acting Assistant Adjutant General
Big Horn and Yellowstone Expedition
Sir: ·

In compliance with revised Army Regulations and the verbal instructions of the Brigadier General Commanding I have the honor to submit the following report of the part taken by my command in the engagement with Sioux Indians on the 17th instant.

The Battalions of the Third Cavalry were upon the south

bank of the Rosebud river, that of the second being upon the opposite side, when the alarm was given by allied Indian Scouts. Shortly after, firing was heard upon the high crest north of the river and receiving orders to cross, deploy as skirmishers, charge and occupy the hills in the possession of the enemy, those instructions were promptly obeyed. The battalion of the Second Cavalry had already deployed and charged and with Captain Mills' battalion (except Captain Andrews' (I) Company) and Captain Van Vliets squadron of the Third Cavalry, were not under my immediate command at any time during the engagement. Capt. Mills' battalion deployed and Captain Van Vliets squadron occupied a crest in rear, but the latter was subsequently removed by the Brigadier General Commanding.

I now found myself upon the extreme left with Captain Andrews' company and Captain Henry's battalion of the Third Cavalry (consisting of companies D, B, L and F commanded respectively by Captains Henry and Meinhold and Lieutenants Vroom and Reynolds of that regiment) the Indians occupying the series of ridges in our immediate front. They were steadily charged and retreated from one crest to another, my instructions at this time being to slowly advance. But few shots were fired the men being mounted. In this manner was reached the ridge lying adjacent to but separated by a wide canon from the main crest, which, the men being dismounted and deployed and the horses protected upon the contiguous slope, I occupied by instructions from an Aide-de-Camp of the Brigadier General Commanding, who informed me that a charge would be made upon the enemy's left flank by the Battalion of the Second Cavalry. The enemy occupied the crest in my immediate front and were promptly engaged. They also lined a battle upon the left distant about six hundred yards from which they obtained a plunging and enfilading fire. Capt. Andrews whose company had advanced upon the extreme left, was withdrawn for better protection and a flank and rear movement by the enemy being observed, it was promptly checked by Captain Henry's company which took possession of a rocky ledge to my left and rear.

Immediately subsequent to the delivery of the preceding

instructions, I was directed by the Brigadier General Commanding, through an orderly, to extend my right and connect with the left of the main body occupying a remote portion of the highest crest and I detached Captain Meinhold's company for that purpose. I now received an order to withdraw delivered by an Aide-de-camp of the Brigadier General Commanding which I proceeded to obey by gradually retiring my led horses under the protection of a line of skirmishers which movement being perceived by the enemy, they began to close in upon us in large numbers and the ground being favorable for that purpose we were now subjected to a severe direct flank and rear fire. The advance points of the main crest which had before been occupied by troops, had by their withdrawal fallen into the possession of the enemy, observing which, knowing that my successful withdrawal was greatly endangered thereby and my experience in Indian warfare warning me that protection would be necessary in crossing the last defile which separated me from the main command, I dispatched my Adjutant to the Brigadier General Commanding requesting such assistance, but before it was furnished, the enemy (being elsewhere disengaged) was upon us in full force and I was compelled to direct the company commanders to rejoin the main body as rapidly as possible. Thus far my casualties had been slight, but in effecting the crossing the firing was exceedingly severe and my loss was quadrupled. For protection in the passage I had directed Lieutenant Vroom and company to precede and line a crest which covered it; but by this time every Sioux in the engagement was surrounding this single battalion and the position assigned was too exposed to be even temporarily occupied. The only killed were in this battalion under my immediate command and numbered nine. There were thirteen wounded including Captain Guy V. Henry 3rd Cavalry, a total of twenty two casualties. In the companies of the 3rd Cavalry not with me during the engagement, there were two men wounded and also two in the Battalion 2nd Cavalry making at total of twenty six casualties in the cavalry. The officers under my command were 2nd Lieutenant Henry R. Lemly Adjutant 2nd Lieutenant Charles Morton A. A. Captains Guy V. Henry and William H.

Andrews. 1st Lieutenant Peter D. Vroom and 2nd Lieutenants Bainbridge Reynolds and James E. H. Foster all of the Third Cavalry, their conduct and that of the enlisted men was commendable in every respect. Mr. R. B. Davenport of the New York *Herald* accompanied me throughout the entire engagement. The report of Major Andrew W. Evans 3rd Cavalry and Captain H. E. Noyes 2nd Cavalry are appended.

> Very Respectfully Your Obdt. Servt.
>> (Sigd) W. B. ROYALL
>> Lieutenant Colonel 3rd Cavalry Commanding.

Official copy.
(Sgd) A. H. NICKERSON
    Captain 23rd Infy A.D.C.

OFFICIAL REPORT OF CAPTAIN CHARLES MEINHOLD,
Co. B, 3rd Cavalry

> Camp on South Fork of Tongue River W. T.
> June 20, 1876

To 2nd Lt. H. R. Lemley, 3rd Cavalry.
    Adjutant Cavalry Command Big Horn & Yellowstone
    Expedition.
Sir:

I respectfully enclose herewith Col. Guy V. Henry's report of the part taken by his Battalion in the action on the 17th inst. As the report in its main points only relates to companies D and F, 3rd Cavalry, I may add that on the morning of the 17th inst. when the order to saddle up was given, companies B and L, 3rd Cavalry (Capt. Meinhold and Capt. Vroom's) received orders from you to follow Col Royall, 3rd Cavalry, and we left camp in the order stated above. We formed lines. Col. Royall's escort in front, my company next, Capt Vroom's in my rear, and charged across the open space to the left and front of the camp to a knoll, thence to an adjoining one, opening fire upon the Indians, who seemed to fall back before us. At this moment, I received orders to move with my company (B) rapidly up a ravine to our right, to join Major Noyes 2nd Cavalry at a distance of about 800 yards, and at a place where the cañon widens out. I received a very severe sweeping fire from Indians on a bluff facing the canon, killing a horse and wounding a man of my company.

On joining Maj. Noyes, I was ordered to take position in his Battalion. While doing so Major Evans 3rd Cavalry ordered me to follow him. I remained with him until the command concentrated and returned to camp. Capt Vroom's company, L 3rd Cavalry was during the entire day under the immediate command of Col Royall. His casualties are as follows

Killed 5 enlisted men

Wounded 3 enlisted men

Very Respy Yr Obdt Svt.

CHAS MEINHOLD

Captain 3rd Cavalry Comdg Batt 3rd Cav.

Through Col. A. W. Evans, 3rd Cav

Comdg Batts 3rd Cav.

OFFICIAL REPORT OF CAPTAIN GUY V. HENRY, 3rd Cavalry.

Camp on South Fork Tongue River Wy
June 20, 1876

2nd Lieut H. R. Lemly, Adjutant Cavalry Command

Sir:

On the morning of the 17th inst my battalion consisting of companies B, D, F and L 3rd Cavalry being in camp on Rose Bud, fire by hostile Indians was heard and the order to saddle up given at once. Major Evans had ordered me to take D and F Companies to the left some 500 yards to form line to prevent the Indians from turning our supposed left: this broke up my battalion. I therefore can only relate the operations of the two companies during the day. (D and F).

Having taken position as ordered, I reconnoitered personally and found Indians some distance to my right on the bluffs. While starting to change my position accordingly, Colonel Royall ordered me to follow him. We took position behind a knoll about a half a mile from General Crooks left. While waiting there with his consent, I made such dispositions of my two companies as to prevent the Indians from getting in rear of us, which they were trying to do. The order then came to retire and to connect with General Crooks left. While doing so we were subjected to a very heavy fire from three different points, the Indians having turned our rear as I supposed they would when we retired. They evidentally intending to capture all the lead horses which had been sent to the rear.

It was impossible and unwise under the heavy fire from three directions to keep the men in position they were ordered to retire rapidly with the intention of being rallied under cover. During the retreat we were saved from greater loss by the charge of two infantry companies from General Crooks left, which I personally observed. While doing so I was wounded and taken to the rear to have my wound dressed intending to return but the Surgeon forbid me doing so. I may add that upon joining Colonel Royall I found Captain Meinhold and Vroom Companies over whom I exercised no immediate control, they being under the immediate orders of Colonel Royall. I personally observed however that the officers themselves, Captain Meinhold and Vroom. Lieutenant Simpson and Reynolds were cool and kept their men well in hand and carried out such orders as they received in an efficient manner.

Very respectfully Your Obedient Servant

Guy V Henry Capt 3rd Cavalry Comdg Batt.

By Chas Meinhold

Capt 3rd Cavalry

OFFICIAL REPORT OF CAPTAIN WILLIAM H. ANDREWS
Co I, 3rd Cavalry

I Company 3rd U.S. Cavalry

Camp of the Big Horn and Yellowstone Expedition

Goose Creek W. T. June 20, 1876

To Capt Andson Mills Comdg Battn 3rd Cavy.

Sir:

I have the honor to make the following report in regard to the part taken by I Co 3rd Cavy in the affir of Rosebud Hills on the 17th of June 1876. The Battalion, Capt Mills Cmdg, was moved from the position they were in on the south bank of Rosebud Creek, at about 8 A.M. 17th inst in the following order, A, E, M and I Cos, the first named leading. Taking the trot and passing the creek we dismounted in line in rear of the 2nd Cavalry. In a moment we were again mounted and moved by the flank in the same order at a trot. Three Companies of the Battalion, after gaining a valley, went left front into line, but as I gave the command to my company to conform to this movement, Lt. Col. Royall 3rd Cavy directed me to deploy and carry the ridge on our left which at this time was occupied by the enemy. I did so and then ordered the Company to charge, this deployment being made at the trot. After pushing to the front some considerable distance driving before me and away from the ridge a strong body of the enemy, I halted the company and directed Lieut Foster to take the 2nd Platoon, numbering eighteen (18) men—and "clear those people on the left away" meaning a part of the enemy who threatened to enfilade our line. Charging as foragers under a sharp fire Lieut Foster drove the Indians from three positions in succession and away from the ridges to the left of the ridge along which the balance of the battalion were moving. As soon as Lt Foster had started, I moved forward at a sharp gait with the remainder of the Company, getting at the same time a terribly strong fire from a rocky point on my right. I took possession of this point and held it until ordered back. As long as I held this position I kept the fire in front of me well under. In accordance with orders I sent Private Weaver I Co 3rd Cavy to Lt Foster, who by this time was far in advance of our line, with orders to fall back at once to the Company with the 2nd Platoon, this he did under a very heavy fire from his rear and flanks, marching at a gallop but in good order and having two men and one horse wounded. After some little time I received orders to again fall back, which I did to another point in our rear and received in doing so a heavy fire from the enemy who had occupied the ridge just abandoned. After remaining here for some time and aiding in checking the enemy who charged our line three times and were each time repulsed with loss, we were ordered to mount and retreat to the high crest upon which the Infantry were posted. In falling back from this position the company suffered its greatest loss, though it had men wounded further to the front. After reaching the crest upon which the Infantry were posted, I was ordered by Lt. Chase, Adj. to Col. Evans to halt until further orders. Subsequently, being so directed by Col Royall, I marched down from the crest and brought in the dead of my company, who were brought into the camp that evening and buried. The men of the Company behaved in the most gallant manner throughout the day, and where all did so well it is difficult Matter to particularize, but I desire to mention the very gallant conduct of 1st Serg John Henry; his bearing conduct and bravery I wish specially to commend to the consideration of the General Commanding.

In closing this report I desire to mention the distinguished gallantry of 2nd Lieut J. E. H. Foster who acted throughout the whole affair in the most efficient manner, displaying courage and bravery of a very high-order.

Casualties

Killed	Horses
Private Wm W. Allen	Wounded, six (6)
Do Eugene Flynn	

Wounded

Sergt Andrew Groesch, Pvts
John Socciborski, James
O'Brien, Francis Smith,
Chas W. Stewart, James
Riley

Force of Company engaged 2 commissioned 46 enlisted.
Capt Wm H. Andrews
2nd Lieut. J. E. H. Foster

Very Respy Yr Obt Sert
WM. H. ANDREWS
Capt 3rd Cavy

OFFICIAL REPORT OF CAPTAIN VAN VLIET,
Co. C, 3rd Cavalry

Camp on Goose Creek W. T.
June 20th 1876

Major A. W. Evans
Comdg. 3rd Cav. Battalion
Major:

In compliance with instructions I have the honor to make the following report of the part taken in action of the 17th inst with hostile Indians. Companies C and G 3rd Cavy, at commencement of action were ordered to gain a commanding ridge in rear of our camp and hold it until further orders. This ridge was gained just in advance of the Indians who were striving hard for it. These companies remained in this position until about Eleven o'clock when they were withdrawn and joined the main command. No casualties.

I am Major

Very Respectfully your Obt Servt
F. VAN VLIET
Capt 3rd Cav Comdg.

OFFICIAL REPORT OF CAPTAIN ANSON MILLS,
Battalion Commander 3rd Cavalry

Head Qrs 1st Batt: Cos A E I and M 3rd Cav.
Big Horn & Yellow Stone Expedition
Goose Creek Wyo June 20th 1876

Lieut. Geo. F. Chase
Adjt Batts 3rd Cav.
Sir:

In compliance with instructions, I have the honor to submit the following report of the part taken by my command in the battle with the hostile Sioux on the 17th inst.

About 8 A.M. while bivouaced in line on the right bank of the Rosebud (between Maynadiers Camp 8 & 9 where the stream runs from west to east) facing the stream and being the right of the 3rd Cavalry. (The other troops and Indians occupying the opposite bank) skirmishing commenced between the Crows, Snakes and the Sioux. It soon became apparent that we were attacked in force and I received orders from Col Evans to mount, cross the stream and charge and drive the Indians from the opposite hills.

The superior force of the Sioux who now appeared on the hills in large numbers, had driven the Crows and Snakes pell mell into camp but the Battalion 2nd Cav and 9th Inf. had promptly thrown out dismounted skirmishers who held them in check on the first ridge. The Batt. being formed and about ready for the charge, Col. Royall detached Capt Andrews Co I further to the left and he remained so detached during the engagement.

The 3 remaining companies being our extreme right charged the first ridge in our front about 800 yards distant and drove the Indians from it but they immediately formed behind a second some 600 yds. from the first and this also being taken the greater portion of them formed around a large cone shaped mount and when about to move on this I received an order to advance no further but to throw out dismounted skirmishers and hold the position.

The General Commanding soon appeared and informed me that he did not want the engagement pressed any farther then, but that he had ordered all the troops to assemble there when he intended to move the whole command on the village which his information led him to believe was only a short distance below on the stream, that my Batt. should lead pushing as rapidly as the stock would stand it and pay no attention to the assaults of the Sioux as the friendly Indians would flank us (and to charge the village as soon as I got sight of it) 20 men from Co A Lieut. Lawsons, being detailed to accompany the friendly Indians and keep up connections.

I moved out with Co E Capt. Sutorius deployed and soon gained the stream, (driving some 30 or 40 Indians from the hills in our former rear and between us and the stream) followed by Noyes' Batt. 2nd Cav. We passed rapidly down the stream, which turns almost due north, for 6 or 7 miles where the bluffs are high, rugged and rocky (Lieut. Bourke Aid to the Comdg Genl and Guide Girard accompanying me with the advance) when I received from Capt. Nickerson the General's order to divert my column to the left and try and gain the rear of some Indians who were making a demonstration in our former front with difficulty we gained the position only to find the Indians had fled and thereupon were ordered into bivouac on the battle field for the night.

My command consisted of:

Co A 3rd Cav Lieut. Lawson Comdg 1 off and 49 men;

Co E 3rd Cav Capt. Sutorius Comg with Lt Von Leuttwitz 2 off and 54 men.

Co I 3rd Cav Capt Andrews Comdg with Lt Foster 2 off and 46 men

Co M 3rd Cav Lieut. Paul Comdg with Lt. Schwatka 2 off and 51 men

Total 7 off: and 200 men

The casualties were Co A 1 horse killed, 1 horse wounded. Co E Pvt Herold wounded. 2 horses wounded. Co I Pvt Allen and Flynn killed. Pvt. Sosciborski, O'Brien, Smith, Stewart, Riley and Serg. Grosch wounded 6 horses wounded. Co M Trumpeter Snow wounded. 1 horse wounded. Total 2 enlisted men killed and 8 wounded.

All the officers and men behaved with patience, coolness and courage. Messrs Finerty and McMillan, correspondents respectively for the Chicago *Times* and *Inter Ocean* accompanied Co E and A respectively and participated in the engagement throughout.

I submit herewith reports of Company Commanders.

I have the honor to be Very Respectively Your Obed. Servt.

Anson Mills Captain 3rd Cavalry

Comdg Batt.

OFFICIAL REPORT OF LT. JOSEPH LAWSON,
Co A 3rd Cavalry

Camp on Goose Creek. W. T. June 20, 1876

Captain Anson Mills,

Commanding First Battalion. Third Cavalry.

I have the honor to submit the following report with reference to the engagement on Rosebud Creek, Montana Territory, June 17, 1876. Company A participated occupying through the first charge the left center and during the Second charge the left. It was while A Company was on the left of the skirmish line that Sergeant John H. Van Moll acted courageously in advancing to the enemies lines, supported only by a few friendly Indian allies, by whom he was rescued and brought to our lines. One horse was killed, and one wounded in action. No casualties among the men occurred. Private Leonard acted in a commendable manner during the engagement. The company non-commissioned officers and privates deserve credit for their efficiency and bravery.

I am Sir Very Respectfully Your Obedient Servant

JOSEPH LAWSON
1st Lieut. 3rd Cavalry
Commanding Co A

OFFICIAL REPORT OF LT. AUGUSTUS C. PAUL,
Co M 3rd Cavalry

Camp on Goose Creek Wyo T.
June 20th, 1876

Capt Anson Mills 3rd Cavly
Commanding 1st Battalion Captain

I have the honor to report that M Company 3rd Cavalry participated in the engagement against the Sioux Indians June 17th near the head of the Rosebud as a part of the 1st Battalion. In the charges both mounted and dismounted the Company behaved handsomely. Sec Lieut Frederick Schwatka throughout the entire fight acted very courageously. Trumpeter Snow while in the extreme advance in the charge made by the 1st Battalion was badly wounded through the right and left arm.

I have the honor to be very respectfully Your Obedient servant

AUGUSTUS C. PAUL
1st Lieut. 3rd Cavy
Comdg Co M 3rd Cavalry.

BIBLIOGRAPHY

(Major Sources Only)

Beyer, W. F., and Keydal, O. F., *Deeds of Valor*, 2 volumes, Detroit, 1903.
Bourke, John G., *On the Border with Crook*, Charles Scribner Sons, New York, 1891. Reprint Edition, 1950.
Bourke, John G., *Diary*, U.S. Military Academy Library, West Point, New York.
Brady, Cyrus Townsend, *Indian Fights and Fighters*, Doubleday Page & Co., New York, 1904.
Capron, Cynthia J., *"The Indian War of 1876, From Letters of Lieut. Thaddeus H. Capron,"* Journal Illinois State Historical Society (January, 1921), pages 476-503.
Crawford, Lewis F., *Rekindling Campfires*, Capitol Book Company. Bismarck, North Dakota, 1926.
Daly, Henry W., *Manual of Pack Transportation*, Washington, D. C. 1910.
Daly, Henry W., *"The Warpath,"* American Legion Monthly (April, 1927).
DeBarthe, Joe, *Life and Adventures of Frank Gruard*, St. Joseph, Mo., 1894. Buffalo (Wyoming) Bulletin Reprint Edition, N. D.
Finerty, John F., *Warpath and Bivouac*, Published, Chicago, Illinois, 1890.
Grinnell, George Bird, *The Fighting Cheyennes*, Charles Scribner Sons, New York, 1915.
Hebard, Grace Raymond, *Washakie*. Arthur H. Clark Co., Cleveland, O., 1930.
Kennon, W. V. Lyman, *Diary*. Army War College, Carlisle Barracks, Pa.
Linderman, Frank B., *American: The Life Story of a Great Indian*, World Book Company, New York, 1930.
Marquis, Thomas B., *A Warrior Who Fought Custer*, The Midwest Publishing Company, Minneapolis, Minn., 1931.
Mills, Anson, *My Story*, Privately Printed, Washington, D. C., 1918.
National Archives, War Records Branch, Washington, D. C.
Neihardt, John G., *Black Elk Speaks*, Published, New York, 1932.
Nickerson, Azor H., *Major General George Crook and the Indians*, Army War College, Carlisle Barracks, Penna.
Parsons, John E. and du Mont, John S., *Firearms in the Custer Battle*, The Stackpole Company, Harrisburg, Pa., 1953.
Ricker Interviews, Nebraska State Historical Society, Lincoln, Neb., 1906 and 1907.
Sandoz, Mari, *Crazy Horse*, Alfred A. Knopf, New York, 1942.
Schmitt, Martin F., *General George Crook: His Autobiography*. University of Oklahoma Press, Norman, Okla., 1946.
South Dakota Historical Collections, Volumes 2, 6, and 15. Pierre, South Dakota.
Vestal, Stanley, *Warpath*, Houghton Mifflin Co., Boston and New York, 1934.
Vestal, Stanley, *Warpath and Council Fire*, Random House, New York, 1948.

PERIODICALS

Annuals, Association of West Point
  Graduates.
Army and Navy Journal.
Army and Navy Register.
Billings (Montana) *Gazette.*
Cavalry Journal.
Chicago *Interocean.*
Chicago *Times.*
Frank Leslie's Illustrated Newspaper.
Hardin (Montana) *Tribune Herald.*
Harper's Weekly.

Helena (Montana) *Herald.*
Helena (Montana) *Independent.*
Military Service Institution Journal.
New York *Graphic.*
New York *Herald.*
New York *Tribune.*
Rocky Mountain News (Denver,
  Colorado)
United Service Magazine.
Winners of the West, St. Joseph, Mo.

INDEX

The names of "Brigadier General George Crook" and "Crazy Horse," together with the various regiments and army organizations, are omitted from this Index because of the frequency with which they occur. Appendix A, which contains the names of the soldiers in the campaign, is aso excluded.

241

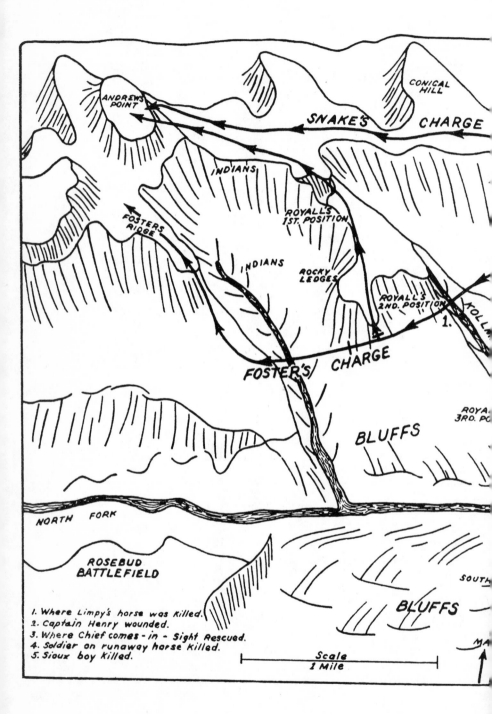

CONICAL HILL

ANDREWS POINT

SNAKE'S CHARGE

INDIANS

ROYALL'S 1ST. POSITION

FOSTERS RIDGE

INDIANS

ROCKY LEDGES

ROYALL'S 2ND. POSITION

KOLLM

1.

ROYA 3RD. PC

FOSTER'S CHARGE

BLUFFS

NORTH FORK

ROSEBUD BATTLEFIELD

BLUFFS

SOUTH

1. Where Limpy's horse was killed.
2. Captain Henry wounded.
3. Where Chief comes-in-Sight Rescued.
4. Soldier on runaway horse killed.
5. Sioux boy killed.

Scale
1 Mile

MA

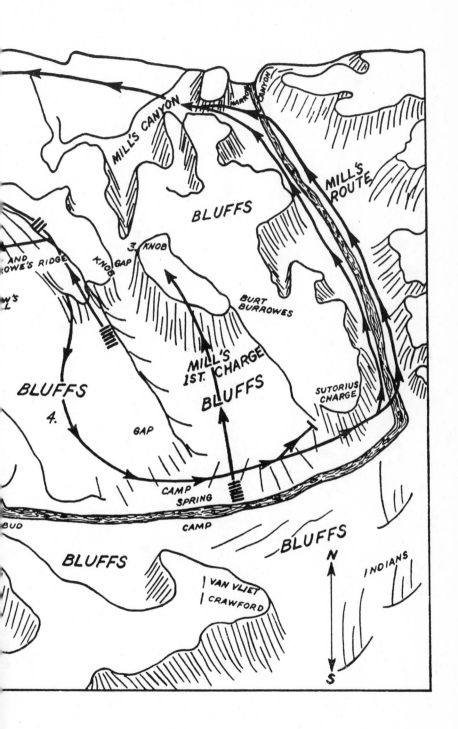

THE CUSTER LIBRARY

The Custer Myth
by W. A. Graham

⁓

Legend into History and
*Did Custer Disobey Orders
at the Battle of the Little Big Horn?*
by Charles Kuhlman

⁓

*The Reno Court of Inquiry:
Abstract of the Official
Record of Proceedings*
by W. A. Graham

⁓

The Story of the Little Big Horn
by W. A. Graham

⁓

Troopers with Custer
by E. A. Brininstool

⁓

With Crook at the Rosebud
by J. W. Vaughn